Harry Van Arsdale Jr.

Harry Van Arsdale Jr.

LABOR'S CHAMPION

Foreword by
Theodore W. Kheel

Gene Ruffini

Routledge
Taylor & Francis Group
LONDON AND NEW YORK

First published 2003 by M.E. Sharpe

Published 2015 by Routledge
2 Park Square, Milton Park, Abingdon, Oxon OX14 4RN
711 Third Avenue, New York, NY 10017, USA

Routledge is an imprint of the Taylor & Francis Group, an informa business

Library of Congress Cataloging-in-Publication Data

Ruffini, Gene.
    Harry Van Arsdale Jr. : labor's champion / Gene Ruffini.
        p. cm.
    Includes bibliographical references and index.
    ISBN 0-7656-1044-2 (alk. paper)
        1. Van Arsdale, Harry, 1905–1986. 2. Labor unions—United States—Officials and
    employees—Biography. 3. Labor movement—United States—History—20th century.
    I. Title.

HD8073.V36 R84 2003
331.88'092—dc21
[B]   2002075859

ISBN 13: 9780765610447 (hbk)

Contents

Foreword

Simply to say that Harry was a labor leader is to overlook this remarkable man's wide interests.

His business card simply identified Harry as the business manager of Local 3 of the International Brotherhood of Electrical Workers, a major affiliate of the AFL-CIO. But Harry saw his role as the leader of Local 3's 30,000 members extending far beyond the statutory duty of unions to represent their members on wages, hours, and working conditions. Harry's concern included the total existence of their lives, their families, their housing, health, education, and retirement.

It also included the well-being of their employers. As a practical realist, Harry knew that the contractors could not provide the benefits he wanted Local 3's members to receive if they could not afford them. No wonder they responded generously to the demands he made of them.

Harry was also concerned about New York, the city in which his union's members lived. Every day, his secretary would give him a typewritten list of his appointments. They began at about 7 A.M. and continued well into the night on such matters as the way the city was being managed, the affairs of the many charitable organizations he supported, and the problems of unions affiliated with New York's Central Labor Council for which Harry was serving as president.

Harry introduced me to Bert Powers when his union was striking New York's newspapers. Together we spent days and nights assisting in the resolution of that 114-day strike. When President Kennedy denounced Powers in a nationally publicized press conference, Bert turned to Harry for advice, and, as a result, wisely responded by simply saying that he did not believe the president had been adequately informed.

Harry's interests extended far beyond the boundaries of our city. I was with him in London where he spoke about the four-hour day with British labor leaders who had yet to achieve the forty-hour week. But little did they know that this unusual proposal he had on the bargaining table with the electrical contractors in New York was part of his well-conceived plan to open the door to a major infusion of minority workers into the ranks of Local 3.

In Rome we hosted a dinner for Father Arupi, the leader of the Society of Jesus, with whom Harry participated in an extended discussion of race relations. Harry was equally at ease in our meeting with Israel's Prime Minister Golda Meir in Jerusalem.

Harry greatly admired Governor Nelson Rockefeller and their friendship was mutual. The governor had given Harry his private telephone number to use whenever he thought it necessary. Such an occasion arose shortly after the end of the crippling eleven-day subway and bus strike that began on January 1, 1966, Mayor John Lindsay's first day in office. But for Harry's intervention, the settlement might have come apart.

Michael J. Quill, the fiery leader of the Transport Workers Union, had died of a heart attack and Matthew Guinan, a thoughtful leader, had taken his place. Guinan immediately faced a major crisis. The settlement had been challenged by a taxpayer who claimed that it violated the Condon-Wadlin Act prohibiting workers who participated in a strike against a public agency from receiving a wage increase. The Supreme Court justice hearing the suit told the mayor that he had no choice but to set the settlement aside and the mayor relayed the news to Matthew Guinan. Another strike was out of the question. But what could Guinan do? He turned to Harry for help.

Harry quickly reached the governor on his private number and explained Guinan's dilemma. The governor respected Harry's concern and immediately had legislation prepared repealing retroactively that portion of Condon-Wadlin invalidating the wage increase. The state legislature passed the bill the same day and the city, thanks to Harry, was spared another transit crisis. Yes, indeed, Harry was a man for all seasons.

Theodore W. Kheel

Preface

As a reporter in New York working for a major newspaper, I often covered stories involving Harry Van Arsdale Jr. I knew him as the most powerful labor figure in the city; a man who was always active in key negotiations either to head off or settle strikes. These included work stoppages of extreme personal interest to me, such as strikes within the newspaper industry (in which I was one of the workers on the picket line). Once Van Arsdale became involved, I knew the dispute would soon be settled to the satisfaction of the strikers.

But I, like others, knew little of the man himself. He was a figure of the headlines or an image on the television tube, a voice on the radio, and a presence in the city like the Empire State Building, seen and appreciated. But the man behind the image was relatively unknown.

As I began to research this book, I found that Van Arsdale preferred it that way. He abhorred self-aggrandizement. He was modest and unassuming to a fault. Many tried to interview him or even to write his biography, but he demurred. Let the next guy shine, not me, was his motto. He just wanted to get the job done. He preferred to be just a worker in the field of labor organization, or, as he would have put it in his earlier days, "a woiker"—in the New York accent he never completely outgrew, although his self-education made him more scholarly than most.

Another part of the equation was his extreme wariness of the press, which as a rule, he considered to be in the service of big money interests inimical to labor.

Van Arsdale, as I came to learn, was unique as a labor leader. He shared the sense of altruism, dedication to humanity, toughness, and charity incumbent on all good labor leaders, but he went beyond this. His was a life of total devotion to the working man and woman. He served the interest of others so single-mindedly that people were in awe of him and his accomplishments. His work was not just an occupation. It was a calling.

He is such a legend that members of his home union, Local 3 of the International Brotherhood of Electrical Workers (IBEW), who knew him, speak his name with a special reverence. He is accorded the respect of a saint. That sounds like hyperbole, but it is not, because Van Arsdale did not just rebuild a union local: he created a genuine fraternity. And to him brotherhood was not just a term to describe fellow members. It had a deeper meaning to Van Arsdale. He lived to help those who needed help. It was a philosophy he imbued in his membership. He called upon them and they responded to help other unions in their disputes by picketing and by providing financial help or other necessities. In turn, the members felt a selfless loyalty to Van Arsdale because of everything he had done for them. In reconstructing Local 3, he sculpted what amounts to a workers' utopia for men and women of all races. He was a strong advocate of civil rights and counted A. Philip Randolph, Dr. Martin Luther King, Jr., and Bayard Rustin among his friends.

He not only provided good wages for the members of the various divisions within the Local but also responded to the members' needs for good, affordable housing by building the cooperative apartment complex of Electchester. He developed quality medical and dental care, comfortable pensions and annuities, and broad educational, cultural, and social programs.

He accomplished these gains by pioneering a unique alliance with management through the Joint Industry Board of the Electrical Industry of New York City (JIB) through which management and labor have formed a partnership to their mutual benefit. Management provides a fair wage and benefit package in return for a fair day's work, one of the credos of Van Arsdale. The JIB model has been studied and copied by other labor organizations around the nation and the world. It was an illustration of his belief that capitalists and workers are symbiotic by necessity and that workers can gain the most benefits by working cooperatively with employers. Van Arsdale, who had studied communism, was strongly against it because of the strictures it placed on workers' choices and individual freedoms. The model he had established with the JIB and the philosophies he had practiced with Local 3 of the IBEW, he carried over to the New York Central Labor Council (CLC) as its president from 1959 to 1986. As CLC president, he had not just one union to be concerned about, but scores of others, with more than a million members, and he worked tirelessly on their behalf as well. He became a confidante and friend to the powerful of his day and used his relationships to ensure fair settlements and fair treatment of employee and employer.

He could have worked to become president of the IBEW, or state or national president of the AFL-CIO, but titles and self-enhancement were not in his character. As a pragmatist, he felt he could do more for people and achieve tangible results within his native environment, which came to encompass the immensity of New York City.

His work ethic (and practice) astounded everyone who knew him. He managed on four or five hours of sleep, sometimes less. He was famous for calling people at two or three in the morning with thoughts, propositions, or requests for help. He was indefatigable in attending meetings and joining strikers on picket lines.

Although far from unsophisticated, he lived life almost as an ascetic. He did not smoke, and only on rare occasions did he take a drink. He lived extremely modestly. He had few suits. He had no automobile in later years, preferred to walk or take a subway, and exhorted his union officials to do the same. He had plain tastes and eschewed luxuries, adding to what amounted to a mystique of union brotherhood in a religious context with Van Arsdale as chief proselytizer.

This tempering of idealism with the realities of contract negotiations, this mixture of mammon and myth led Theodore Kheel, who knew Van Arsdale well as a friend and colleague, to suggest that the title of this book include the term—"pragmatic idealist." He was that and more.

A Tribute

John Fitzgerald Kennedy, Martin Luther King, and His Eminence Terrance Cardinal Cook were among his friends. Meany, Reuther, Shanker, and Quill were his contemporaries. Thomas Jefferson, Franklin Delano Roosevelt, and A. Philip Randolph were his heroes. His union was his life. He was a giant. I saw him on television; he always led the Labor Day parade and the men would yell, "Harry, Harry, Harry." He always called me lad, and I always called him grandpa. They say he was a visionary, yet he never took credit for anything. It was always his associates and the electrical contractors whom he thanked for contributing to so many of the wonderful programs he initiated.

He ascended from the streets of New York to a seat at the table. The captains of industry and banking were in awe of his stature. They did not just tolerate him, they sought his counsel. Chase Manhattan's David Rockefeller and his brother Nelson, New York's governor, Senator Jacob Javits, and Mayor Robert Wagner were all close associates. Labor's role in our city, the city he loved, was respected and Harry's integrity had everything to do with that.

Harry's life was full and satisfying; he accomplished so much for the people he served. He taught me that, "the only purpose of the union was to serve the membership," and they loved him. Helping those less fortunate was his creed. The plight of working men and women was what drove him. His compassion was evident as he marveled at a child's joy while attending the union's summer camp at Bayberry Land or as he shared in the pain of the PATCO worker who took his life over his indebtedness after having been permanently replaced by Ronald Reagan for daring to go on strike.

The mid-1980s were difficult times for the Trade Union movement, and Harry was dying. Labor was being challenged, there were strikes at

J.P. Stephens, Greyhound, and TWA. He cautioned us about those who strove for a union-free environment, saying, "They employed the best minds money could buy." Harry would always remind us of what was important, "What chance could a worker have for a better life without an education?" he would ask. He compelled his members to continue their education as he negotiated scholarships and educational benefits, and ultimately established a Labor College. Harry encouraged people to persevere and to achieve goals that were unthinkable, and they did. Harry was proud of their accomplishments and he let them know.

This book is about a special person—one who is truly missed, and someone I hope you will get to know in reading this book. For those of us who did know him, we take comfort that his story is finally being told and that maybe, just maybe, more people will take his advice. He posed a challenge to all of us, "To join the human race," as he did, and, for this, we are most certainly better off today. Thank you, grandpa, thank you, Harry Van Arsdale Jr. You truly are labor's champion.

Christopher Erikson
Assistant Business Manager
Local Union No. 3
International Brotherhood of Electrical Workers

Acknowledgments

This work could not have been completed without the help of many. I must thank all the members of the Harry Van Arsdale Jr. Memorial Committee for allowing me to work on the book, and, in particular, members of the book search committee who included: Hy Greenblatt, Chris Erikson, Brian McLaughlin, Vincent McElroen, and Dr. Jerry Finkel. Thanks also to Thomas Van Arsdale, Madeline Van Arsdale, and Larry Jacobson for their approval of the project. A special thanks is also due to Barry Lipton for introducing me to all of them. Invaluable research assistance was provided by Lizette Aquinaldo, Janet Greene, Debra E. Bernhardt, Dr. Lois Gray, Laurie Finkelstein, Ted Jacobson, and Dr. Bernard Rosenberg. I also want to acknowledge the fine work of the Apprentice Committee in 1973 chaired by Robert Oberstein. The interviews conducted by Dr. Julius C.C. Edelstein and Renee Epstein were also integral to fleshing out the portrait of Van Arsdale. Thanks also to Mary Jamison for her liaison work. And special gratitude is reserved for all those who gave of their time to be interviewed. A special thanks must be given posthumously to Armand D'Angelo who pushed this project from the start, and, in spirit, from beyond the grave.

Harry Van Arsdale Jr.

1

From the Revolutionary War to Hell's Kitchen

The morning of Tuesday, November 25, 1783, was cold, crisp, and bright in New York City, a bracing day for marches, speeches, and joyous, even raucous, celebration. It was Evacuation Day, when the British were finally to leave New York in defeat.[1]

And as the British were to leave at noon, the Continental Army, under the command of Major General George Knox, was to advance into the vacated areas. The procedures had been carefully worked out by the British commander, Sir Guy Carleton, and General George Washington during the spring of 1783. But the disgruntled British had a nasty and petty surprise for the victorious colonists, and it delayed Washington's triumphant entry into the city.

As had been agreed, the British had dismantled Fort George at the tip of Manhattan, removing cannon and ammunition and disabling those guns they could not carry away, but they had spitefully not taken down their flag, even though this had been part of the agreement. It still flew defiantly on a staff over the fort.

"On a closer view it was found that the flag had been nailed to the staff, the halyards taken away, and the pole itself besmeared with grease, obviously to prevent or hinder the removal of the emblem of royalty, and the raising of the Stars and Stripes," wrote historian James Riker.

Many tried and failed to climb up the slippery pole. Guns were fired at the flag in an attempt to bring it down, but that too was unsuccessful. Happening on the scene was John Van Arsdale, an ancestor of Harry Van Arsdale Jr. and grandfather of historian Riker, and his exploits that day were to furnish his descendants with a story they still tell. They are justly proud to be members of a family that not only extends back into the genesis of American history but also boasts an authentic hero.[2]

Van Arsdale had served with distinction in the war against the British, enlisting at the age of 19. He had fought in Canada, been wounded and taken prisoner in the battle of Fort Montgomery, suffered in foul British dungeons and a prison ship in New York before his release, and then had gone on to serve in several Indian campaigns. He was in New York that day as the captain of a packet boat following his discharge from the Continental Army at the beginning of the year.

Van Arsdale tried to climb the pole sailor-fashion, but failed. Then it was proposed that cleats be nailed to the pole. Onlookers ran to Peter Goelet's hardware store in Hanover Square and returned with boards and cleats, which they proceeded to nail onto the staff. Van Arsdale got up a short distance with a line to which the Stars and Stripes were attached.

Finally, a ladder was secured, enabling him to reach the top of the staff, tear down the British flag, and install the halyards that allowed the American flag to fly over the scene. Even General Washington heard of this exploit and joined with others to contribute money when a hat was passed to reward the young hero.

"Though taken quite aback, Van Arsdale modestly accepted the gift, with a protest at being rewarded for so trivial an act. But the contributors were of another opinion; he had accomplished what was thought impracticable and the occasion and the emergency made his success peculiarly gratifying to all present."[3]

After his soon-to-be-legendary deed, the young Van Arsdale returned to his New Windsor, New York home in Orange County, and to his wife of six months, Mary (Polly) Crawford Van Arsdale, the daughter of David Crawford, a minister in Goshen, New York. They subsequently moved to New York City where John continued his seafaring trade as a captain. He had another run-in with the British during the War of 1812 when they tried to capture his ship outside Mamaroneck Harbor on September 17, 1813. But he evaded them and as bullets flew around him, shouted to the enemy to "fire away"— it was not the first time they had wasted powder on him![4] His son David served in the army in the War of 1812. John died in 1836 at the age of 81 in his Manhattan home at 135 Delancy Street.

Thus, the family's roots in New York—both in New York City and upstate—go back to the seventeenth century, and their remains are buried in cemeteries in Montgomery and Bullville.[5]

It was Harry's grandfather and grandmother who returned his branch of the family to New York City at the turn of the century. Alanson Van Arsdale and his wife, Margaret (née Daugherty), began a wholesale milk and cream business in the city, operating out of a house they purchased at 202 West 40th Street. They advertised "Milk in Bottles A Specialty."[6] Margaret remained a country woman at heart, never forgetting her bucolic roots and striving when she could to resurrect them to soften the concrete edges of the city. She had a love for horses and drove a sulky in races on land now occupied by Yankee Stadium.

They had nine children, of whom five survived: Willis (born 1873), Bertha (1878), Harry Sr. (1883), Alanson (1887), and George (1894).

Harry Sr. married Kathryn Plunkett in 1903. Their first child, Edward, did not survive. Harry Jr.—Henry Joseph Van Arsdale, according to the baptismal records of the Sacred Heart of Jesus Church—was born on November 23, 1905, and a year or so later his sister Abbie was born. By that time, Harry Sr. and Kathryn and Bertha and her husband, Charles Lawrason, were living in a building in Hell's Kitchen.[7]

The area in which Harry Jr. spent his early years was tough and hardscrabble, and its polyglot population and economic deprivation were major factors in fashioning his character. Harry Van Arsdale Jr. would always champion the kind of people he grew up with. There is a certain cachet for some in saying that they were raised in Hell's Kitchen, making them quintessential New Yorkers whose strength was tempered on the hot streets within a crucible of adversity. Most of the residents were hard-working folk for whom hardship was a spur to achievement and the respectable celebrity they coveted.[8] But poverty also breeds crime and rebellion for others, and those aspects, exaggerated by lurid newspaper accounts, helped to paint the neighborhood as unsavory, despite the fact that most of its residents were law-abiding. As it is in other economically deprived neighborhoods, the criminal element preyed on themselves or strangers, or exported their talents, while the honest people kept to their own circles and tried to help each other get through the hard times. The poor have a great sense of community and commonality, and it is this aspect of cooperation that helped, one can believe, to inspire unionism. In other words, each working together can achieve more than one alone and a community can soften the rough times.

Ironically, the area that became known as Hell's Kitchen was originally called *Bloemendael* or "Vale of Flowers" by early Dutch settlers in the city. It was an area of streams and grassy meadows but then came the influx of European immigrants. By the start of the Civil War, the population of Hell's Kitchen had soared to more than 350,000. With population pressure came turmoil.

At the turn of the century, Hell's Kitchen was the home of many gangs, many of them small—barely more than a circle of friends who gave themselves fanciful names to improve their social standing—but others more formidable and dangerous, one such being a gang called the Gophers, so-called because of their propensity for hiding in basements. A legendary story has it that the Gopher leader "One Lung" Curran blackjacked a policeman to steal his coat and give it to his girlfriend who had complained that she needed a coat for the winter. Other gang members, goaded by their chilly female companions, did the same with other officers so that coatless cops were common in the area. Notorious gangster Owen "Owney the Killer" Madden was a Gopher. The gang became known as the Arsenal Gang later to give way to the Westies, a tough Irish gang that kept things percolating in Hell's Kitchen in the 1970s.[9]

The Reverend Philip Carey, a good friend of Harry who was active in the labor movement, tells a story about Monsignor Joseph F. Mooney, chancellor of the Sacred Heart Parish during Van Arsdale's youth, that gives a sense of the neighborhood's character. "He gave his report to the parishioners and said, 'Oh, we had a very good year. Nineteen were ordained at Dunwoodie (a seminary in neighboring Westchester County) and nineteen were executed at Sing Sing."[10]

Irish were the predominant ethnic group when Harry was a child, although Germans, Italians, and Poles were also amply represented. Many of the men worked as longshoremen or in the slaughterhouses, breweries, and stables in the area. They lived within acres of tenements with black iron fire escapes. These tenements were usually of the old law type, mostly of the "railroad" variety with one room strung out after another in linear style. The front door opened into the kitchen and there was a series of small bedrooms on either end, one of which led to the parlor. From the parlor one saw a vista of tenements and crowded streets with cobblestone gutters, worn blue-slate sidewalks, and stretches of red brick laid during the Civil War. It is likely that the Van Arsdales lived in such an apartment.[11]

The loose boundaries of Hell's Kitchen were from 23rd to 59th Streets and Eighth Avenue to the Hudson River. In Harry's youth, Eighth Avenue was noted for its movie theaters, particularly Ye Olde Drury Lane, the Arena, and the Gem. Piano players would tinkle classical or popular melodies under the mute screens while ushers marched up and down the aisles spraying perfume from squirt guns to neutralize the pungent odors of some patrons.

Ninth Avenue was marked by the black and rusting girders of the elevated train. The noise from the trains, along with that of the horse-drawn trolley cars (on every avenue except Eleventh) raised the noise level of the neighborhood to the point where housewives, making purchases from horse-and-wagon peddlers located at the curbs, had to shout to make their orders heard.[12]

A freight railroad ran along Eleventh Avenue, making it difficult for children, perhaps including Harry's sister, to reach Clinton Park, a playground that opened in 1905. Adventurous boys climbed over and through lines of parked freight cars to reach the playground. Another, more dangerous activity, hitching rides on moving freight cars, sometimes resulted in injury or death.[13]

Harry's father worked in the electrical industry, then in its infancy. By all accounts, he was a feisty and independent man and a fighter for the rights of the working man, characteristics he was to keep all his life and pass on to his son. Harry Sr. soon became involved in the labor movement and the organization of electrical workers. What was to become Local 3 of the International Brotherhood of Electrical Workers reportedly originated in 1887 with a group of journeymen who met secretly at the home of the mother of William A. Hogan, an electrician who became known as the "Grand Old Man" of the local.[14] They formed the Electrical Mechanical Wiremen's Union and affiliated with the Knights of Labor as Local Assembly 5468. Samuel Gompers was then busy building the American Federation of Labor (AFL) and Local Assembly 5468 moved into its camp.

It was a stormy time for the young Harry Sr. and his family. There was constant internal and external strife in the local and on the union scene in general. Although members of Local Assembly 5468 (LA5468), the forerunner of Local Union 3, attended the convention that established the National Brotherhood of Electrical Workers (NBEW) in 1891, they did not remain members because of a dispute over payments. They operated independently as the Brotherhood of Electrical Workers, LA5468, Local 3, AFL, and, as such, signed their first contract with the Electrical Contractors Association of New York City a year later.

It was a time of depression in the nation and the agreement reflected that. It merely maintained standards that had been established in 1891 that called for $3 a day. Working hours were nine hours on weekdays and eight hours on Saturday. The union was so weak, however, that it could not even get that renewed in 1895, and wages returned to their lower rate.

The next six years were scarred by strikes, lockouts, conflicts with company unions, associations and disassociations with other units of electrical trade workers, and jurisdictional disputes with three other rival unions in the city established by the NBEW, which was still smarting from the snub Local 3 had inflicted at the 1891 convention. It was not until 1901 that the NBEW softened its position and allowed Local 3 to become part of the AFL national organization.[15]

And that was just in time for another turbulent era for unions that later was to have a severe effect on the Van Arsdales. In 1902, in the Danbury (Connecticut) Hatters case, employers sued a striking labor union for alleged conspiracy to restrain trade. Restraint of trade had been banned by the Sherman Anti-Trust Act of 1890—originally aimed at businesses, but now being broadened to include unions. The case itself was not decided until 1908, when the U.S. Supreme Court ruled in favor of the employers. However, the willingness of the courts to try the case encouraged other employers to increase their attacks on unions.

This is where the Van Arsdales and others within Local 3 entered the picture. In 1904, the year before the birth of Harry Jr., the New York electrical contractors initiated a citywide lockout of Local 3 members. Not one of the 1,800 men then in the Local was to be hired. The lockout lasted until 1907—at which time another financial panic added to the burden of the beleaguered Van Arsdales and other working families.

Harry Jr. recalled that his father bitterly told him later that only 400 men stayed with the union and refused to give up their cards during that period.

"My Dad happened to be one of the men who remained loyal for the whole 33 months. They could tell you what fellow stuck it out one year and who stuck it out a year and a half. I recall when we had our first scroll celebration at Madison Square Garden; it was Old Timers Day [and some said] 'why that fellow gave up after two years and I can't understand why you are honoring a man who gave up after two years.'"[16]

The stalwart, who by strength of will, energy, oratory, the granting of favors, and just extraordinary leadership ability, held the 400 diehards together was William A. Hogan, who had by this time in 1903 become Local 3's financial secretary. It was a time of extreme hardship for Harry Sr. and his family. Times were so bad that Harry Sr. had to stuff cardboard into his shoes. His grandmother gave him an overcoat so he would not be without one in the winter.[17]

Finally, facing the need for skilled electricians, the employers softened and gave some work to Local 3 members, but, reluctant to lose face after ordering a boycott of the Local, they turned a blind eye and hired them under the aegis of Local 534 (actually Local 3 sandwiched between different numbers). It was not until 1917, when America was on the brink of entering World War I, that the Local was allowed to return to its proper name and work out a contract with the employers whose animosities were softened by time. Nevertheless, the employers still bargained for and won an open shop, forcing Local 3 members to work alongside nonunion members.[18]

However, Harry Sr. never lost his militancy and outspokenness in the union cause. And that continued to cost him and his family dearly. Harry Jr. recalled: "I remember when I was still in school, my dad would come home and throw his tool bag under the bed. He had been fired again for union activity. My mother would go into another room and cry and on my next trip to the butcher or the grocer I would have to notify them that my pop was out of work again. Then when dad would find another job, we would start paying off the bills. Many times before the bills were paid, he would be out of work again."[19]

A good friend of the elder Van Arsdale was William McSpedon. "Many's a beer we had in Max's after work or when we weren't working," he said. "He was not 100 percent, but 1,000 percent union. If you had a hat on that was non-union, he would go over and tear it up on you. And he could fight. He didn't take any bull from anybody. And he used to call Harry 'the kid.' 'The kid is upstairs,' he would say." [20]

McSpedon also had fond memories of William Hogan: "One of the kindest, greatest men that God ever made," he said. "He helped fellows that were losing their homes, that couldn't pay their dues. And Bill dug in his own pocket [to help them]. He was a father to everybody. They called him Pop Hogan. What a wonderful, wonderful man."[21]

Thomas Van Arsdale, Harry's son who was destined to succeed him one day as business manager of Local 3, relates that his grandfather took pride in his ability to install lead cables, handling it in such a way that it looked like smooth conduit. His grandfather often had to sit in a boatswain's chair to place the cable into shafts.

Thomas also gave insights into his grandfather that indicated how difficult it must have been for him to take charity for his family. He would not, for instance, accept unemployment insurance payments when he was out of work in later years. "He never even applied," Thomas said. "He would say, 'I'm okay. I don't need it.'"[22]

The senior Van Arsdale also had a high regard for education and books. Harry Jr. recalled: "My father went to electrical school on his own and when I got his books, there was a great deal in them about gas lighting. There was a time when the electrician's biggest job [was in converting gas lighting fixtures and outlets to ones utilizing electricity]."[23]

In many ways, Harry Jr. had been much like other youngsters in the neighborhood, playing street games or hanging out with his friends. He also liked sports, especially boxing. Nevertheless, there was a discernible difference between Harry Jr. and his peers. He was a frequent visitor to the Columbus Branch of the New York Public Library at 742 Tenth Avenue, opened in 1909 at 52nd Street, and he was brighter than his companions. He was quick to grasp facts, to see the "big picture," and quick to act on what he saw. As he grew to manhood, he displayed an ability to organize and lead others, so much so that his peers called him "the manager." "Where's the manager? Where's the manager? We used to say," recalled his cousin Chris Plunkett, who grew up in the same neighborhood.[24]

In his early school years, Harry Jr. attended the Sacred Heart of Jesus School on West 52nd Street where discipline was maintained by tough Catholic brothers and nuns not averse to cracking a student across the knuckles with a ruler. The education was also rigorous. "All [students] remembered that reading writing and arithmetic were drilled into them and agreed that such preparation gave them a sound basis for further schooling."[25]

He transferred to Public School 5 at 141st Street and Edgecomb Avenue and the Van Arsdales lived nearby at 220 Bradhurst Avenue. Harry Jr. graduated in 1920. The school authorities were evidently unconcerned about mixing church and state in a public institution inasmuch as the scriptures were read to the young graduates followed by the singing of the hymn "Holy, Holy, Holy."

Faced with his family's poverty, Harry Jr. suggested to his father that he be allowed to go to work and add to the family's income. His father resisted that idea, particularly because Harry Jr. had shown himself to be a superior student. In later years, Harry Jr. was to recount a story about his father and school. He said: "This great man said, 'Son, while I have these two arms'— and they were quite some arms in those days—'you go to school and I will take care of work.'"[26]

Harry won entry to one of the most prestigious secondary schools in the city: Townsend Harris High School. Considered equivalent to the Boston Latin School, one of the top schools in the nation at the time, it was meant to be a preparatory school for college. Two degrees were offered, one in the arts and the other in science.

Both degree programs included classes in mathematics, English, history, drawing or manual training, physics, physiology, and oral English. However, those who opted for the arts degree were obliged to take classes in Latin, Greek, French, or German. Students in the science curriculum were required to take only French and German.[27] It is unclear in which curriculum Harry Jr. was enrolled, but science would have been in keeping with his practical bent.

However, he was not destined to graduate from Townsend Harris. In 1921, after he had been in school for two years, another financial depression struck and the family was once more in dire financial straits. Harry was thus able to overcome his father's objections and left school at 16 to go to work to help support his family. He did, however, continue his education in night school while hoping to enter Local 3, but because his father opposed the leadership in Local 3, Harry Jr. was not allowed to become a member. Instead, he worked in a variety of other jobs, holding a position in the Museum of Natural History, working as a stock boy at Wanamakers Department Store, and then as an apprentice in the sound studio unit of the Western Electric Company.

In 1922, he married Mary (Molly) Casey. Within six years she had presented him with four children: Harry Jr. found himself with a large family to support at an extraordinarily young age. He took whatever work he could find. And then he learned through a friend that Local 3 was opening its books and he went before the membership committee to try to gain entrance. Van Arsdale recalled:

> There was great friction in the union. There were factions. They spent all their energy from my observation . . . fighting each other rather than closing ranks and using that energy to have the employers understand that they were entitled to a better life. So, I went down and one fellow said, "Are you the son of Harry Van Arsdale?" And I thought, Oh, boy, there's the end of my chances because I knew they were on different sides of the factions . . . [but] they all had respect for each other even though they differed. So I was given what they called a temporary card. And you could find a job [but only if] you went from job to job. You stood outside and whenever they needed men, they called whoever they would like to have. If you had a temporary card, you were allowed to work providing there was nobody with a regular helper's [apprentice's] card . . . but if a helper came by he would replace anybody with a temporary card and you went looking for another job.[28]

Van Arsdale officially joined Local 3 in 1925. His career as a union activist, nurtured by his feisty and forthright father, had begun.

2

Making His Mark

Early Struggles in Local Union 3

By all accounts, the union that Harry Van Arsdale Jr. joined on August 13, 1925, as an electrician's helper (after passing the helper's examination on May 1, 1925) was a labor scandal. Along with other building trades unions in New York City, the Local came under the close scrutiny of the Lockwood Committee, a state investigative panel established in 1921. It found that the Local's finances were in a shambles with almost nonexistent bookkeeping. There were three cashiers receiving money but no one was responsible for keeping track of it.[1]

The Local president would receive packets of cash from the treasurer and place them in a safe, and, not surprisingly, some would be unaccounted for. Because of this, treasurer William Hogan was indicted and jailed. He was charged with stealing $21,675 from the union between August 1918 and July 1921. It was alleged that Hogan had deposited an average of $11,000 annually in his bank in 1919, 1920, and 1921, and had constructed a $13,000 home in Mount Vernon, New York. Local 3 raised a $19,000 defense fund, but it failed to save Hogan from conviction. He was sentenced to serve from eighteen months to three years in Sing Sing prison in Ossining, New York. But many in the union thought that Hogan was just a victim of the Lockwood Committee witch-hunt singled out for blame. The support he enjoyed within the union was shown when he was once again elected financial secretary after his prison term was over. And during that whole time he had also continued as treasurer of the IBEW.

Hiring practices were also criticized. "Even for a full-fledged card-carrying journeyman there was no guarantee he would be hired when he shaped up at the job site. The jobs were handed out by the foreman on the spot and all the old timers agree that race and religious affiliation governed."[2]

IBEW vice president Howell H. Broach said:

> Each faction had a club—social, political, religious or fraternal. The Jews had their Jewish Welfare Club, the Catholics their Anchor Club, the Masons their Square Club. Then came the Triple Club, etc. All striving to elect their candidates. All set up in hostile camps. All pulling and tugging at the heart of the organization. Each clamoring for its share of the spoils. Men got their jobs through the strongest clubs. The Business agents passed out jobs at the club meetings. Favoritism, clubism, ruled.[3]

The clubs divided the city with each staking out a borough largely its own. Catholics—primarily Irish—prevailed in Manhattan. Masons predominated in Queens and Jews made their mark in Brooklyn and the Bronx. "It was very difficult for the Jewish boys to operate in Local 3," recalled Joseph Jacobson.[4]

Moreover, helpers undercut journeymen in gaining work by offering to do a journeyman's job for a helper's pay. The practice was so beneficial that some helpers never sought an upgrade because they were employed more steadily as they were. They became "permanent boys."[5]

Another Local practice that troubled the Lockwood committee was the selling of "privilege cards" to nonunion men at $2.50 a week for a journeyman and $1 for a helper. This was the reason the committee offered to explain why the Local had a membership of only 3,800 in an industry employing 12,000.

In 1926, the IBEW took action against the Local. Vice President Broach was assigned to take custody of Local 3, superseding its officers. Charges were also filed against the top officers and they were thrown out of their positions. Broach moved to New York to take personal charge as the Local's overseer, and he ran the Local's affairs for the next six years, operating out of an IBEW office a few blocks from the Local's headquarters.

The IBEW had picked the right man for the job. Broach was brilliant, self-righteous, indefatigable, and ruthless, and he was to have a great effect on the life of Harry Van Arsdale Jr. A native of Beaumont, Texas, Broach entered the trade in 1906 when he was only 13 and quickly began a campaign to educate himself by reading extensively on a broad range of subjects. Politically ambitious, he set his sights early on rising within the union, and, with that in mind, studied parliamentary procedure and practiced oratory with marbles in his mouth, in the manner of ancient Greek orators, as a way to sharpen his diction.[6]

He soon became a national organizer for the IBEW and its vice president in 1920. He had a strong hand in a number of strikes, including telephone operators and mechanics in Minneapolis-St. Paul and Cleveland, and utility workers in Des Moines, Milwaukee, and Minneapolis.

But New York became the site of his shining hour. Here, in part, is how he described what he found in a report made to the International convention in Miami in 1929. His tone was that of an evangelical preacher berating the works of the devil. And in his fervent and even vitriolic vision, he painted a vivid picture of a corrupt landscape.

> Here we found a situation that challenged the very principles upon which the Brotherhood of Electrical Workers was founded. One can search the entire history of labor organizations in this country, or any other, but would fail to find any situation that was so disgraceful or which paralleled that existing in New York.
>
> Here we found a Local Union whose officers were positively rotten. They would do almost anything for $10. Service came last. Politics first. Everything was measured by the political yardstick. An election of officers resembled a day at the circus. Streamers, signs, banners, barkers—all blazed forth in the meeting halls. Campaign managers were selected. Souvenirs were distributed by the candidates on jobs and at meetings in their mad campaign for votes. . . .
>
> The union was completely demoralized. Meetings ran wild, lasting until one and two in the morning. Dice shooters jammed the aisles, drinking went on freely, drunks played merrily—all while the meetings were in progress. Little business could be transacted. Order and discipline were unknown. The Local Union was shaken to its foundation. The city was wide open. Conditions were shot. As a typical example, we found at 315 West 26th Street, 20 electrical contractors all in one and the same building and only four were union.
>
> Men worked below the wage scale. Both union and nonunion men worked in the same shops and on the same jobs. Union shops, having an agreement with the Local, were found employing two crews—a union and a nonunion crew—all with the knowledge and consent of the officers. Union men roughed in the jobs. Nonunion men did the finishing work.
>
> Nonunion shops that had no union men in them at all, and who never had any agreement with the organization, had their correct names and addresses in the printed Directory of Electrical Contractors employing members of the Local Union. This was a directory in use and of current date, and was compiled, printed and distributed by the local officers. A shop-to-shop check of this directory disclosed that only two out of every ten employers listed therein employed Union members exclusively. There were practically as many contractors in the territory as members in the Union. Its membership totaled 5,124.

When the nonunion shops obtained strictly union jobs the Business Agents furnished them our members to do the work, while the nonunion employer continued working his nonunion men on other jobs. In other instances, nonunion employees were allowed to shift their nonunion crews to union jobs on Saturday afternoons and Sundays before the return of our members on Monday morning and nothing was done about it. A ten dollar bill left in the cabinet box usually turned the trick.

Union shops owned and operated nonunion shops—and vice versa. Nonunion contractors were allowed to continue working their nonunion men on strictly union jobs, while our members walked the streets.

A Business Agent would go on a job, as in Brooklyn, obtain the cards of our members on this job, then rent them out to a nonunion contractor who would take his crew and use these cards to work on a strictly Union job over in the Bronx. Fixtures were hung on a piece work basis at the rate of 50 cents a fixture. Instances were found where wiring was done at so much an outlet by our members, also where members would contract with their employers to do all the labor on the job on a lump sum basis.

Men bought their way into the organization as they would buy tickets to a show and what a show it was. Truck drivers, mail clerks, soda jerkers, night watchmen, locksmiths, sewing machine mechanics, janitors, pool room owners, all went dashing through. Such men passed into the organization.

Helpers were brought in at the rate of almost four to every one journeyman admitted. There was a ratio of one helper to each journeyman in the shop. In addition, one apprentice was allowed to each shop which had five journeymen and five helpers.

Journeymen were forced to loaf while helpers worked. That's why helpers did not want to become journeymen. Often a journeyman had both a helper and an apprentice working with him. Friends of friends, friends of anybody's friends, all flowed into the organization. These helpers received little or no schooling or training whatever. They were all paid a flat rate of $7.00 a day, regardless of the time spent in the business. The resultant load on the industry was terrific. The effect on the Union was disastrous.

Helpers ran wild. They attended all meetings and voted on all journeyman's questions. They practically controlled. Officers and politicians feared [them] and catered to them. There were as many helpers as journeymen. All had votes.

Boys 18 and 19 years of age made speeches at leisure, telling how things should be done. The helpers' bloc sat as in a permanent grandstand before which all the politicians would parade. Men seeking office appeared to go mad and made all sorts of silly, ridiculous statements and impossible promises to helpers in a desperate attempt to gain their votes.

The organization was a splendid training ground for "orators," communists, nuts and phrase makers of all sorts. Anyone with an idea or bellyache had the floor. "Democracy" was the cry and they were drunk and staggering with their particular brand of democratic dope.

The International had plenty of evidence. We pleaded with the Local officers again and again to attempt to correct conditions. We offered to aid them. We gave them every chance. But all in vain. Charges were then filed by me against them before the International Executive Council in Washington. They refused to appear for trial. They were expelled.

The doors to meetings of the Local Union were closed to them. They refused to turn over the property of the organization and tried to continue to function. Records were burnt and destroyed. They surrounded the headquarters of the Union with police and refused to allow auditors to enter. They called upon the courts to aid them. They obtained numerous injunctions. They started numerous suits. They made numerous efforts to have receivers appointed. They remained seated in the Building Trades Council.

All their injunctions and suits were based and obtained on untruthful affidavits and later when called upon to appear in person and support their claims before a referee appointed by the Supreme Court to hear and determine the issues, they refused to appear. They dared not face examination. In his decision, Mr. Justice Black stated: "These men did not see fit to appear and deny, exclaim or excuse the conduct complained of."

Their friendly police raided the New York office of the International every few days, hoping to discourage and drive us from the city. Every contemptible scheme imaginable was tried to block us in our efforts to cleanse and rebuild the organization. We had a job to do. We had a responsibility we could not escape and we refused to "get out."

But critics, of which there were many, charged that Broach's methods were so draconian that he was called "Little Caesar." Broach's apparent Calvinistic horror at the misadventures he found in Local 3 still did not deter him from calling on Hogan to help him in cleansing the Local. Broach also saw the New York situation as a lever he could use in strengthening his ambition to become president of the IBEW, some said.[7]

In the meantime, young Harry Van Arsdale was making his voice heard in the Local. He had a strong, fervent belief in unionism because of the influence of his father and his father's good friend, William Hogan, with whom the senior Van Arsdale had long discussions about the state of the union in Hogan's kitchen.[8]

A worker has no chance without a union. He has a little chance if he has a union and he has a better chance if it's a good union. But without a union, he has no chance. Now there are a lot of our members that do not realize that; they do not understand that. . . . I was very fortunate because I worked with a lot of older men who were involved in a lot of the early struggles of labor. And they used to coach myself and other young fellows. And they were not intellectuals and they had not been to college, but they had been involved in struggles in different parts of the country and they would tell you about them.[9]

And their whole message was: "Build your union strong. Build your union strong." I remember one of them I idolized and he told me: "There are only two things I ever pray for: Hills to climb and strength to climb them." [10] And lots of times when you go up against impossible situations— you couldn't learn more than that. Hills to climb and strength to climb them was the training to know how to overcome an obstacle. He also quoted a former New York City Central Labor Council treasurer, William Bowe, as saying: "A quitter never wins. A winner never quits."

Joseph Jacobson recalls that Harry became quite vociferous during union meetings as the leader of those rank and filers who were unhappy with the union's shortcomings, including its cliques, clubs, shape-ups and other questionable hiring practices. Van Arsdale earned the affectionate nickname "the kid," a reference as much to his age as to his combativeness and a reflection that he was the militant son of a stalwart father who had also dubbed him "the kid."

Van Arsdale also was critical of the cavalier attitude taken by some of the union members who saw the meetings as an opportunity for revelry, mischief, and pompous speechmaking, which stalled meaningful action.

When I first went to a union meeting, you went every Thursday; you went from 8 P.M. [and] they amended the laws so that the meeting had to be over by 11 p.m. [because often] they went on till midnight or 1 A.M. as everybody made his own speech.

And during those years, there would be a crap game outside of quite some size and then when a vote was being taken on some occasions, they'd stop the crap game and come in and vote, then go back to the crap game. There were some fellows who thought the union meeting was the place to come when they were hilarious and drank more than they should have. Incidences like that had a long tradition which had to be turned around. And with the help of a great many serious minded people, it was.[11]

He had also earned the respect of supporters not only as an orator and battler for reform but also as a skilled craftsman. Still employed by the Western Electric Company, he had become an expert installer of telephone machine switching equipment, and, when sound movies began to supplant silent films, Van Arsdale's talents were of special value to theater owners keen to be among the first to install the new technology in their auditoriums. Van

Arsdale's base salary then was $66 a week, but overtime often increased his pay to more than $200 a week.

Meanwhile, he became an admirer and champion of Broach. Broach was unstinting in his praise for himself in outlining his achievements in his 1929 report:

> Today this Union—now the largest in our International Brotherhood and one of the very largest in America—operates, amazing as it may sound, without internal politics and red tape. There are more enmeshments, no trading, no bickerings, no "grandstanding" or theorizing. Popularity contests, ballyhoo and wild scrambles for office have gone into the dead past. Helpers are not allowed to attend meetings or do any voting. They are brought together every two months for instruction and for educational purposes only. Meetings are orderly, short and businesslike. Everything is systematized and today the organization operates much the same as any successful business corporation.
>
> From a corrupt, demoralized, disorganized and floundering organization living in the dead past, with its officers going around like bats in the darkness, from a slow-moving, cumbersome and irresponsible organization, seething in politics and turmoil, it has become, I believe, one of the most modern labor unions of our times. Labor students and historians agree on this. Though much remains to be done, this local Union is now certainly one of the most responsible, powerful and respected labor organizations in America, operating smoothly, quickly and efficiently. . . .
>
> It is an institution of considerable size, one of nearly 8,000 members. . . . The Union has its own five story office building at 130 East 16th Street, Manhattan. It has a branch office in Brooklyn . . . the headquarters are modern and operate as such.[12]
>
> A private telephone switchboard with twenty trunk lines and numerous extensions is operated by an experienced operator. She also serves as an information girl. Formerly there were two telephones. The one upstairs was used to conduct a betting pool in baseball. Certified public accountants audit, examine, supervise and direct the keeping of all records. No dead wood, no relatives of members are employed. Only trained clerks, secretaries, officers and trained employees and assistants function throughout the various offices.
>
> The internal clubs are through. There are no more streamers, signs, banners, barkers or literature. All election literature of any nature is forbidden. The last two annual elections, held with the utilization of voting machines, were the most orderly and businesslike ever known in the history of the organization. Not a single piece of election literature, cards, handbills or anything else appears. . . .

In New York City today one never hears of both union and nonunion men working together in our field. No longer do we hear anything about "two-crew" shops. Our members do all the work on the job, both roughing and finishing. No longer do we hear of any of our men working below the union scale or on a piece work basis. One never hears that a union shop is interested in owning or operating a nonunion shop, or vice versa. No longer can truck drivers, soda clerks, sewing machine artists, umbrella makers or locksmiths buy their way into [the] organization. The doors are not closed, but each man must prove his qualifications.

This Local Union has jurisdiction over all of Greater New York, including the five boroughs and Nassau and Suffolk Counties, with a combined population of approximately 7 million. Its jurisdiction covers 1,494 square miles. The jurisdiction of our Chicago Local 134 is less in size by 561 square miles. . . .

There is a field staff of 19 Business Agents covering and patrolling the large territory under the direction of the Business Manager's office. The Business Agents are all furnished automobiles by the organization and are allowed a fixed expense account for repair, garage and upkeep. They are required to report to headquarters by telephone four times a day.

The Local Union has a business manager. He is elected for a period of three years—but provisions are made for his removal at any time his conduct and actions warrant it. He is held solely responsible to the organization for results in the field. The Business Manager operates the same as the head of any modern business institution.

He makes his own appointments of an Assistant Business Manager, of Assistant Business Agents and office assistants, as the head of a business corporation does. His appointments must be confirmed by majority voice of the Union. The assistants are held solely responsible to the Business Manager and he may discharge them at once, without notice to the Union.

Retaining their positions depends entirely on conforming to rules, on their conduct and on efficient results obtained. Changes in the staff have been made in an effort to get the best results possible for the money spent.

The Business Manager's office deals with all complaints and disputes of various kinds in the field, brought or telephoned in by members, employers, builders or anyone else. This central office makes all agreements with and handles all situations involving employers. Interference by the President, Executive Board or any other officer or member is strictly forbidden by law. No officer or member can inject himself into such matters. Each officer has his own duties and powers clearly defined in the bylaws. . . .

Under the present Business Manager system, the Agent must be on the job, conform to certain rules and be a business-getter rather than a vote getter. He can have no interest in getting votes. He must get results. . . .

> The officers and agents are required to co-operate effectively and work in complete harmony, regardless of their likes or dislikes for each other. Petty quarreling or quibbling is not permitted. No fighting or fussing or breach of discipline or rules is tolerated—this [is] because, when officers and Business Agents of a Union quarrel or fuss among themselves or strive for popularity or petty advantage over each other, the organization invariably suffers, dissension grows, efficiency is decreased and the members must foot the bill incurred by such jealousy or quarreling. . . .

Many of Broach's changes remain in place today, but he was not one to follow his own advice when it came to politicking. He was deeply involved in his own political maneuvering within the IBEW. At the end of 1929, the Executive Council appointed him president of the IBEW. He remained in New York until 1932, when he returned to Washington.

Before Broach left, however, he took one of his most important actions. Sponsoring the young battler, Harry Van Arsdale Jr., Broach induced Emil Preiss, whose election as business manager he had engineered, to select Van Arsdale as a business agent.

Even though the sound-movie industry was booming in 1931, and Van Arsdale, then 26, was earning a premium salary, the union meant more to him and he accepted the job as business agent at a salary of $100 a week. His admiration for Broach also played a strong part in his decision.

"Broach was one of the greatest brains that we ever had in the labor movement and particularly in a rising market," said Van Arsdale in an interview. "He came into the city when there was friction; most of the energies that people had were being used up in politics. He more or less got the union going in one direction. . . . He was just a terrific guy. Then he became the International president. He started out to do some great things across the country, like he did in New York. He was an idol to me."[13]

But Broach's high plans for the Local and the International were sidetracked by the Great Depression. Twenty-five percent of the workforce was unemployed, and, in most cases, without any safety net. With the exception of food stamps issued in some parts of the nation, there were no public or private resources including unemployment insurance, "home relief," or other forms of welfare, to keep a man and his family from deprivation or starvation.

It would be some time before the administration of President Franklin D. Roosevelt and his New Deal would initiate the Works Progress Administration and start to put some people back to work.

Men took to selling apples on street corners to try to bring some money home to their families. Other men faced with financial ruin leaped from windows to their deaths so that their wives and children might live off their life insurance. A Sunday edition of the *New York Times*, which today requires some athletic effort to lift and carry away, had a mere twelve-page news section at Christmas 1931, because of the lack of advertising, and on each of those pages was a story of another desperate suicide by a bankrupt financier or middle-class executive.[14]

More and more the people of the country turned to movies as a way to escape the painful reality of the depression. "Talkies" (sound motion pictures) were all the rage and movie theater owners vied with each other to install new sound equipment to pull in the customers. And Van Arsdale, the fledgling business agent, saw this as another way to get work for the men of Local 3. His biggest obstacle was the Electric Research Products Company (ERP). It was the major manufacturer of the equipment, which it sought to have its own nonunion employees install. Local 3 men, supposedly untutored in the fine points of cinematic sound, would take care of the fringe work of connections and minor wiring.

Not so, believed Van Arsdale, who, knew that Local 3's members could learn all the intricacies involved. The ERP Company refused to believe him and continued to ship its equipment to theaters with nonunion men assigned to install it. Van Arsdale countered by having Local 3 men refuse to place any cables in the theaters, rendering the new equipment useless. The equipment sat unused in the theaters while despairing theater owners lost tens of thousands of dollars.

This stalemate lasted for twenty-eight weeks until Van Arsdale proposed a solution. Let the men of Local 3 do the complete job at one theater and if all worked well, then let them do the work in each theater in their jurisdiction. The theater owners agreed. After all, they had nothing to lose. ERP also felt confident that the Local 3 men would fail and the issue would be settled in favor of ERP.

But Van Arsdale had an ace up his sleeve: education. He used his connections in Western Electric to train the men of Local 3 secretly in the installation of the equipment. When the day came for the test of equipment installed by Local 3 members at the Astor Theater, ERP inspectors checked the work and "found" scores of supposed errors. But when the switch was thrown, everything worked smoothly and Local 3 had made its case. Training to do a specific job was a tactic that Van Arsdale was to use throughout his career.

Meanwhile, more and more banks were forced to close their doors. One of the first things Roosevelt did after his inauguration on March 4, 1933, was to order a "Bank Holiday" and propose the Emergency Banking Relief Act. Congress acted overnight to pass it. Federal auditors would examine the banks and allow them to reopen and receive federal assistance if they were shown to be strong enough. If not, federal "conservators" would aid them to regain solvency. Also shuttered were the great stock exchanges and many commodity exchanges. An estimated 15–17 million men were unemployed and many municipalities could not meet their payrolls. Municipal employees, including thousands of teachers, paid in warrants (pledges to pay) instead of checks, were often forced to sell them to lenders in order to get immediate cash.

Most Local 3 members felt themselves lucky to work two days a week, even if it was for rates lower than they had earned in the late 1920s. Matchsticks became a bargaining symbol for a day's rate of pay. If a man showed up at a job site with one wooden matchstick in his hatband, a foreman knew that he would work for $1 below scale. If he had two matchsticks so displayed, it meant he would work for $2 off. Men over 50 found that their age had advanced them out of the job market altogether. They could not "match" youth.[15]

In his inaugural address, Roosevelt, who had become a hero to Van Arsdale, declared that it was his "firm belief that the only thing we have to fear is fear itself, nameless, unreasoning, unjustified terror which paralyzes needed efforts to convert retreat into advance." He placed the blame for the nation's travails on the heads of bankers, speculators, and financial promoters whom he chastised as "the unscrupulous money changers" whose practices "stand indicted in the court of public opinion" and who "have fled from their high seats in the temple of our civilization." The nation's most pressing need, "our greatest primary task was to put people to work," he said, and the program he outlined of governmental action toward that end was a preview of the key features of the early part of his administration.

Local 3 had initiated its own program of helping its suffering members by handing out a bare-bones payment of $15 a week in unemployment benefits. However, by 1932, even this had so drained the Local's treasury that the Local could only offer a waiver of union dues for those out of work—which was most of the membership.

In addition to the external problems of the depression, Van Arsdale and other unionists faced internal battles. The dire times provided a fertile field of opportunity for the American Communist Party to try to improve its position in the union. Nor were they the only outside influences that attempted to move in. The other chief faction was organized crime. Racketeers Louis ("Lepke") Buchalter and Jake ("Gurrah Jake") Shapiro were at the forefront, often aided by political cronies and corrupt law-enforcement officers.

Lepke and Shapiro were said to be so fearsome that ordinary citizens shook in fright when they set eyes on them. They did not rely on underlings to do their dirty work for them: they did it themselves, apparently for the sheer joy of it. Buchalter was later the head of the notorious and bloody Murder, Inc., the enforcement unit of the national crime syndicate, for six years. He reportedly killed as many as 100 men and ordered the deaths of perhaps 1,000 more.[16]

Before he joined the Mafia, however, Buchalter specialized in labor racketeering, focusing his efforts in Manhattan's garment district. He branched out from there to other union locals, including bakery delivery trucks. He taxed bakers a cent a loaf to insure that their goods made it to shelves on time. Otherwise, the loaves might meet with "unfortunate delays" because of the inopportune destruction of trucks and injuries to their drivers.

Lepke and Shapiro had similar plans for Local 3. They would tax the Local a certain sum for each member as payment for inducing nonunion workers into joining the Local or risk loss of livelihood through broken arms, legs, heads, or other vulnerable parts. Employers would be threatened and told to hire only Local 3 men. And there were neither money-back guarantees nor promises that the collections would stop once they went to work. Their track record, in fact, showed the opposite.[17]

"Dutch" Schultz (born Arthur Flegenheimer), another famous mobster of the Prohibition era (known as "The Beer Baron of the Bronx"), was said to have offered his services to Local 3. In an interview, Harry Van Arsdale recalled that when Local 3 had been under the control of the IBEW, "There were some people creating problems within the union. It was not just the communist faction. There were other groups. And I understand that one of them suggested that Dutch Schultz wanted to meet with [a representative of the IBEW].

"So, when Dutch Schultz wanted to meet, you generally made it a point to go to see him. So [a representative of the IBEW] went to see him and the way he described it, it was like a movie, a movie setting. You know they had the black curtain across and the guy [apparently Schultz] was to tell [the IBEW representative] that 'I have settled the difficulties in many organizations.' And people had been to see him and 'I can settle your troubles for you.' [The IBEW representative subsequently] left New York. It was not through fear; it was through the use of better judgement," Van Arsdale said. But before the Local replied to this overture, Schultz's enemies succeeded in removing him from the scene, Van Arsdale continued. "You know if it had [continued], somebody in a key position might have been injured or insulted or something," Van Arsdale added dryly.[18]

The American communists used different—and more legitimate—tactics to effect a takeover. They wanted power and economic leverage, but not for monetary gain—they wanted control. To weaken the locals, they set up rival, avowedly communist, units in what they called "dual-unionism." When that gambit failed, because of paucity of membership and the strength of their competitors, they formed the Trade Union Unity League, the members of which were designated to infiltrate established AFL locals and then gain power from within. One of their chief techniques was to disrupt meetings by arguments and parliamentary intricacies until opposition was worn down. Then they would move to pass their favored proposals.

Broach noted that the communists "practically wrecked" the furriers and cloakmakers union in New York "and it was only natural to find them attempting to get control of Local Union 3 and other building trades organizations."[19] At meetings they passed out handbills and issues of the communist newspaper, the *Daily Worker*, instructing members how to capture and control Local 3. They also created as much "havoc and disturbance as possible," Broach said. "Meetings were again put in a state of bedlam. Long tirades on how to cure the 'ills of the working class' were the order of the day. . . . Little business could be conducted. The situation became serious."[20] But the communists failed to win control when their ideology was rejected by the majority of the rank and file.

Bertram Powers, former head of Local 6 of the Typographical Workers Union, gave this insight into Van Arsdale's attitude toward communists. In a conversation with Van Arsdale, he said:

> I have some Communists in my union. They're not bad union guys. I get along with them. I do not agree with them, but I get along with them. Harry took exception to that. He said, "You can't get along with them. None of them are any good."[21]

Because of Van Arsdale's rank and file record, during the period that Broach was reorganizing Local 3, he was officially named a business agent by business manager Emil Preiss. As alluded to previously, Van Arsdale worked primarily as foreman of crews involved in the installation of sound equipment in studios and theaters. He also worked for such firms as Thompson and Starrett Construction Company, the Reflex Engineering Company, the E.J. Electric Company, and the Halco Company.

After he gained entry into the union as a helper, for a short period, he was part of a cadre of organizers soliciting nonunion companies to work with the union, but that effort washed away on the incoming tide of the Depression.

"I was on a staff to undertake them [nonunion firms] to hire our people," Van Arsdale said in an interview. "And then, of course, that petered out because when your market goes down, your funds go down. I went back to work. And then on a later occasion, you know, I was called on to come back to employment with the union and I was on the staff. As a matter of fact, I was asked to take charge of the sound equipment."[22]

With the help of friends, Harry Jr. and Harry Sr. built a house in Ozone Park, Queens. This was done over time as they could afford materials in some periods, and not in others. Harry Jr. was very optimistic and had envisioned another home on the adjoining lot. This never materialized, however, due to the crisis-prone nature of his early career.

For a brief interval when he had a personal life, he enjoyed gardening and raising homing pigeons, a hobby learned from his Uncle George.[23] Much later he returned to this for relaxation, setting up a coop on the roof of the union's Manhattan building.

He continued to follow the New York Yankees, Babe Ruth, and to watch boxing matches. He sometimes would go with friends to jazz clubs in the city, or to Irish entertainments in the Rockaways, although he did not sing or dance. A friend Joseph Cuty observed, "He just went along for the ride, and he never drank much either."[24]

But the main focus of Van Arsdale's life, then and forever, was the union. As he got deeper into local politics, he made enemies, and this ultimately led to his conviction on a charge of first-degree assault for which he and a codefendant were sentenced to prison.

3

A Fight to the Top

The year 1933 was a particularly turbulent one for Van Arsdale. Broach's achievements at Local 3 were eroded by the Great Depression. Four years previously, Broach had pointed with pride to some of his accomplishments. Local 3 had been the first union in the Building Trades Council in New York to receive $12 a day, and in February 1929 it won a five-day, forty-hour week and $13.20 per day. The Local further extended its jurisdiction to encompass members in "motor shops, fixture shops, excavation and foundation jobs, work in connection with hoisting and concrete mixers, temporary work for light and motors, maintenance work, work in subways, work on new and old schools, movietone and sound equipment and transformer vault work."[1] In 1930, the Local had 7,034 members.[2] These consisted mostly of construction workers, plus about 200 fixture assemblers and wirers who had previously belonged to Local Union 261 (which had merged with Local 3 in 1928).

In November 1930, Local 3 members also voted to work only a four-day week in cooperation with a national "Share the Work" plan as unemployment rose. The following year, the members voted to restrict themselves to a three-day week as the effects of the Depression deepened.

The situation posed particular dangers to unions faced with diminishing coffers and disgruntled members, and Broach decided to tighten his control of the IBEW. In 1930, Broach succeeded in getting the IBEW's constitution revised in order to restructure and centralize the organization along more business-like lines. This weakened the Local's autonomy and established the foundations for the modern-day Brotherhood.

But his ambitions for the International and the Local were shredded by continued widespread unemployment and the often bitter competition for work. Broach also faced growing opposition from left-wing critics in the IBEW and from emboldened opponents in Local 3. This opposition was engendered not only by the left, but also by Broach himself, who was often outspoken, egotistical, and impatient with those whose views did not coincide with his. This led to bitter antagonisms, even hatred, and a desire for revenge.

The almost Byzantine politics of the Local and the IBEW can be seen in the controversy over the alleged activities of a group of right-wing reactionaries and anti-union forces that sought to discredit Broach and his supporters around the nation and in New York. The IBEW's official publication, *Journal of Electrical Workers and Operators,* printed nine "unique and startling exhibits [of] a nation-wide spy plot against the union [but] dealing mainly with attempts to break up the New York local" in its June 1932 issue. All of the exhibits—letters—bore the signature of "G. Edgar Applegate," alias George E. Anderson, and bore the letterhead of "The American Financiers-Investigative and Protection Bureau (Industrial Division)." The letters, some containing anti-Semitic remarks, outlined an apparatus of informers and agitators aimed at undermining the local union's leadership and crippling its operations. One letter, dated April 16, 1932, was addressed to the Building Trades Committee in New York City and took the form of a report of the bureau's activities on behalf of the committee. It told of eight "informers" in Local 3, most of whom had been operating for eight years or more, who were paid small salaries and bonuses to issue circulars, spread stories, make motions, and speak at meetings. According to the letter, every attempt was being made to get the men into "important positions" in the Local. It also added that a thorough investigation of the Local's present leadership had yielded nothing that "would be favorable to our side."

There was no indication in the article or in an accompanying analysis by G.M. Bugniazet, IBEW secretary, of how these documents came to be in the possession of the IBEW. But Bugniazet focused on a lawsuit by fifteen members of Local 3 seeking reinstatement after they were thrown out of the Local by Broach and his supporters. He also lashed out at circulars issued by the "New Deal Group," which opposed Broach and his methods. (Almost equally vocal was another faction calling itself the "Rank and File.")

Bugniazet's documents were attacked as "phony" by the New Deal Group and other opponents in new barrages of circulars. Among other things, these pointed out that the IBEW leadership had failed to submit their findings to impartial investigation. They also noted that all the "letters"—ostensibly composed in different cities—appeared to have been written on the same typewriter. They also indicated that no proof could be found of the existence of either the Bureau or the "Building Trades Committee." In addition, Broach, Bugniazet, and Hogan were sued for libel.

There is no doubt that the spurious letters and revelations, clumsy and careless in their execution, were a reflection of the blunderbuss style of Broach's opponents. They furnish vivid examples of the bitter political battles being fought in the International and the Local, especially in the months preceding Local elections scheduled for June 1932.[3] As part of the mud-slinging, Broach was pilloried as a "Mussolini" because of his high-handed tactics. It was also alleged that he embezzled money from the Local and accepted bribes from contractors to steer work their way. All of the lawsuits eventually came to naught.[4]

But words were not the only things that were thrown in meetings. A New Deal newsletter decried the events of a meeting held on May 26. "Never before, as far back as some of the old-timers can remember, was such a scene of chairs, knives and black-jack swinging against people who dared to speak their mind, seen. That the officials had cold-bloodedly contemplated this bloody orgy is amply demonstrated by the fact that all the gangsters were seated on single chairs which could be easily brought into action. The chairs which the rest of the members sat on were combination chairs for six people and could not be used for this purpose."

Both sides accused each other of instigating such battles and eventually Broach's supporters proved stronger by winning the election. With the fire of opposition at least diminished—but hardly extinguished—Broach left to combat home fires in Washington, leaving Local 3 in the hands of Business Manager Emil Preiss and other loyalists, including Harry Van Arsdale Jr. The situation was further complicated by the growing illness of Preiss, who was deteriorating under the pressure—and constant epithets—within the Local. He made known his desire to resign, but Van Arsdale visited him at his home and prevailed on him to stay, at least in name only, until he and other Broach supporters could strengthen their positions.[5] Hugh Morgan stepped in to assume Preiss's duties on a temporary basis.

In another gambit to counter the barrage of inflammatory verbiage being fired by the New Deal Group in their Circular Letters, Van Arsdale organized the "Committee of 100," which issued newsletters of its own after the election. The committee was composed of those men close to Van Arsdale, chosen not only for loyalty but for tactical abilities—and a willingness to match the long hours Van Arsdale put in! The original committee members included many who would go on to high office in the Local. Among the names listed as committee members were Howard McSpedon, a Local 3 business agent and later president of the New York City Building and Construction Trades Council, whose son, Dennis, would later serve as president with business manager Thomas Van Arsdale; Jeremiah P. Sullivan, committee chairman and future Local president and International treasurer; Al J. Mackie, who would become assistant business manager under Van Arsdale; John J. Kapp and Michael Siegel, who also became assistant business managers; Dennis Crimmins, who rose to become the executive secretary of the Joint Industry Board; and Edward Cleary, whose son, Edward J. Cleary, became Local 3's president and eventually president of the New York State AFL-CIO.

The first newsletter, addressed "To All Members of Local Union No. 3," began:

> Having seen the disastrous effect of internal dissension, mud slinging and vicious slander that has weakened our Union considerably in the past year and realizing the crisis which this Local Union is facing . . . we should stop this foolishness and proceed to strengthen our Union so that it will be able to withstand the attack of certain contractors that are organizing and determined to reduce our wages even if it is necessary to declare another lockout. . . .
>
> If we stop and try to picture what our condition would be, if we did not have as strong a Union as we have, we would realize the necessity for keeping a cool head and instead of finding fault with everything that is done, we would devote our time and effort to maintaining the conditions and benefits we still have left and attempting to better them if possible . . . more progress could be made than slandering the officers and attempting to disrupt our meetings and causing the outside world to feel that we are wrecking our own Union.
>
> Following these thoughts we have formed a "Committee of 100." The platform of this Committee is to work for the good of our Union and against anything or anyone who is detrimental to our Union. All we are interested in are suggestions and ideas [so] that we will be able to work out [sic] some constructive and progressive measures to put forward for your approval.

The tone of this and succeeding committee letters reflected Van Arsdale's pragmatism: he always put personal feelings about individuals aside in order to get the job done and to issue constructive, not destructive, proposals.

The second bulletin lauded the membership for approving the recommendation of Broach and the International Executive Council to cancel a scheduled national convention in order to save money.[6] In order to help relieve the financial burden on men whose age was a further impediment to finding work, members were also urged to amend the by-laws to lower the age from 65 to 60 for those exempt from paying dues. "It is unfortunate that something more beneficial cannot be done for the older members at this time." Van Arsdale was always concerned about the older member, perhaps remembering the difficulties his own father faced in similar circumstances.

Another recurring theme in those early newsletters was encouragement to strive for education and self-improvement. Members were exhorted to acquaint themselves with proposed federal and state laws that would benefit labor. The committee also proposed extending invitations to AFL officials to lecture the membership on those bills and other aspects important to labor.

The letters that followed charted a path of relative calm within the Local, but only for a short time. Emotions still ran high between leftists and the Van Arsdale faction, and despite exhortations of Van Arsdale and his committee to allow reason to prevail, sometimes violence erupted. Police often had to be called in to quiet bloody battles. Alfred Terry, an opposition member, brought charges of felonious assault against Van Arsdale and others in 1932. The charges were reduced to disorderly conduct and then dismissed. But more serious charges loomed.

Van Arsdale and member Max ("Rosey") Rosenberg were charged with assault in the first degree in the shooting of opposition leader William Sorenson on February 24, 1933, in the Local's headquarters on 25th Street. Both men pleaded innocent and Van Arsdale testified that he had been accosted by his old nemesis, Alfred Terry, and others, who pushed him into a corner on the fifth floor and began to punch him—continuing a dispute that had allegedly begun in a membership meeting the night before. While they were so occupied, he said shots rang out. Everybody, including him, ran, and he subsequently called the police. But police believed others who said it was Van Arsdale and Rosenberg who had shot Sorenson. Committee of 100 Bulletin No. 4 described the incident:

> After being defeated on local issues at our regular meeting Thursday, February 23, 1933, they [i.e., consolidated "Rank and File" and "New Deal" members] decided to take the law into their own hands either to Rule or Ruin our Union. On Friday, February 24, 1933, seventy-five [percent] or three-fourths of their followers attempted to take over the union headquarters at 125 East 25th Street. We have been informed from reliable sources that their intentions were to start at the fifth floor and go right through the building to the street, by fair or foul means. Their intentions of sabotage and felony were self-evident when they appeared in working clothes wearing gloves and carrying pieces of lead in their hands. Their intentions were realized when they attacked an officer of our Local Union. We believe one of their members was mysteriously shot. We believe one of their own followers shot the Brother in his haste and anxiety to shoot Brother Harry Van Arsdale Jr. We deeply

regret the whole episode that any group of men should resort to mob violence to settle any grievances and differences in our union.

But despite such arguments, Van Arsdale and Rosenberg were convicted on January 29, 1934, and sentenced on February 8 to serve six to twelve years in prison by Judge Joseph E. Corrigan (who had earned a reputation as the city's most notorious "hanging judge"). However, the case was appealed and reversed on the grounds that the identifications made were inconclusive. Sorenson, Terry, and three others subsequently signed a statement that absolved Van Arsdale.

In an attempt to stabilize the volatile scene, Local 3, with Frank Wilson as president, voted on February 23, 1933, to have the International take full control of the Local, but with no supervision of the Local's funds. Clair Killen was designated as the IBEW representative to handle the Local's affairs. On March 9 he formally announced the resignation of Emil Preiss as business manager. Preiss explained that he was stepping down on advice from his doctor. Killen then announced that Robert Bryan had been appointed as temporary business manager, succeeding Hugh Morgan.

But Killen's choice of Bryan brought immediate repercussions from Broach who sought to remain very much in control of the New York situation. He summarily ousted Killen on the grounds that Killen had overstepped his authority by making the appointment. He said he had instructed Killen not to fill any vacancies but to defer those to the Local Executive Board until told otherwise. Broach replaced Killen with IBEW vice president Charles D. Keaveney and Hugh Morgan was restored as temporary business manager.

Broach's own position was uncertain, however. He had become battle weary from the internal wars, and, on July 10, he submitted his resignation, insisting that it be accepted. He declared that he had suffered a "nervous and physical breakdown" previously. "It was a long struggle to regain my health as you know," he stated. "Since then I have been up and down. The strain has been especially heavy and depressing in these times and if I continue to carry on as President of this organization, another breakdown is inevitable. This would benefit neither the organization nor myself." After expressing his gratitude to his friends, he also said he would be "happy to advise, counsel and aid whenever called upon."[7]

His words were prophetic and would have a great effect on Van Arsdale in the future. Although removed from the spotlight, Broach would remain a "gray eminence" behind the scenes and maintain a lasting interest in New York. Van Arsdale's fortunes, partially through Broach's interventions, continued to rise.

The faction supporting Van Arsdale took over Local 3 on April 6, 1933. Frank Wilson, who had been president of Local 3 since the mid-1920s, resigned. Bert Kirkman was elected to serve out Wilson's term. After a see-saw battle in which opposing factions maneuvered to position themselves for the appointment of a new business manager, Harry Van Arsdale Jr. and William Reuter were put up for a vote on October 16. Van Arsdale won the appointment three to one. One year later the entire membership elected him business manager.

"The kid" had arrived.

4

Dealing with the New Deal

Franklin Delano Roosevelt and Van Arsdale had much in common when they took office. In 1933, each was new to his respective position and faced the same task: to restore dignity and decent living standards to the people they served. Both were responsible for constituencies that were impoverished and desperate; both took strong and fast action and in doing so imprinted their vibrant images on a new era. It was Van Arsdale's good fortune to step in as business manager of Local 3 coincidental with the start of the New Deal because the Roosevelt administration furnished a new and more hospitable arena for labor leaders like Van Arsdale to do battle. The ground had also been prepared by the Norris-La Guardia Anti-Injunction Act of 1932, which underscored for the first time that labor had a right to strike without interference from the federal courts. The act, co-authored by Fiorello La Guardia, always a friend to labor, also banned the so-called Yellow Dog contract under which, upon being hired, an employee agreed to be discharged if he joined a union.

The soil of adversity was fertile for the growth of the labor movement. There was a new philosophy in the land—helping the working man who may have a blue collar, a white collar, or no collar at all. Social reform was in the air, much of it promulgated by progressive intellectuals who were drawn to Washington, DC, and FDR like iron filings to a magnet. The programs initiated by Roosevelt spearheaded or paralleled many of the initiatives that Van Arsdale introduced, but Van Arsdale would also establish programs that preceded federal actions, in fact providing examples for them to follow. Van Arsdale, even in those early days of his assumption to power, showed himself to be a man of vision. He was also a man with a heart and a hand to help the needy and the downtrodden, ideals which ran parallel to the man in the White House. Both were men for the times, one in Washington, the other in New York. The light from the New Deal reflected on Van Arsdale's work, which, in turn, added to the progressive reforms emanating from the White House. An examination, in that context, is in order.

In Washington, with his administration only a few hours old, Roosevelt had his cabinet members sworn in and ordered them to begin work at once. Frances Perkins was the secretary of labor and the first female cabinet officer in the history of the nation. An informal "brain trust," part of the famed "Kitchen Cabinet," helped to lay the groundwork for the remarkable first hundred days of the administration, which saw a flood of new legislation and programs, unprecedented in U.S. history.

The first step was to get money moving again. Within twenty-four hours of his inauguration, Roosevelt issued an executive order to close all banks in the nation for four days to get the country's financial house in order and allow Congress, meeting in emergency session, to deal with the administration's proposed Emergency Banking Bill. At the end of the four-day "Bank Holiday," Congress passed the bill, which included a provision allowing sound banks to reopen. By March 15, 1933, 90 percent of the nation's banks were again in operation and the money panic was over. On the heels of this, the Economy Act of 1933 authorized the president to cut the salaries of administrative officers up to 15 percent and to streamline government agencies.

To combat unemployment, the Civilian Conservation Corps (CCC) was formed, eventually providing work and vocational training for an estimated 2 million young men. Earlier in May 1931, the Federal Emergency Relief Act created the Federal Emergency Relief Administration (FERA), under the helm of Harry Hopkins, a former New York City social worker. The FERA provided direct and substantial aid to the states for welfare. This was followed in October by the creation of the Civil Works Administration (CWA). Some 3 million people were soon put to work, although much of it was "make-work" to keep them busy and justify a salary—some critics called it "leaf-raking" or "boondoggling." The CWA was closed down after six months, having spent $900 million. But the lessons learned paved the way toward more substantial work makers as the Public Works Administration (PWA) and the Works Progress Administration (WPA).

In those first hundred days, Roosevelt's administration took steps to aid farmers and to further regulate the stock market. The Tennessee Valley Authority (TVA) was established to provide cheap electrical power and improve social and economic conditions for millions of people. But the program that would have a particular impact on Van Arsdale and all of labor was the National Recovery Act, passed in June 1933, providing for planned and controlled production in industry and the end of destructive competition in wage and price cutting. An ambitious public works program was initiated with a start-up budget of more than $3 billion. Labor and industry were to be aided by shorter work days and minimum wages. Section 7a of the act guaranteed employees the right to collective bargaining through representatives of their own choosing, the first time labor's right to organize had been part of a statute. Codes of practice were drawn up regulating wages, hours, and prices. Roosevelt said the act was probably "the most important and far-reaching measure ever enacted by the American Congress."

The National Recovery Administration (NRA) was created to administer the code provisions and its Blue Eagle emblem was seen all over the country. More than 500 national codes were put into effect immediately and 22 million workers were affected. But the NRA proved to be a double-edged sword: it put a yoke on labor as well as management by controlling collective bargaining.

Many of the NRA's provisions were to be nullified by the U.S. Supreme Court, which held, in 1935, that the NRA codes were unconstitutional. But a friendly Congress responded by passing the nation's first national labor relations law, the Wagner Act, which became a great liberating force for labor. The new law went farther than the old Section 7a. It set up a new National Labor Relations Board (NLRB) consisting of three members empowered to administer the law through investigations, hearings, and the supervision of employee elections for choosing bargaining units.

Later Roosevelt also pushed through the Fair Labor Standards Act (1938), which set a minimum wage of 25 cents per hour for adults and a forty-four-hour workweek. The act included a provision allowing revisions of the minimum wage (to 40 cents per hour) and the workweek (to forty hours), as well as mandating overtime pay beyond forty hours. Labor had been given new muscle and began to use it. Bloody strikes erupted around the nation, particularly in the steel and automobile unions. There was also growth in unionization among general laborers and industrial workers as well as craftsmen. This led to controversy in the American Federation of Labor (AFL) over the issue of organizing workers in industry across craft lines: a so-called horizontal union as opposed to the vertical union that represented workers of a single craft. The dispute resulted in the expulsion of the Committee for Industrial Organization (CIO), led by John L. Lewis of the United Mine Workers, from the AFL in 1936. Lewis then founded the Congress of Industrial Organizations, in which workers in an industry were placed under one union roof horizontally, regardless of craft.

This was particularly relevant to Van Arsdale, who was to fashion Local 3 into a hybrid industrial/horizontal and craft/vertical union. The various divisions encompassed the entire industry, thus giving it the advantages of a horizontal union in which local members honored and supported the actions or strikes of their brother divisions. It was a remarkable and inventive structure and just one of the many far-reaching innovations Van Arsdale and his associates were to make.

But Van Arsdale's immediate task on taking office was to heal wounds in his fractured Local while easing the financial burdens on the members. As for the Local itself, its finances were so anemic that occasionally there was as little as $16,000 cash in the treasury—roughly $3 for every member. Assets balanced debits by including $200,000 in back dues (owed by nonworking members) and the value of the 25th Street headquarters. However, there was very little chance the unemployed members could pay up, and the headquarters could not be sold, thus there was no way to balance the books. Furthermore, Local 3 members saw no work and were withdrawing from the Local in large numbers. Only a fraction of the Local's 5,000 journeymen worked full time; some managed just two or three days a week and felt lucky to do even that.

To find work, Local 3 men would straggle from job site to job site and often accept less than scale pay. The search for a job was more often than not determined by public transit routes—a job seeker trying to get as much value as possible from a five-cent fare visited contractors or job sites along the line. If he failed to find work, it was back to the union hall on 25th Street for free coffee and sympathy.[1] Van Arsdale described the situation thus:

> This is what you used to do when you were unemployed. You would go around for a nickel and get to most of these places. [But some] fellows would walk across the Brooklyn Bridge to save the nickel because with that nickel you could go into a bar and get a beer and then you also had access to the free lunch counter. And then there were some saloons—this is a very important part of labor history—some saloons that catered to working people. And when they were on strike or when they were out of work, you know, they used to put food out there that you would have to pay Longchamps [a relatively expensive restaurant] prices for today. But in those days, having that nickel to get that beer to have access to that free lunch counter was a very important part of a man's carrying forward.[2]

In order to provide immediate financial help for the members, Van Arsdale proposed bold decisions, and, in his view, eminently practical actions. They exemplified his talent for direct, clear action. In a way, they were part of his own first hundred days, and, like Roosevelt, he often had to overcome bitter (and sometimes violent) opposition.

First, Van Arsdale proposed and won acceptance for the elimination of the Unemployment Fund, under which each working member was obliged to contribute 15 percent of his wages. He further proposed that each member not pay any dues for the first six months of the coming year. To cover the loss of such funds, Van Arsdale and his fellow officers negotiated a mortgage on the 25th Street headquarters.

In addition, in a typical display of dedication to the Local, Van Arsdale and the officers said they would work for nothing if the Local could not afford to pay them. As Van Arsdale put it: "The officers have made known the fact that they will take their chances for their pay when all unnecessary expense is eliminated."[3] Moreover, he was scrupulously honest in his dealings and made sure that his business agents were, too. He wrote to contractors to ask them not to give any gifts to his officers at Christmas. And he told his men that if they received gifts they were to return them.[4]

In order to spread the work as much as possible among the members of Local 3, Van Arsdale, even before he became business manager, introduced a resolution on August 24, seeking a six-hour day. The resolution was unanimously approved and the Local wanted to go on strike to achieve it. But union rules mandated that strikes could be authorized only by the International. IBEW President Daniel W. Tracy rejected the strike plan on October 11, 1933, saying that the Local had not exhausted other alternatives.

The Local's position was later amended, on Van Arsdale's recommendation, to strike for a seven-hour day, $11.20 per day for journeymen, and $7.60 per day for helpers with four years of seniority.

The battle between electrical industry contractors and Local officials was finally heard by the NRA's Regional Labor Board. Van Arsdale noted that the Local's earlier demand for a six-hour day was at a time when all government work called for a six-hour day and thirty-hour week, and FDR was suggesting that shorter working hours per day in a shorter workweek was not unreasonable.[5] The regional board, however, refused to allow a strike. But Van Arsdale would continue to fight for a shorter workday in order to give more men a chance to work.

The Local's finances had been an extremely sore point in the past and one that Van Arsdale meant to bury forever. Van Arsdale introduced quarterly financial statements, and newsletters that showed in detail how the members' money was being spent, including $25 a week for coffee and $15 for the business agents' automotive expenses.

Van Arsdale further required that financial reports be read at monthly meetings, a practice not appreciated by all members—many of whom thought they were boring—but Van Arsdale prevailed, reasoning that the members had a right to know how their hard-earned money was being spent.

Van Arsdale put it this way: "Are we going to steal or be honest?"

In the first financial report issued to the members on April 9, 1934, Van Arsdale wrote:

> Since assuming the duties of Business Manager on October 16, 1933, one of the many problems has been to keep the membership informed of the developments, changes and progress that have taken place in our jurisdiction. Approximately 1,500 men attend the regular meetings. There is seldom time for as complete a report of the activities of the Field Staff as is necessary to acquaint the membership with the work being done.
>
> Being a firm believer that every member in a trade union should have the knowledge of everything that is done and should be done to better conditions in his particular craft, I intend, when the circumstances warrant, to notify the membership of all developments and opportunities for progress.

This was part of his mission to modernize the Local and put it on the sound, stable, and democratic footing that helped establish its reputation as one of the best locals in the nation. Other unions would not be required by law to do the same until 1959.

Van Arsdale told the members that he was keeping business agents up to the mark by having a bulletin board placed in the executive board room showing their success or failure in signing up nonunion contractors and by requiring business agents to report to him monthly. He also reported on new organizing activities by the Local. This was a critical endeavor, because Van Arsdale intended to bring the entire industry into the Local.

He asked for volunteers to aid in the organizing work and spoke of the volunteer picketers outside shipyards who were successful in bringing marine electrical workers, switchboard manufacturing shops, and department stores into the fold. In Bulletin No. 9 of the Committee of 100, possibly written by Van Arsdale, it was observed that: "One of the more recent proofs of the caliber of this organization has been the way a large number of men have attempted to meet the common enemy by picketing, in spite of the most unfavorable weather conditions. We know of no other more difficult or discouraging job than picketing. In many instances, the picketing is being done by men with empty stomachs, insufficient clothing and worn shoes, but with the indomitable courage to carry on in spite of all this. These are some of the things that prove this organization is capable of winning its fight for a shorter work day."

But Van Arsdale would not only rely on volunteers for picket lines. If he saw men gathered around the free coffee table or the day room at the Local's headquarters, he would tell them: "For every three days work that anyone gets, there will be three days on the picket line from the same man and anyone who doesn't show up for picketing needn't bother coming around for work."[6]

The switchboard industry was an early target: construction electricians were being denied work as switchboard firms shipped finished switchboards ready for installation. The work was being done by nonunion men and women at cut-rate wages, 40–65 cents per hour, thus denying work to the higher paid union members.

But, as always, Van Arsdale faced opposition from forces within the union. When he began the campaign to organize the switchboard workers, his opponents accused him of seeking to pack the membership with new supporters that would cast their ballots for him in the elections of union officers (scheduled for the following year). They were too shortsighted or too politically motivated to appreciate Van Arsdale's goal of getting every aspect of the electrical industry in the New York area under Local 3's banner. But Van Arsdale, showing his political shrewdness, countered his opponents' arguments by pointing out that no switchboard worker would be a paid-up member of the union, paying dues and an initiation fee and thus able to vote in a union election, until he or she was covered by a union contract.

This was another of Van Arsdale's innovations in labor practice. Other unions signed up members, collected their dues and then tried to negotiate a contract with employers. Van Arsdale's tactic was more appealing to prospective members who had nothing to lose by being organized. Van Arsdale's creative practice became standard in every division of Local 3.

Van Arsdale cleverly found a way to "sweeten the pot" for the switchboard manufacturers and make it easier for them to sign a contract with their workers. Manufacturers had argued that they could not raise wages because it would mean they would have to raise prices and this would put them at a disadvantage with those manufacturers who paid less. They opened their books to Van Arsdale and the Local to show that big competitors like Westinghouse and General Electric could outbid them on jobs and this would deny work to Local 3 members.

But Van Arsdale told switchboard manufacturers that if they signed up, the Local would put its label on their products and protect them by refusing to install switchboards that did not display this label. This gambit would be one of the most significant the Local would ever undertake, as well as a tactic Van Arsdale and his cadre would use in creating other divisions within the Local and enticing contractors to sign agreements. However, it also caused antagonisms and brought charges of monopoly from the federal government.

On another front, Van Arsdale had Local 3 tackle department stores. The Local had signed up sixty-four maintenance electricians in fourteen of the larger stores, including Gimbels and Macy's. As Van Arsdale noted in his

April 9 report to the membership, "Our survey showed deplorable wages and conditions existing in this branch of our industry. The average wage was approximately $26.00 for 46 hours work." The men were also called on to do construction work, he continued, and, if necessary, more men were hired at the same low wage. When the work was done, the men were released. But even so, the labor costs were too high for Gimbel Brothers. They decided to hire nonunion electricians to do a large electrical installation in the store in December 1933. Van Arsdale responded by placing pickets in front of the door exhorting would-be buyers to "pass 'em by" as being unfair to labor. Gimbels held out for four weeks and then caved in.

Van Arsdale continued in his April 9 report: "Because of the efforts of members who volunteered for picket duty, a total of 97 jobs that had been started nonunion were turned over to our members. Numerous other jobs in the vicinity of those picketed were done union because of this militant display." (The specter of a picket line being erected around Macy's, brought Percy Strauss, Macy's CEO, to the table with Van Arsdsale two years later. Strauss noted that Macy's had had an open shop for the seventy-eight years it had been in business. Van Arsdale's answer: "It's time for a change." Strauss agreed to a union shop.)

The April 9 report also listed a series of organizational gains in about a dozen other companies including New York Edison Company, United Electric Company, and large street-lighting and sign-making firms, such as the Broadway Maintenance Company. Van Arsdale also told of a campaign to inspect and replace electrical installations suspected of being unsafe as well as to organize all contractors involved with large housing projects.

All in all, it showed that the Local's new business manager had hit the ground running and had the energy for a long run.

In his report to the membership on June 18, 1934, Van Arsdale explained what he felt a business manager was supposed to do and showed how he was putting the Local on a sound business footing. He was also mindful of an upcoming election and his present position as an appointee: "The membership should realize that the Business Manager's Office is similar to the Sales Force of a private concern," he began. "The Business Agent is the Salesman for the Union . . . [selling] business people on the advantages and efficiency of Union Labor. A campaign of picketing nonunion jobs and establishments not fair to our Union has been carried on. This has brought many satisfactory results and much work to our members which otherwise would have been done by nonunion people."

He went on to praise volunteers who helped his office and the business agents who researched the F.W. Dodge Building Reports on all construction jobs starting in the city, which resulted in an increase in unionized work, "far greater than at any time previous to our activity in spite of the present economic situation."

One of the construction jobs to be started was the Lincoln Tunnel, then known as the Mid-Town Hudson Tunnel, and it showed that Van Arsdale did not shrink from taking on governmental agencies when it came to getting work for his men. The Lincoln Tunnel was a federal PWA project, but the Mason and Hanger Company, the successful bidder on the job, planned to operate as an open shop employing union and nonunion men.

After negotiations failed to change the contractor's mind, Van Arsdale struck the company. He also sent business agent Howard McSpedon to Washington to plead the union's case. McSpedon was successful in his arguments and negotiations resumed on his return. To further tighten the screws, Van Arsdale also arranged a mass demonstration at the tunnel's ground breaking ceremonies protesting the planned use of nonunion labor. Van Arsdale knew of the effectiveness of this kind of public pressure on an entity dependent on public favor. As it had with Gimbels, it worked with the tunnel project. The job became a Local 3 closed shop.

At the same time, Van Arsdale and other state and local leaders, under the guidance of (then) New York AFL President George Meany, won approval from Mayor La Guardia to farm out all city work funded by the PWA to members of unions belonging to the Building Trades of New York, including Local 3.

La Guardia, always sympathetic to unions and the plight of the working man, was prevailed upon by Van Arsdale to have the city's Department of Water Supply, Gas, and Electricity license stores and dealers selling electrical equipment. Unlicensed equipment could not be installed in the city.

On the state level, Van Arsdale, in partnership with Meany, convinced Governor Herbert Lehman to use only local contractors on state projects. This provided more jobs for Local 3 men. Van Arsdale was also instrumental in getting the state legislature to have safety devices placed in neon signs, which not only made it safer for his men but also gave them additional work.

In all of this, Van Arsdale worked closely with Meany who was at the forefront of the campaign to mold the rules of the WPA around a union form. Meany, Van Arsdale, and other building trades unionists led a successful strike to enforce labor's protests against WPA wage controls, and New York's victory became the standard for the rest of U.S. labor to emulate.

As mentioned previously, however, Van Arsdale had internal problems to deal with. One of the most obvious signs of Van Arsdale's success was the formation of another division within the Local.

On June 14, Class E was established, consisting of men employed in the manufacturing and processing of electrical equipment. Many more classes were to be added in years to come. "The creation of this class (E) will benefit our union in several ways by increasing numerically our economic strength and increasing future earning opportunities for our members," Van Arsdale wrote.

Van Arsdale again thought of easing the burden upon the older worker who had difficulties competing with younger men for work. He exempted members 60 years of age or more who had at least twenty years in the union from paying dues.

Early in 1934, he hit on a plan to get more work for the older union member. He beckoned a number of senior men sitting idle around the day room of the union headquarters and said, "Let's go visiting." The men accompanied him on a call to John Flagg, president of the New York Electrical Contractors Association and head of the firm of Watson, Flagg, and Company. He recognized many older men who had worked for him in the past. "Isn't it a shame," said Van Arsdale, "that these good and experienced men cannot find a job because of their age." Flagg seemed shocked and readily agreed with Van Arsdale who then offered a solution, to which Flagg agreed on May 9, 1934. He stated that all of the Contractor Associations represented on his association's Trade Agreement Committee had adopted Van Arsdale's proposal that one man out of every ten employed should be above the age of 55. Flagg wrote "I sincerely trust that the effect of this action will be to find employment for many of your older and deserving members," and Van Arsdale quoted him in his June 18 report to the members.

Van Arsdale also had occasion to address the issue at a later date:

> At first in those early years of the Depression, there was no Social Security and later when it came into existence it provided very little and the employers were pressing and pressing that we—the union—should stop requiring them to hire older men and we felt that common justice demanded and required that we insist that if the employer wanted the services of our members he should accept the services also of those men who had grown old.
>
> I recall once some employers came to the union to complain that one of our older business representatives had sent to work a man [who] was quite elderly to work at a bench and I remember that old-time business agent saying to the employers: 'You feel the man is too old to work? Why don't *you* [emphasis by Van Arsdale] take him out in the back yard and shoot him. You don't want us to be the ones to do it [do you?].[7]

Van Arsdale's diligence and accomplishments were weighed in the election of local officers held on June 30. Van Arsdale, who had served as an appointee business manager, received 1,539 votes out of 3,803. Finishing second out of ten was Harry Gilroy with 1,199 votes. Bert Kirkman was also reelected president. Henceforth, Van Arsdale would be regularly reelected.

That same year, the victorious Van Arsdale led his men out on strikes, including one against Edward F. Caldwell and Company, one of the largest lighting fixture equipment firms in the nation and against the DeLuxe Theater in the Bronx.

Van Arsdale's willingness to use force when words failed was crucial to his milestone achievements. Beginning in late summer 1934, Van Arsdale began his fight for a seven-hour day and thirty-five-hour week without any reduction of wages. This would be another victory that would be a beacon for other unions. In his end-of-the-year report to the members on December 17, Van Arsdale noted that the victory had been accomplished only "because we stopped quarreling over petty differences."

It had been a two-year battle, he continued, but in the end, separate agreements had been reached with Master Electrical Contractors of Brooklyn, the Lighting Fixtures Employers Association, the New York Electrical Contractors Association, and the Long Island Master Electrical Contractors Association. Van Arsdale was given a standing ovation at a membership meeting.

Almost in passing, Van Arsdale reported the most historic event of all: the establishment of a Joint Conference Board in July 1935, consisting of three employer and three union representatives. As part of that agreement, the contractors and Local 3 signed a Voluntary Local Code of Fair Competition with the aim of preventing "a return to those unfair business practices, the effect of which is to lower the standard of wage scales and working conditions of employees and promote ruinous business practices between employees and employers."

The practices mentioned included kickbacks and phony bids on jobs. The position of Director General of the Joint Conference Board was established to investigate and adjudicate any discrepancies with the code. Findings would be submitted to a Code Committee of the Board, which could either censure, fine, or suspend a transgressor. The Board would be funded by an assessment of 1 percent of the cost of construction labor on a job.

"One of the many duties of this board is to plan ways to better our trade," Van Arsdale continued in his report to the members. The Board was a precursor of the Joint Industry Board established in 1943, and reflected Van Arsdale's deeply held belief that management and labor working together without strife can achieve goals that would benefit both of them.

Van Arsdale was establishing himself as a rising star among the city's union leaders, a man whose presence was felt in City Hall, the state legislature, Congress, and even the White House.

But in all this time, he drew a salary of only $85 per week (albeit $10 more than any other officer), when he felt he was able to take it at all. The hard times felt by his members were felt equally by Van Arsdale and his other officers. Thomas Van Arsdale, then approaching adolescence, remembers those times. "I would refuse to go to the grocery store because we had a charge account and during those years we couldn't pay the bills on time," he said. "I was embarrassed to ask for groceries that we couldn't pay for and ask that it be added to the bill. I told my dad and mom that I would only go when they had the cash."[8]

Van Arsdale's practice of dedicating himself almost exclusively to union business at the expense of his family and personal life was becoming more and more entrenched. Peter Brennan, president of the New York Building and Construction Trades Council, recalls Van Arsdale saying, "Look, I care for my family, but if it's not done who's going to do it? You can't tell people to do it if you don't show them the way."[9] Thomas said that his father spent long hours on union business in Manhattan and it became more and more onerous for his father to commute to and from Ozone Park.

"In those years, transportation was slow and many times he would find himself coming home late at night and have to leave early in the morning," Thomas said. "So, early on, he established the practice of staying in Manhattan, at the Shelton Hotel in a room provided by the union. Later, he took a place in the George Washington Hotel across from the 25th Street headquarters."[10]

His father would return to his midtown office late at night after attending various affairs related to the union and then do more union work, such as signing checks. It was also his habit to get an early edition of the *New York Times*. After a few hours sleep, he would be ready to do it all again.

His family would see little of him.

"It was as though he was never there," Thomas continued. "He would only return on weekends and big occasions, birthdays and of course holidays, Christmas, Easter, and such. And when he did come, it would always be a big event. But mainly it developed into him not being there and with the kids being raised by my mother and grandfather and grandmother."

Van Arsdale's youngest child, Kathryn, echoed this. "Grand-dad was the father figure. My father was extra. I was lucky to have both grand-dad and dad. But I used to wonder why wasn't my father home more. Everybody in my neighborhood had both a father and a mother. It was like we didn't have a father. But momma was always there when you opened the door. She was a wonderful woman."

She recalled too that her mother pampered her husband and tried not to burden him with the everyday problems of the family: "My mother was very protective of him. She would tell the kids not to upset him. He can't cope with a lot of things, she said, because he had so much to do. We understood that because we knew he was an important man. I was in awe of him."

Which is not to say that Van Arsdale abdicated his role as father entirely. "He tried to show us how to do things in the right way, the moral way and in ways that made good sense. And mother would support him," Kathryn said. "'He's always right,' she would say. And that was true. He was always right."[11]

Van Arsdale's life was his work. Everyone who knew him realized it, and remarked about it. After his first wife, Molly, died in 1966, Harry remarried in 1969. His second wife Madeline observed: "He was always on the job. . . . His life was his work. The utmost thing in his life was people. He was an extraordinary man. I never heard of anybody like him. He was dedicated to the union and had a good life doing what he liked to do—work, work, work, work, work, work for people."[12]

Madeline also said her husband was a religious man who received the sacraments of his Roman Catholic faith regularly and who attended Mass with her each Sunday and on Holy Days.[13] Armand D'Angelo, a former union official and good friend of Van Arsdale (and later commissioner of the Department of Water Supply, Gas, and Electricity in New York), said Van Arsdale "was very attached to the Church" and he and Van Arsdale went to services often, even while on out-of-town trips.

"[In spirit], he was a very religious man with strong moral values," D'Angelo said. "The teachings of the Church were well known to him."

Van Arsdale's religious beliefs helped to shape his life as a union leader along with the philosophies of unionism, inculcated in him as a youth by his father, which stressed brotherhood, mutual help, and sympathy for those in need.

Van Arsdale's goal was a better life for those not born wealthy and an even playing field for everybody. One of labor's goals, he said, was "to make a contribution in whatever way it can to the rest of the community. . . . I don't think too much of people who have goals [but] don't make any sincere effort to reach their goals. A goal has kind of an empty meaning if an individual or an organization makes no sincere effort, [or is not] willing to make the necessary sacrifice of time and effort and money when necessary to attain the goal and be willing to face and overcome whatever obstacles might be in the path of accomplishing a worthwhile goal."[14]

5

Growing Pains

Starting in 1935 with a massive show of force, Van Arsdale, Local 3, and labor were unafraid to take on public entities and were capable of enduring pressure from the press and the public in order to win what they felt was a fair deal.

The issue was the projected city-owned Independent Subway line. It had been announced on July 16, 1934, that the city's Board of Estimate had awarded the General Railway Signal company a $2,827,500 contract for the all-electric system. Federal Public Works Administration (PWA) funds had been allocated to the city for the completion of the system. In the May 21 newsletter and financial statement, Van Arsdale noted that his office had been "untiring" in its efforts to obtain electrical work on the subway project for his members who were enrolled in a new Class F division for municipal electrical workers.

But General Railway wanted the work done by a rival union that set rates a great deal lower than those won by Local 3. As far as Van Arsdale was concerned, this was virtually a nonunion job, and if Local 3 allowed public funds to be used for such work, it would compromise its attempts to organize and bargain with the private enterprises.

The La Guardia administration could not see any way to change or ameliorate a contract that had already been awarded. Local 3 and Van Arsdale were told by a mournful Francis X. Sullivan, the labor representative on the Board of Transportation, that it was useless to try to change the situation.

Angered at this turn of events, the men of Local 3 met in a turbulent session at the Central Opera House.[1] At first, a motion was made for a general strike of the entire electrical industry in the city—which would have the effect of practically shutting the city down—as a lever to win the subway dispute. This was amended to a proposal to strike only PWA jobs in Local 3's jurisdiction. This was further narrowed in another amendment that directed the strike solely against the subway system, although the general strike and the PWA walkout would be held, like the sword of Damocles, "until such time as it was necessary to put it into effect."

Thus, at 8 A.M. on March 22, the strike began. Local 3 men, with Van Arsdale at the forefront, turned out in massive numbers in front of the company's Park Avenue offices and at the subway construction site at Houston Street and Second Avenue.

Sixteen men were arrested in front of the company offices and seventy-four others were taken into custody for picketing the subway and the home of Bernard Deutsch, president of the Board of Aldermen. Deutsch was picketed because he publicly questioned why Local 3 members could not accept the $15 a week wage the nonunion signalmen were getting. All those arrested were freed and their cases were dismissed.

On the second day of the strike, nearly all of the 8,000 Local 3 membership showed up again at the East Houston Street and Second Avenue site. Across town,[2] the rival union working on the subway was holding a membership meeting. Van Arsdale and other Local 3 officers either were invited or invited themselves to challenge and debate the merits of their arguments at the meeting with the other union's leadership.

"The membership of their alleged union, after hearing our representatives state our case, were receptive to our cause," Van Arsdale wrote in his laconic, formal prose.

The blandishments of Van Arsdale and other Local 3 leaders were apparently so successful that it was reported in the press that twenty members of the rival union refused to go to work the following day in a show of support for Local 3 strikers.

Meanwhile, the contractors used the press to lambaste the union and attempt to sway public opinion against the strikers. One of their arguments was that the men of Local 3 did not have the expertise to handle the intricacies of subway signal work. Van Arsdale countered by pointing out that Local 3 had wired the original Interboro Rapid Transit (IRT) line thirty years earlier as well as having done similar work at Pennsylvania Station.

In addition, Van Arsdale, with the help of Francis Sullivan, who was the Transportation Board Commissioner, started special courses for members at the Board of Transportation offices in order to make sure his men could do the job when called for. Local 3 men were given daily instruction on signal wiring, working amid actual railroad ties and rails in a facsimile of the subway.

Van Arsdale also launched a public relations campaign of his own. "We had a gigantic job before us of making the people of the City of New York 'Local Union No. 3 conscious,'" Van Arsdale noted. One aspect of the campaign was the distribution of 250,000 circulars to the public and to General Railway Signal Company employees. The circular outlined the achievements and public-spiritedness of Local 3. Among other things, the circular mentioned Local 3's welfare benefits for its elderly or sick members and insurance payments to the families of deceased members. It reminded readers of the Local's willingness to cut its workweek and take lower wages at the start of the Depression in order to give jobs to more of the unemployed. And it pointed to its educational efforts for members to teach them how to be better at their jobs. "The members of the Union have made these things possible only by sacrifice and suffering and have now reduced themselves to the point of exhaustion. . . . We now appeal to the public to support us by only patronizing stores and merchants that employ members of Local 3," the circular stated.

If readers of the circular had any suggestions or comments, they were invited to address them to Van Arsdale at the union headquarters. Finally, the circular urged a boycott of businesses that were unfriendly to Local 3.

In conjunction with the distribution of the circulars, Local 3 members roamed the streets in Queens and Manhattan shouting out their contractual positions to the public with the use of a sound truck donated by Motion Picture Operators (Local 306). Aid also came from all the unions of the Building Trades Council, Central Trades and Labor Council, various civic leagues, and community clubs.

On March 26, 1935, 4,000 members marched down Second Avenue, across East Houston Street, and down Centre Street to a rally at Foley Square. The marchers, carrying banners and placards, were led by a band. World War I veterans wore blue armbands with the gold word "veteran" across them. Fifteen members carried the large service banner of the union, which bore 618 stars, representing each member of the Local who were veterans. A loudspeaker also blared the Local's message to the onlookers along the way and for blocks around. Van Arsdale and other Local leaders spoke at the rally at Foley Square. Then he led a strike delegation to nearby City Hall to present the union's position to Mayor La Guardia.

Van Arsdale used the power of the airwaves: Local 3 official John K. Lapham gave radio addresses over station WEVD. Meetings were also held with various public officials, the Board of Aldermen, Board of Estimate and Apportionment, and the Board of Transportation.

As a result, a resolution was introduced before the Board of Aldermen and the Board of Estimate and Apportionment calling for an investigation into the practices of the Signal Company. Bronx Borough President James J. Lyons also voiced support.

Van Arsdale and Local 3 took the case into federal jurisdiction. Several hearings were held before the NRA Compliance Board in the city, which delivered rulings sympathetic to Local 3, although the Signal Company immediately appealed to the NLRB.

The dispute neared an end after Transportation Board Commissioner Sullivan was accepted as a mediator by both sides. Mayor La Guardia also worked hard behind the scenes to achieve a settlement and worked out a plan whereby a portion of the original contracts would be re-let to open the door to union-approved contractors. After several meetings, a tentative agreement was reached and subsequently ratified by the membership at a rousing meeting on May 9 at the Central Opera House. Also as part of the agreement, the city's Board of Aldermen agreed it would never again approve nonunion or open-shop contracts.

Van Arsdale and the Local were to have their difficulties in getting contractors always to abide by the hire-union rule. Nevertheless, the settlement was a major victory not only for the men of Local 3 and Van Arsdale but also for labor throughout the nation, which had watched the strike. Local 3 members gained about $400,000 in wages and the IND's Sixth Avenue[3] branch became the first subway in the nation to be constructed completely by union workers—and eighteen days ahead of schedule in the bargain.

The lot of the membership was also improved by another Van Arsdale negotiation that increased wages to $11.90 for a seven-hour day, an increase of 70 cents per hour. The number of helpers was capped at five per job, eliminating the contractors' practice of loading their payrolls with helpers at the expense of journeymen. The agreement was ratified by the membership on August 23 and was to go into effect on January 1, 1936.

But the higher wages were contrary, ironically, to a new federal program created to help the working man. Under the Emergency Relief Act of April 1935, the WPA replaced several works and relief programs for the unemployed. As mentioned previously, it was a "make-work" program, providing jobs for the unemployed as its predecessors had done. Laborers, including artists and writers, received wages ranging from $15 to $95 per month. It would be the primary work/relief program until the start of World War II.

The problem for labor was wage scales below those sought or enjoyed by union members. Employers would cite the WPA codes and standards, as they had done in earlier New Deal programs, as reasons to pay less.

The New York Central Trades Council urged strong action by its member unions against the proposed $93.50 wage on federal projects. In his report to the membership on September 7, 1935, Van Arsdale noted that the Local's new pay increase came in the face of employer demands across the nation for cuts in wages, fanned by WPA limits on pay. He praised the membership for the militancy they had shown in battling for higher pay and better working conditions and predicted additional "major achievements" in the future.

Thus, with the WPA now the enemy, the Local 3 membership authorized a strike against the WPA on August 8, 1935. Van Arsdale's disenchantment and disappointment with FDR, whom he had admired, was evident:

> After the hardship, suffering and sacrifices our members have made throughout the last five years of this Depression, it is certainly a sad state of affairs. The Roosevelt administration, that promised to help "the forgotten man," now is responsible for the Works Progress Administration which we all realize will destroy the wages and conditions of building trades unions and bring about the introduction of an open shop movement by private interests in the building industry which has been union for more than 50 years in New York City. It is hoped that President Roosevelt will realize the great mistake that has been made and the misery and doubt that has been caused by the attempt to coerce and force men to work for half the legal prevailing rate and that he will take the necessary steps to correct this condition.

Van Arsdale urged the president to exempt New York from WPA regulations and pay rates. But, despite an intense lobbying campaign by Van Arsdale, there was no exemption. On the other hand, neither was there a demand for a rollback.

The WPA strike, overlapping the subway walkout, again illustrated Van Arsdale's ability to keep several balls in the air at once, including areas of special interest to Van Arsdale: schooling and benefits.

In his September 7 newsletter, he pointed out that the sign industry offered an opportunity for increased employment, and urged members to attend a new school to learn neon sign work and maintenance. Moreover, the industry was ripe for organization and Van Arsdale urged his members to be as diligent and as tireless as he was in that endeavor.

"You are requested to take an active interest in the organizing of this field by visiting every store of which you are a customer and ask the owner who maintains the [neon] sign [remember that no sign is too small] and in the event that it is a non-union maintenance company, urge him to hire a union concern," Van Arsdale wrote.

In his efforts to improve life for Local members, Van Arsdale reestablished an affiliation with the Union Health Center, which would provide each member and his family with medical care at a small fee. It is worth noting that the Electrical Workers Benefit Society and Union Cooperative Insurance paid out death benefits totaling nearly $69,000 in the first eight months of the year.

Van Arsdale's emphasis on education as an avenue of self-improvement was not limited to industry classes, but spread into the arts. This would be seen in many vast and dramatic enterprises in the years to come. The labor play *Let Freedom Ring*, by Myra Cohn Livingston, opened on Broadway in 1935, and Van Arsdale urged members to go to the Broadhurst Theatre to see this fine play which is in itself an education.

"It is important that members of labor unions encourage this type of play. Arrangements can be made for theatre parties by groups of our members. Unemployed members can attend matinees for admission of as low as 50 cents."

Theater, books, and films of the day echoed other serious social concerns including the growth of Nazism in Germany. This was also addressed in the Local. Local members protested against the purchase of steel from Germany that was to be used for the Triborough Bridge, under construction in 1935 with public funds. This was in keeping with an earlier resolution in which the Local supported an AFL action urging the boycott of German industry and products because of its persecution of Jews. But on the other hand, on a noneconomic issue, the Local members apparently felt that sports and politics did not mix: they rejected a proposed resolution to join with other metropolitan area unions to protest against the participation of U.S. athletes in the 1936 Olympics in Germany, even though the AFL had issued such a protest.

Nevertheless, the social and political conscience of the Local was always strong and progressive. At a meeting on August 8, 1935, members approved a motion to endorse a bill introduced in Congress by Representative Vito Marcantonio, an avowed communist, calling for a Workers Rights Amendment to the Constitution. (The amendment, however, failed.) Two days later, Marcantonio spoke at a general membership meeting of the Local on the problems facing organized labor. According to the minutes of the meeting on October 10, he commended Local 3 for its progressive activities, which had attracted national attention. He also declared that labor could not count on elected officials to give them justice that could be achieved only "if they continued to fight for better conditions themselves."

At that same meeting, it was announced that Van Arsdale had been appointed by IBEW President Tracy as a delegate to the AFL's Building Trades Council, a post that would give Van Arsdale a greater opportunity to influence other unions nationally.

Van Arsdale used the appointment to make peace—apparently—between rival factions in the Council. In his report to the membership on November 8, he said he was "pleased to report that the dispute which splits the Building Trades Council into two factions will be settled in the near future."

That same newsletter contained the admonition—virtually a credo of Van Arsdale—that "a labor union must go forward or it will slip backward— there is no middle ground."

Events at the end of 1935, however, not only threatened that forward movement, but also posed the possibility of severe regression, and they would have far-reaching ramifications for years to come. The events had their roots in what had been one of Van Arsdale's greatest organizing victories, when he won contracts with local manufacturers in the switchboard and panel board industry. Van Arsdale used a union boycott of any equipment that did not bear his Local's label, in other words, that was not put together by Local 3 workers. The metropolitan area manufacturers, freed from the competition of outside units produced at a lower price, signed up to gain the label—and the profits it promised. Van Arsdale was to use that maneuver in other organizing drives.

But the outside manufacturers, including some of the biggest in the nation, did not sit still when faced with the loss of much of the New York market. On December 9, 1935, the National Electrical Manufacturers Association (NEMA) and ten firms each brought a suit in federal court seeking an injunction against what they charged was an illegal restraint of trade.[4] Over the years, this took many shapes, and bedevilled Van Arsdale. At first, the suit was known as the "Allen Bradley" case, named after one of the firms in the litigation. The plaintiffs, seeking $1.35 million in damages, alleged that Local 3 "had built a Chinese Wall" around New York in creating what amounted to a monopoly in violation of the Sherman Antitrust Act. The director of the Association stated that "By means of strikes, boycotts, threats and intimidations, the local union had thrown an economic wall around the 10 million or more people residing in the New York metropolitan district.[5]

The case was a cause of deep worry for Van Arsdale because he knew that recent court decisions had gone against labor. Van Arsdale urged his troops to stand firm against the attack. "Injunctions by hostile employers against labor still remains one of their most effective weapons, used to break down the morale of a progressive union. Just so long as we stand together, the attacks by our enemies will have little, if any, effect," he said.[6] He also told union attorney Harold Stern: "If it is decided against us now, we're dead. Five or six years from now it won't matter." Stern was told to stall the case as long as possible.[7]

Stern and Local 3 countered by denying that a boycott existed and stating that the Local's action was intended to improve its members' financial status, which was out of the purview of the antitrust laws. The dispute was not an antitrust matter but a union-management conflict because the plaintiffs had refused to bargain with the Local. Moreover, the Norris-La Guardia Act barred the federal courts from issuing injunctions in labor disputes. Finally, the defense contended that this was a local and not a national dispute and federal courts did not have jurisdiction.

In a report to members, Van Arsdale said it was his accusers who were guilty of maintaining a monopoly and the real reason for the suit was retaliation for the gains it had achieved for its members. The plaintiffs sought not only to discredit the union but to drain its resources through legal fees. He castigated the greed of his antagonists in strong proletarian terms. "We still have with us 'powerful interests' who consider our Union is interfering with their desire to amass huge fortunes which in many instances does not bring to them and their families as much genuine happiness as our members enjoy when they receive a small increase in their weekly income. How much improved the world would be if these powerful men could prevent their greed from blinding them just long enough to realize this simple fact."

He added that NEMA and the plaintiffs represented a group so rich and powerful that they constituted something out of "a nightmare." He urged the membership to stand strong and remain informed about the case. He also pointed out the growing power of the Local, which had doubled its membership in the past several years to 13,800 and predicted (accurately, as it turned out) that if that pace continued it would have 25,000 to 30,000 members.[8]

The case went before Special Master John Kirkland Clark and hearings lasted two and a half years with 400 witnesses heard, 24,000 pages of testimony taken, and approximately 1,700 exhibits presented.

Some of the testimony bordered on the absurd. A witness for the plaintiff, for example, testified that although he did not have firsthand knowledge of the alleged event, "someone" told him that a stench bomb had been thrown through the window of a hostile contractor and had landed in his infant daughter's crib, blinding her. Investigation showed that his story was false.

While the case was being deliberated, the United Electrical, Radio, and Machinery Workers Union, chartered by the rival CIO, joined the battle in 1939 and made the same charge as the employers: the IBEW, Local 3, and Van Arsdale had created a monopoly. In published reports, Van Arsdale made light of this development. He was quoted as saying that "he was not greatly worried about the final outcome because the spirit of unity manifested by our members and their willingness to make sacrifices would overcome any ill effect coming from this suit."[9]

In 1942 Clark ruled against the Local, which promptly appealed. Two years later the Appeals Court ruled and reversed the special master's decision. Now it was the turn of the manufacturers to appeal. In a ruling that set a precedent in monopoly law, the U.S. Supreme Court declared in 1947 that the union could undertake a boycott—even though illegal—as long as it was not in collusion with employers.

In general, Van Arsdale's tactics had been successful and his hopes had been fulfilled in the stalling of the action. The union's victory would be even greater than anticipated. The decision influenced Congress in its passing of the Taft-Hartley Act on June 23, 1947, which included a section dealing with boycotts such as Local 3's. As far as Local 3 was concerned, however, the growing cooperation between the Local and employers made the law moot. The goal of organizing thousands of manufacturing workers had been achieved.

But that would be later. Van Arsdale was wrong in his assessment that there would be no ill effects from the suit. The suits were expensive and put a strain on the depleted union treasury. Local members were assessed an additional 10 cents an hour in 1940 to help defray the costs. Van Arsdale voluntarily cut his wages from $150 to $100 per week.

The press, which was largely antiunion, attacked Van Arsdale and the Local, and claimed that the consumer was paying the price for the alleged monopoly. Knowing a hot political issue and a headline when he saw one, the ambitious Special Rackets Prosecutor Thomas Dewey announced on January 14, 1937, that he had opened an investigation into Local 3's books. Van Arsdale and Local 3 lashed back with a coordinated counterattack.

First, the Central Trades and Labor Council and the Building and Construction Trades Council protested to Governor Lehman and the New York State Legislature against Dewey's action. A mass protest rally was held and others were planned. A delegation was sent to Albany for meetings with Governor Lehman and leaders of the State Legislature to protest Dewey's investigation.

Two weeks after Dewey's announcement, at a January 29 meeting, Van Arsdale told the membership: "Let Dewey spend your money and mine to investigate the reasons for people leaving the straight and narrow path. In the flood districts, looting has become general. Why? Because people want to be clothed and they want to eat. This same reason is the cause of vice, crime and racketeering throughout the country. Get to those who are responsible for low wages and long hours. He will then find a racket that will be worthwhile investigating." Dewey turned a deaf ear to the protests and the battle of headlines continued.

In contrast to his announcement of the investigation, Dewey quietly closed his investigation several years later after finding nothing amiss. "Knowing Mr. Dewey's reputation, one may be sure that if the records had revealed the slightest evidence of irregularities, action certainly would have been taken," Van Arsdale said in a press statement. "The return of our records without comment speaks for itself. When these records were requested by Mr. Dewey there was a fanfare of publicity which tended to create the impression that there was something wrong with our organization. The most significant aspect of the return of our records is that no action has been taken." He added, "it is about time that ambitious public officials stopped using so-called investigations of labor for witch burning purposes. . . . It is regrettable that many otherwise splendid public officials permit themselves to be used as screens for labor-baiting drives."

Legal investigations did not end with Dewey, however. The Justice Department opened an investigation of Local 3, Van Arsdale, and the nation's building trades unions in 1939. A federal indictment on monopoly charges was filed by "trust-buster" Assistant Attorney General Thurman Arnold of the U.S. Attorney's office against Local 3 and five New York City electrical manufacturers in what was essentially a reprise of the Allen Bradley case.

Van Arsdale publicly lambasted Arnold and warned him against allowing his ostensible aim of lowering building costs to become "the rallying point for all the labor-baiting forces in the construction industry." He called on Arnold to probe price-fixing in steel, cement, and other building materials.

"Our union, one of the largest single locals in the American Federation of Labor, stands ready at all times to cooperate with Mr. Arnold's office, but we must insist that organized labor will not permit an antitrust drive to degenerate into an attack on the American standard of living."[10]

Van Arsdale met with Arnold to try to explain how his actions were intended to help members of the Local, and reported that Arnold would allow him to continue his alleged antitrust practices if he would just sign a decree to cease and desist. He quoted Arnold as saying, "Van Arsdale, you don't understand this, all you have to do is to sign a decree, go on doing everything the way you have been doing it and you will be making a great contribution." Van Arsdale said he asked himself "What the hell kind of a representative is this of government?" He said he reported this conversation to several of the president's aides and they told him, "We don't approve of what he is doing, but he's got the President sold on this method. And until the President realizes it's not going any place, there's very little we can do."[11]

With the Justice Department roasting him in the press and the courts, Van Arsdale resigned his post as business manager on June 28, 1940, to seek a vote of confidence in a new election. He got it. He was returned to office by a landslide—9,169 to 1,823.

The issue disappeared quietly when Arnold, its prime advocate, left the Justice Department and more friendly hands took over. But the bogeyman of monopoly was to raise its head yet again in a future intra-union dispute.

After the start of the Allen Bradley proceedings in 1935, Van Arsdale told his membership in his February 10 report, in his recurring patriarchal tone:

> In these momentous times, I feel you should be warned and be ever vigilant of our rapidly changing social system. Political leaders, leaders of industry and labor, are assailing each other's theory of economics. Political office seekers are burning the radio airways and the public press with cure-alls for our economic ills. Social and labor legislation is being bitterly attacked in the courts.
>
> It seems that the Anti-Boycott League and the League for Industrial Rights have been recreated under the colors of the American Liberty League, sponsored by the Chamber of Commerce, the National Manufacturers Association, the National Electrical Manufacturers Association, bankers and industry to combat labor. Labor leaders in conventions and elsewhere are still debating Industrial Unionism versus Craft Unionism.
>
> The trend of the working people is constantly toward organization. Regardless of what may develop in national politics and in the policy of the American Federation of Labor, the solidarity of our membership must be self-evident to assure our intelligent progress. Many things remain to be accomplished to fortify the progress made in the past.

Van Arsdale then went on to list some of the events since the distribution of the previous report. These included not only the Allen Bradley case but also the successful pressuring of the city Board of Education to overturn a number of contracts for electrical work in schools given to nonunion firms and also to agree in the future to protect union interests in the letting of new contracts. The board's action removed the threat of a strike by Local 3.

The strike weapon was also used successfully in 1936 in actions against Brooklyn Edison Company and Bronx Gas and Electric Company, in disputes to force the hiring of union workers to replace nonunion employees. That same year saw the men of Local 3 strike against Macy's, exerting the kind of pressure that Van Arsdale knew would be especially harmful on a firm so dependent on public good will. The action ended successfully, as reported earlier.

Van Arsdale's zeal and success in organizing drew kudos from IBEW President Tracy. He spoke before a membership meeting October 8, 1936, and praised the organizing of the fixture, switchboard, cable boxes, and low-tension equipment manufacturers. Then he added:

> I want to congratulate you on the very fortunate selection of Brother Harry Van Arsdale as your Business Manager. . . . I have the highest regard for him personally as I find him to be a man of integrity and his modesty is

worthy of attention. His regard of the interests of others and especially his inexhaustible energy, his masterly understanding of the labor movement in general makes him a man whose merits equal his reputation. I should have to think a long while if I were asked to name one who had done more valuable service to the International Brotherhood, always with responsive interest and cooperation in matters concerning the brotherhood as a whole.

It is not hard to imagine a blush coming to the cheeks of Van Arsdale when he heard that. He was never one to seek celebrity, but would always say that others were responsible or had shared heavily in the responsibility for much that was accomplished on his watch. Tracy's position regarding Van Arsdale was to change in later years, as will be shown in a later chapter. But at this time, all was wine and roses between the two as the Local's campaign of organizing the industry rolled onward. The next group to become the focus of the organizational drive was the Signal Appliance Manufacturing Industry.

"The wages, hours and conditions of employment in this industry are in a deplorable state," Van Arsdale wrote in his March 1937 bulletin to the members. "It is found that skilled workers earned as little as $18 or less per week. The organization of the miscellaneous branches of our industry is necessary and essential to fortify the progress we have made. Electrical manufacturing plants have been an incubator for nonunion electrical workers. A labor organization must forge ahead to maintain its advances. Other branches of the industry will be reported on [at] a later date," he continued, a harbinger of his intention and ultimate success in organizing every facet of the electrical industry in the New York metropolitan area within Local 3.

To accomplish this, Van Arsdale applied to (and received permission from) the IBEW to amend the Local charter. This allowed him to create divisions within the Local and remake the organization as a combined craft and industrial union. "This will be helpful in organizing the various branches of our industry," Van Arsdale noted in his March 11, 1937, bulletin to the membership.

The amendment allowed the Local to bring Class B members into its fold. As defined by the IBEW, there are two basic classifications of all members: A and BA charter members. The first group includes the more skilled, and, therefore, more highly paid, craftspeople, who also pay a higher percentage of dues. They are thus also eligible for welfare and pension benefits from both the IBEW and the Local. BA charter members have no say or vote on IBEW pensions and death benefits. However, BA members can enter the A class as their wages rise. The broadening of the net to include Class B members into Local 3, already a de facto accomplishment with the organization of the panel board and switchboard industries, would continue to swell the

Local's membership, making it even more of a force to be reckoned with.

Life was improving for the electricians. Local 3 members had capped work at three days per week in order to spread employment, but Local President Bert Kirkman declared: "The expected business improvement, while slow, is steadily on the upgrade and should it gather momentum, as I am positive it will, we may confidently look forward to a four- and perhaps a five-day week before many more months have passed. During the past three years, we have gone through the most trying period in our history with flying colors and each and every member should feel proud of his accomplishment for Local No. 3 and the International Brotherhood."[12]

In a special meeting on August 13, the membership happily approved a five-day schedule and gave Van Arsdale the mandate to strive for a six-hour day. The proposal was then put to the New York Electrical Contractors Association and approved. The regular working day was to be from 8 A.M. to 3 P.M. (with a seventh hour apparently included for lunch), with a top rate of pay for Class A Journeymen at $2.00 an hour, and with healthy increases for apprentices, something that had not been achieved before. Overtime rates were trimmed as a sweetener to management. Van Arsdale pointed out that the result of making union work more competitive would be more work for union members. The agreement went into effect on August 27. Van Arsdale wrote in his mid-year bulletin: "We should all rejoice in the knowledge that our Union has succeeded in establishing the six-hour day in our industry and once again has blazed the trail for others to follow. A shorter work day is the only sound solution for the unfortunate millions who are still unemployed." The Local, spearheaded by Van Arsdale, then engaged in a campaign to get the six-hour day, thirty-hour week established nationwide. Van Arsdale won the support of IBEW President Tracy in the endeavor and the six-hour day, thirty-hour week became an official goal of the International's Building and Construction Trades Department.

The entire atmosphere and personality of the Local had changed since Van Arsdale had taken over. There was harmony and a real sense of brotherhood coinciding with a deep appreciation of the business manager. One lively illustration of this could be seen in the renewed interest in the Local's band and glee club. A Local 3 member, Henry Helkin, was so inspired that he wrote a song, "Let's Drink a Toast to the IBEW," to be played in parades, at meetings, or on other occasions. The chorus said in part: "Let's Drink a Toast to the I.B.E.W., the Union that will always lead the way. Now workers' cares are lighter and their skies are brighter." The song was dedicated to Local 3 and certainly, by inference, to Van Arsdale. Another example can be found in the song: "Local No. 3 Forever."

The Local also showed appreciation of Van Arsdale by naming him president of the city's Building Trades Council. Local 3 President Kirkman noted in the August 22, 1936, bulletin that Van Arsdale's elevation to the honorary office would not interfere with his work as Local 3 business manager but "should result in the Council becoming once again of vital importance in the welfare of all union men in the building industry."

However, Van Arsdale would step down from the post in December. A Council reorganization made the post of president a paying position and required the president to devote himself solely to Council duties. Van Arsdale said he could not accept the offered position because he felt a duty to remain with Local 3.

The Council's action, approving Van Arsdale's recommendation to appoint Howard McSpedon as president, however, was another vote of confidence for Van Arsdale who was being vilified in the press because of the Dewey racketeering charges—an opportunistic and antilabor echo of the Allen Bradley allegations. President Kirkman blasted the press reports of the indictment as "libelous."

> Weak, cowardly, bullying individuals always hit below the belt or when your back is turned. . . . How can any victim of an inquisition expect to have a fair hearing in court or an impartial decision rendered, when the minds of both public and jury have been poisoned by these vicious below-the-belt attacks. . . . The reason for these attacks is plain. We have been successful in our effort to obtain fair wages. All these reasons, or any of them, [are] sufficient for big business to use any method to cripple, maim and if possible destroy us. The modern method is to slander us before the bar of public opinion and paralyze our financial strength by subjecting us to legal battles requiring heavy and extra heavy legal expenses.
>
> During the past few weeks, we have visited many other labor organizations and knowing the justice of our case, these organizations have enthusiastically promised moral and financial support. They know it is their fight too and the final outcome of this case will leave us in a still stronger position to meet the problems of the future.[13]

Van Arsdale was to get a respite from day-to-day union matters when he was named by the membership to be a member of a delegation of American trade unionists to visit the Soviet Union for May Day celebrations—and for a firsthand look at the changes occurring there. He was allowed $250 to pay for transportation and $1,000 for expenses during the seven-week stay.

He set sail on the liner *S.S. Berengaria* on April 15, 1937. Van Arsdale kept a diary of the trip, writing in brief note form in his round, careful hand. He wrote about the day's events and the people he met. Convivial and sociable, Van Arsdale, after all, was a people-person.

In his first entry on April 15, he related how gratified he was to have been seen off at the pier by Local 3 officers, friends, and his Aunt Bertha. His "first pleasant surprise" was finding that one of his shipmates was James King, a maintenance man at the *New York Herald-Tribune*. Van Arsdale then went on to scrupulously note all the "bon voyage" gifts he had been given for the journey by relatives, friends, and various Local 3 clubs. These included binoculars from the Spartan Club, a camera from the Kingsboro Club; an eight-day travel clock from the Colony Club; a Parker pen and pencil set from the Allied Union Club; books from the 419 Club; a travel bag and dresser set from the officers of Local 3; and a leather wallet and a pair of spats from his Aunt Bertha.

He spent his time on board mostly reading during the day and watching films at night. At other times he socialized with delegation members and other passengers, always gravitating either to those who were working class or to those who shared his affinity for the working man.

On the fourth day, Van Arsdale was chosen chairman of the delegation of about thirty-five men and women. On the following day a group picture was taken in which Van Arsdale can be seen sitting in the front row, center. When the *Berengaria* arrived in Southampton on April 21, Van Arsdale traveled by train to London. He had an "interesting conversation" with a Russian engineer on a business trip with whom he shared a compartment.

The entry of April 23, 1937, is significant in that, in part, it again shows his essential affability, compassion for the poor, willingness to help people in need—and his practical views as a trade craftsman.

> Rode through London which is a fine city. Everything is being elaborately decorated and the stands are nearly completed for the coronation [of Queen Elizabeth as Queen Consort]. Visited museums, old palaces, historical buildings and various points of interest. Returned to Imperial [hotel] and then went to see some of the people at the Endsleigh [another hotel], mailed books which I had read to N.Y.C. and witnessed bad auto accident. Taxi was hit by delivery truck at crossing and taxi was knocked over on side, helped to pull driver and passenger from cab. Both appeared to be more shaken and frightened than seriously injured. Decided to see London after dinner with several of the others.
>
> London is a very interesting and gay city and a stranger would get the impression that there was little or no suffering and hardship if he does not look below the surface. Many of London's main streets are still illuminated by gas. However they are very bright and they use as many as six mantles in one globe and have three or more globes on a pole. Much of the temporary lighting for the coronation is being done with gas.

Van Arsdale set sail on April 24 aboard the *Felix Dzerzhinsky*, a Soviet ship. Entries were brief and he indicated that he and other passengers were seasick on a rough trip. He read most of the time. He notes that he and others contributed funds to aid "the sufferers in Spain" during the Spanish Civil War.

He arrived in Leningrad on April 29 to be "greeted by thousands of Russian workers who tremendously enjoyed welcoming the delegates of workers from other countries." He arrived in Moscow on April 30 and his entries became reportorial. He described in detail the geography of the Kremlin and the statistics associated with various projects, planned or being built. On May Day, he was assigned a seat to the right of Lenin's tomb and the reviewing stand on which Stalin and other Soviet leaders stood. The available diary records end there. Whatever else he wrote during his trip was apparently lost.

Van Arsdale's frugality in his travel accommodations dismayed some Local 3 members who felt he should have been more generous to himself. David Kass, a member of Local 3 and a friend, who had seen him off at dockside in New York, wrote in part:

> After leaving the dock, I went back to work and from work I met some of our brothers and after telling them where I spent the dinner hour and that you were going second class they all said you should have been going first class or better, exclaiming, "Look what he has done for us. That shows that it is wrong what some old style politicians say: 'There is no use doing anything for the people [as] they don't appreciate it anyway.' They do—and how—they show it on every occasion and—really—there was never one that was so admired, looked up to [was so] encouraging, even loved, all because you, with your leadership, embody honest and progressive unionism."[14]

Kass wrote regularly to Van Arsdale while he was in the Soviet Union, addressing him always as "Van," as those who were close to him did. His letters were accompanied by news clippings intended to keep Van Arsdale up to date with union matters and other items of interest in the city, the nation, and in Europe, including news from Spain and Germany, as well as events in the Soviet Union, which may not have been made public in the local press.

It is interesting to note the contents Kass's letters to Van Arsdale as they indicate what subjects Kass thought would interest Van Arsdale. This may give us some insight into Van Arsdale, who kept his private self unrevealed.

In a letter dated May 5, Kass reveals that Van Arsdale contemplated going to Spain. According to the letter, Van Arsdale had asked William Hogan whether he should go to Spain. Kass, indicating that he knows Hogan would advise against it, urges Van Arsdale to go anyway. "I would certainly not miss it for anything," he wrote. "Probably, the Spanish comrades (this last word must be natural with you by this time) can fix things up for you. It would be great to hear you on the radio at our regular meeting. The Spanish radio is heard very well here." In the same letter, he suggested that Van Arsdale compare the Soviets' "speed-up" methods of increasing worker productivity at their plants, and asked "whether they have places where they do not let anybody go into at all, like in the Ford's forge shop." Kass also sent books to Van Arsdale, including Maxim Gorky's *My University Days*, and a history of Czarist Russia. Kass also suggests that Van Arsdale make an assessment, from whatever he is allowed to see, of the Soviet school system and government, particularly to determine whether government leaders live as plutocrats, as reported in the Western press, and are dictators.

It is not known if Van Arsdale replied to Kass or followed any of his suggestions and one can make only assumptions about how Kass's suggestions were received.[15] But it is worth noting that Van Arsdale kept the correspondence and the clippings in his personal files as mementos of his trip.

On his return, Van Arsdale reported to the membership about what he had seen in the USSR, including its industrial programs, building construction methods and procedures, and social and economic conditions, but there is no record of what he said other than that he delivered the report and touched on the aforementioned points.

George Schuck, Sr., a Local 3 veteran and officer who knew Van Arsdale well, said of the Russian trip:

> When he came back, I listened to him and watched him and I don't think you would have thought he went to Russia . . . and the trip I'm sure opened his eyes to anything that [they] might not have been opened to before that. I'm sure they were wide opened when he left.
>
> He always thought he would like to know everything that is possible to know and he knew that this would make him look maybe like a pinko or a commie or what[ever]. But with him if he wanted to learn something, he was going to go, pinko, red or white . . . wasn't going to make any difference to him; it wasn't going to change him. And he went. And he observed a lot of things while he was over there. And he came back and we never became a communist union.[16]

Bernard Rosenberg, a former business agent and close confidante of Van Arsdale, also throws some light on the Soviet trip. He recalled a luncheon at

Constantine's Restaurant in Queens, which was also attended by a United Nations diplomat connected to the Russian Mission.

> And during the course of the meeting the Russian envoy was talking about Russia, and Harry was sitting next to me. And at that time the Jews were having hard difficulties in leaving.
>
> And I asked him, the Russian envoy, why is it that in Russia it's so difficult for the Jews to leave and go to other parts of the world? And Harry said "You know, if I left this meeting and I went to Kennedy Airport, I can board a plane and go anyplace on the planet Earth, but I could not do it in Russia." So the envoy said "It's a brain drain. We don't allow the Jews to leave because at that time they were a very high percentage of students at the universities. And if they left, we'd be losing a very talented group." And then subsequently Harry and I spoke when we went home together, and he said, "I'll have to tell you about my trip to Russia. . . . I'm riding this train, I looked out the window and I saw all these bayonets as we passed the farms. So I asked my host . . . whether the soldiers were there to protect the farmers or prevent them from leaving."
>
> And then he said, "We had this occasion that I was invited to attend, a big parade, and they had me up on this platform. But instead of standing on the platform, I went down, down below, and I went off the platform to look at the people. And then after the parade was over I came back up and my host said, 'Mr. Van Arsdale, you missed all the important dignitaries.' And I said 'Oh, no, I didn't, I was with the people.'"

Rosenberg believes that the Russian trip had a great impact on Van Arsdale's approach to solving labor's problems and achieving goals for workers. "He turned it around. He became a Conservative after he realized that in order for the labor movement to succeed in America, it had to be business-oriented. Now when Harry went, I guess it was just to expand his knowledge, to get an idea of what it really was like. But he took an opposite view."[17]

The Russian excursion engraved in Van Arsdale's mind the importance of travel as an educational experience, and it led to a program of travel for members, especially Local 3 officers, as a way of meeting trade unionists from other nations and sharing experiences. (In 1951, the membership voted to send two representatives abroad each year with expenses of $5,000 provided. This and discussions with groups on international subjects were part of the many educational programs pushed by Van Arsdale as a means of self-improvement and education of the membership. The programs will be examined in greater detail below.)

On his return, Van Arsdale picked up where he had left off in the Local 3 organizing drive. The electric lamp, lampshade, and electric novelties manufacturers were a new target of organization as the Local and Van Arsdale fought to better the lot of men and women earning as little as $7 in a sixty-hour week. Forty-five shops were struck with additional ones going out each day, Van Arsdale reported in his June 1937 bulletin to members.

Another significant success was the Consolidated Edison Company's signing of a Local 3 contract rejecting the organizing effort of the rival CIO.

One argument undoubtedly used with strong effect by Local 3 was that its organization uniquely encompassed the vertical union philosophy of the CIO, representing more than one trade or skill as opposed to a horizontal union, embracing only one. This facet was further illustrated in 1937 with the establishment of several new divisions in Local 3 as its ranks swelled with the signing of members in broader areas of the electrical industry. The merger of a small, independent union, the United Brotherhood of Electrical Workers, with Local 3 further increased the latter's ranks. Membership was kept apprised of all the doings of the Local, at first through the regular reports Van Arsdale sent to their homes and later through the Local's newspaper, the *Electrical Union World*. Van Arsdale had also encouraged the reestablishment of clubs within the Local reflecting ethnic or racial backgrounds. He felt these served as clearinghouses for information and for effecting solidarity within the membership.

During this period of growth in the mid-1930s, plans were also under way for the projected 1939 World's Fair in Flushing, Queens. Van Arsdale, other Local 3 leaders, and all of the union establishment in the city knew the project would provide many new jobs. Local 3 members, at Van Arsdale's urging, purchased $146,000 in World's Fair bonds. As Van Arsdale noted, it was "the most outstanding effort of cooperation received from any labor organization."[18]

In the midst of all this, another local election was held and Van Arsdale was returned to a four-year term. Those reelected to two-year terms included Bert Kirkman as president and William Hogan as financial secretary.

The most significant victory of the year, however, was the agreement with employers that management would pay the employee's share of the weekly Social Security payments.

Congress had passed the Social Security Act in August 1935. Social Security would be paid for partially by taxes on wages and payrolls. The collections began on January 1, 1937, and the initial charge to employees was 0.05 percent on the first $3,000 of earnings, or a total of $15 a year. Van Arsdale got contractors' associations to agree that pensions were their responsibility, and, on April 1, 1937, they assumed the cost for Class A journeymen, in effect establishing the first employer-paid pension plan (no other union leader had achieved this). Van Arsdale's argument was that it was a small cost to assume, but that was to change in later years as the payment became part of every succeeding contract. This benefit was negotiated in exchange for allowing the employer to pay wages by check instead of cash.

In any event, Van Arsdale and the IBEW had already preempted the Social Security Act: Qualified members each received a $3,000 life insurance policy and a pension of $40 a month on retirement at the age of 65.

It was all part of the Van Arsdale vision that saw not only better wages and working conditions as part of labor's goals, but quality-of-life issues as well, including health, welfare, recreation, and education.

No other Local would ever match the scope of Local 3's welfare benefits.

6

Battles on Many Fronts

The symbol of the 1939 World's Fair in New York was the Perisphere, a huge dome, and the Trylon, a tall triangular spike, which was next to it. Within the Perisphere was Democricity, a model of an ideal world in keeping with the theme of the fair: "Building the World of Tomorrow." Van Arsdale believed that electricity would play a large part, resulting in many jobs in this future world, and, more to the point, in this Fair. The Fair was built on what had been a marsh in Flushing Meadows, Queens, not far from Van Arsdale's home, and close to La Guardia Airport, another prewar project providing employment for Local 3 members.

As the construction of the fair proceeded, Local 3 also carried on negotiations and strikes, some exceptionally tough and long-lasting. These included a seventeen-week walkout against the Stanley Patterson Company, which finally agreed to a 20 percent average increase in wages. BF Division members employed in the wholesale lighting fixture industry struck and won an 18 percent increase, and strikers won all their demands in a walkout against the Circle Wire and Cable Company. Shortly afterward, the last holdout in the wire and cable industry in Local 3's jurisdiction, Bishop Wire and Cable Company, signed an agreement. The entire industry had been unionized.

Mid-1938 brought a dispute at the World's Fair. New York Telephone and Local 3 got into a fight over who would lay the cables at the Fair. Local 3 claimed this as their work, the Building and Construction Trades Council agreed, and a strike was called that lasted for weeks and threatened to postpone the Fair's scheduled opening the following year. Finally, Grover Whelan, president of the Fair Corporation, ruled that all streets within the Fair were private and thus were within the jurisdiction of Local 3. Furthermore, Local

3 also got the nod in the pulling of cables and lines in Fair buildings. When the Fair opened in April 1939, it was with a no-strike, no-lockout agreement between Local 3 and the Fair Corporation.

The goodwill between Whelan and Van Arsdale can be seen in Whelan's appearance with other national, state, and local dignitaries at a special membership meeting of the Local called to honor its pioneer members. More than 7,000 members attended the gala affair, which was broadcast nationally from the Royal Windsor Ballroom on 66th Street, just off Central Park West. Honor scrolls were handed out to the veteran members by Frances Perkins, the U.S. secretary of labor; Frieda Miller, the New York State industrial commissioner; and Elinore M. Herrick, regional director of the NLRB. Others among the 200 guests at this special meeting included such luminaries of public life and labor as: Senator Robert Wagner, Mayor Fiorello La Guardia, AFL President William Green, IBEW President Daniel Tracy, and George Meany, president of the New York State Federation of Labor.

Nevertheless, not everyone was a friend. The heavily Republican press had long ago declared open war on the progressive policies of Van Arsdale and Local 3. Among the chief antagonists was George E. Sokolsky, a columnist for the conservative *New York Journal-American*, owned by the Hearst Corporation. Sokolsky constantly attacked members of Local 3 and Van Arsdale, but it was an article he wrote for *Liberty Magazine* that sparked a particularly angry protest.

The article in the September 2 issue of *Liberty*, entitled "Racketeering at the World's Fair," alleged flagrant labor gouging, featherbedding, and assorted larcenies to the extent that many exhibitors protested and threatened to boycott the Fair in its second year.

In a detailed reply to the article, Van Arsdale stated that the article "was written for only one purpose—to discredit building unions generally and Local Union No. 3 in particular."

Calling Sokolsky's rantings, "a masterpiece of distortion," Van Arsdale methodically refuted the article's points one by one, noting acidly that Sokolsky had not bothered to check them with the Local, but had relied entirely on spurious allegations from employers and individuals with grudges against the Local, and plaintiff's testimony in the Allen Bradley case.[1] Van Arsdale said one of the reasons for the ire of Sokolsky and the rich establishment was the Local's campaign to get the six-hour-day, five-day-a-week schedule adopted nationwide, and concluded: "Every known method has been used to discredit and defame Local Union No. 3. Many stories have been printed in the newspapers, magazines, etc., for this purpose, some with the full knowledge they were prostituting the high ideals of journalism and many, no doubt, without this knowledge, because of the skill of those who are directing the campaign from behind the scenes. I am not optimistic enough to believe that it has reached *the end*."[2]

Van Arsdale was certainly right. The Sokolsky article was followed by an equally vitriolic and inaccurate article by Stanley High in the *American Mercury* in November 1939. Van Arsdale again made a meticulous refutation of the wild charges that had been printed, ending with this comment:

> Essentially, the World's Fair was a spectacular effort in propaganda. It was all facade, stucco, papier-mâché and "front." Without unions like the International Brotherhood of Electrical Workers, the Fair would be nothing, for basically the exhibition was simply so much electrical display. The various concessionaires charged fancy prices for admission, etc. and a dinner at one foreign pavilion cost as high as $10, yet no one charged the concessionaire in question with racketeering.
>
> The International Brotherhood of Electrical Workers, Local 3, has been in existence for nearly 50 years. It is a craft and industrial union with more than 16,500 men and women as dues paying members. It has pioneered for the establishment of insurance benefits for the dependents of deceased members; it has established pension funds, sick funds, unemployment funds and has made serious efforts to solve the unemployment problem.
>
> At present, it is engaged in a nation-wide campaign for the six-hour day, thirty-hour week. It is a militant, hard-hitting union—all of which perhaps explains why it has been subject to a series of violent, unprincipled attacks in the last year or so. However, the benefits which we have won for our members and their dependents enables me and my co-workers to face these attacks with complete equanimity.

Yet, despite all his evidence and arguments, another disparaging article, written by Charles Stevenson, appeared shortly thereafter in the *Atlantic Monthly*. And although he again demolished Stevenson's unfounded allegations, Van Arsdale was somewhat more politic in his overall assessment of the Fair.

> Labor played the all-important part of making possible what at night appeared to be a dream of a wonderland beyond the realm of possibility. The sinewy muscles and the skill of the building craftsmen transformed what had been a swamp and an ash dump into a spectacle of beauty, such as the world has never before witnessed. . . .
>
> The building workers of New York City are proud in the knowledge that they have built this edifice in record breaking time which stands as another monument to their skill. The innuendos [*sic*], insinuations and alleged complaints are picayune [compared] to this gigantic accomplishment.

Again, Van Arsdale stressed the accomplishments of the Local in meeting its responsibilities to its members, saying in part: "Today Local Union No. 3 is one of the largest and most responsible unions in the country and has more members than 32 of the 88 national and international unions within the American Federation of Labor."

Van Arsdale had learned that newspapers think twice about smearing someone if they are sued for libel. He and the Local brought suit against the Westchester Newspapers, Inc. and the McClure Newspapers Syndicate because of an article that appeared in the (Mt. Vernon) *Daily Argus*. The article alleged that Local 3 officials had received kickbacks from out-of-state workers who were then allowed to work at the World's Fair without union affiliation. The case went back and forth in the legal system but in 1943 the Local was awarded $22,500 in damages.[3] A retraction was also printed.

Among other ways Van Arsdale countered the media mud was to establish a radio program for the Local on station WEVD to help spread positive information about the Local to outsiders.

As has been previously mentioned, keeping his members informed about their union was always a priority for Van Arsdale as were efforts to further members' knowledge of and education in their trade. Moreover, Van Arsdale felt that the leisure time gained from a six-hour day should be used for self-improvement and appreciation of culture as a way of gaining more out of life. "The union which negotiates a contract only is not a union. It must go further and try to improve the life and welfare of its members in many other ways too."[4]

After consulting with the other local leaders, a Workers Education Department, "to conduct classes in public speaking and trade unionism," was proposed and approved by the membership at a special meeting on May 11, 1939.

As it was explained in the resolution, in part:

> There are many pressing problems facing the working men and women of this country today and present indications are that the problems will increase. If these problems are to be solved properly, the workers must find the solutions themselves. In order to do this, they must know how to study, analyze, discuss, introduce and put into effect the remedies. . . .
>
> One of the reasons that lawyers, doctors, teachers, engineers, etc. and other professional people hold a dominant position in everyday life is that their education did not stop when they left school or college. The nature of their work made it possible for them to continually study, increase their knowledge and keep abreast of ever changing conditions.
>
> It is quite true, the workers despite their desires, have not had such opportunity in the past because of long hours, extreme fatigue [exhaustion], un-

employment, worry, etc. However, with the six-hour day, thirty-hour week in effect in the electrical industry and the general shortening of hours which has taken place throughout the nation since the introduction of the New Deal under the leadership of our great President Franklin D. Roosevelt, the workers now have the necessary time for self-improvement and adult education. . . .

The active campaign this organization is conducting to establish the six-hour day, thirty-hour week for all workers is in reality a gigantic educational effort.

Members were urged to submit applications for the classes to the director of education at union headquarters. That director was none other than Howell Broach, the former IBEW president who had fallen on hard times and needed a job. He was officially appointed on May 11, 1939, at a salary of $100 a week, equal to that of the Local officers, except for Van Arsdale, who was the highest paid at $165 a week.

Van Arsdale later told an interviewer: "I thought to myself well, he did a lot for the union and we were thinking we ought to have an Educational Director, I went back and talked to the other fellows and they said, 'Harry, this is going to open up all the old sores. This is going to create what we all worked so hard to put an end to.' I said, I agree but I do not see that much harm can come of him being the Educational Director. Who can resent that? So, he came back and did a good job running the classes."[5]

In subsequent newsletters, Van Arsdale chided the membership for being slow to enroll in classes and kept the pressure on to increase the number of participants. Former Local 3 Recording Secretary Robert Reade, a good friend of Van Arsdale, had this insight into Van Arsdale's dedication to education despite his own lack of formal schooling.

I often thought of it. His education never really stopped. He didn't go on to get a formal education, but his education continued on by talking to people, by reading. He was a great reader. Any time he was alone he always had a book or an article or a magazine. He read widely and [because of] the great number of people that he came in contact with—he broadened his views. He was actually a well educated man.

Another thing is Harry Van Arsdale didn't get that formal education because he actually was on the go from morning until night. You know, he's lucky, I guess, if he slept four or five hours a night, and from the time he got up in the morning he was busy until the time he went to bed at night. I think the only leisure moments that he had—and I think he considered it leisure—was when, years ago, when he was out inspecting the street lights with the foremen of the different boroughs.

He would sit and talk to me about the Union. He would talk about what we have to do, propose things, and I think he felt at ease because riding around, he was away from the telephone and work and he didn't have to be on guard like you do in many cases [at a] meeting.

[But] while he just didn't have the time to go for formal education . . . he didn't accept that from anyone else. He didn't accept that. I can remember when, in the early '50s, maybe '50–51, when he told me: "You didn't graduate high school," and I said, "No, I didn't." And he said, "Well, Jerry Waters just got his equivalency diploma and I don't think that anyone who takes an active part in Local Union No. 3 shouldn't be able to say he's a high school graduate. Now Jerry tells me you do have to do some studying for it. Now, he went to Delahanty's [a business school of the day] and . . . I think you ought to go to Delahanty's." And in those days we didn't have the [GED] course ourselves [as made available within the union] so I went to Delahanty's and paid for it myself, of course. I went to Delahanty's and took the course and I didn't have too much difficulty getting my high school equivalency diploma. I think the course was about ten weeks. You went, I'm not sure now whether it was once or twice a week, but I went to the classes. I attended the classes faithfully, and after I finished the course I took the high school equivalency and I really never thought about doing it. But he motivated you.[6]

Veteran union member Joseph Jacobson put it this way: "He wanted an informed membership. He wanted them to know how to think, how to speak and everything else."[7]

Meanwhile, a campaign was under way to sell the six-hour day to all of organized labor, not only in the United States but abroad. A telegram was sent to John L. Lewis, president of the United Mine Workers and founder of the CIO, urging him to fight for a six-hour day for miners. Local 3 President Kirkman was authorized to attend the British Trade Union Congress to advocate the six-hour day and thirty-hour week.

Van Arsdale had another goal—a streamlining of the employment process that would give his membership more security and at the same time improve hiring procedures and efficiency for management. It was an answer to the problem that neither the Local nor the contractors had solved: how to match the supply of labor to the demand. A series of meetings with industry leaders led to the creation of the Joint Employment Board composed of management and union representatives, including Van Arsdale, Bert Kirkman, Hugh Morgan, and Jeremiah P. Sullivan for the union; and A. Lincoln Bush, E.A. Kahn, and Harry Fischbach for the contractors.

The employers agreed to eleven rules of which the key points were:

• Employers shall obtain all men from the office of the Joint Employment Committee.

- Employers shall supply the Joint Employment Committee with a list of their minimum service men.
- Employers shall file a weekly payroll report with the Joint Employment Committee.
- Employers shall furnish the Joint Committee with a list of their foremen and sub-foremen within ten days.
- Employers shall obtain their men either by telephone or by mail, allowing sufficient time in advance to supply such calls.
- Employers shall immediately report to the Joint Employment Committee any men sent out on jobs who are found to be incompetent or not qualified for the job.
- Employers may move men from job to job until their four-week period of employment has expired. Jobs running for a longer period shall have allocations of more men on written application to the Joint Employment Committee.[8]

When the plan went into effect only about half the men in the Local were employed, but a month later practically all had been put to work, due largely to the construction of the World's Fair. One goal of the plan was to apportion the available work so that as many men in the local as possible would be employed. The work weeks would be adjusted according to a formula involving the number of jobs available and the number of unemployed. For instance, by January 1940, when 1,421 men were jobless, the committee changed the rotation plan to ten weeks.

A winning formula for everybody, it led to the creation of the Joint Pension Plan, the first union pension plan administered by both labor and management: the first multiemployer pension plan in the building trades in the United States. The significance of this for those who work for more than one employer in the same industry cannot be overestimated. Previously, pension benefits had to carry over from one job to the next or be lost. Having an industrywide plan, administered by both management and employee, solved that. This seemingly simple idea sprang logically from Van Arsdale's insistence on having management agree to assume Social Security payments.

Van Arsdale pressed employers to pick up the entire cost of the pension plan, but they shied away, realizing that it could prove to be a very expensive proposition. Instead, they and Van Arsdale reached a compromise whereby the pay of apprentices was increased by 15 cents an hour, which would go into a pension fund. This fund would increase by $48,000 a year.

Witnesses at the historic signing of the joint pension agreement included Rev. John P. Boland, chairman of the New York State Labor Relations Board; Congressman James H. Fay and New York State Assemblyman Robert F.

Wagner, Jr., son of U.S. Senator Wagner and later to become mayor of New York and who was always a close friend of Van Arsdale. Wagner and Fay were selected ostensibly because they represented the area that included Local 3's headquarters although undoubtedly the prestige of the Wagner name to the event was also an important consideration. The choice of Father Boland by Van Arsdale in addition provided proper solemnity to the pioneering event.

The pension agreement was signed December 13, 1939, and went into effect January 1, 1941. Under the plan, the 6,500 men of the A Division would receive $40 a month upon retiring at the age of 60 with the prospect of having that sum supplemented by Social Security payments when they reached the age of 65. Death benefits under the Local's insurance plan were also improved to ensure that families would not be strapped when making final arrangements for deceased members.

But all these advancements came while Van Arsdale, his officers, and the Local continued their organizing and jurisdictional battles and conflicts in the court, including the Justice Department suit (discussed in chapter 5). To help in his battle and to augment the flow of information to the membership, Van Arsdale and the Local started a Local newspaper, the *Electrical Union World*. Each Local member was assessed $1.00 from their annual dues for a one-year subscription.

The paper replaced the bulletins that Van Arsdale had included in the quarterly financial reports. The paper's first editor was Harry S. Heustis. The first four-page issue came out on April 2, 1940, and was devoted almost exclusively to the Arnold suit, including Van Arsdale's reply. Also featured was a story of Van Arsdale's radio appeal for the Greater New York Fund: "In these days seething with racial intolerance, the Fund's basic principle of uniting Catholics, Jews and Protestants, people of all races and political and social viewpoints, in one all-absorbing cause, is contributing to the well-being of our country. Organized labor, which must stand or fall according to the ability to achieve such unity within its own ranks, appreciates the importance of such a movement."

Van Arsdale's remarks on race were a reflection of the riots in U.S. cities and Ku Klux Klan activity around the nation. Van Arsdale had long condemned such activities and castigated as "contemptible" any in Local 3 who evinced such prejudice.

Trouble came not from prejudice, but from envy. In 1940, IBEW President Tracy decided to challenge Van Arsdale in his own backyard by chartering a utility workers local and seven new B class locals in Local 3's jurisdiction.

Members of these locals were employed in peripheral areas of the industry. They earned less—and paid less in dues—than Local 3 members who protested that they took work that belonged to Local 3 members. Van Arsdale and his officers felt the chartering of these locals by Tracy was an infringement of the IBEW's constitution. Resolutions calling for the rescinding of their charters were passed by the membership and sent to Tracy, who later agreed that Local 3 had jurisdiction and its members should be doing the work.

Tracy was also chided by Van Arsdale and the membership for not doing more to resolve the jurisdictional differences with the CIO. This split in the family of labor was counterproductive, Van Arsdale felt, and only hampered the goal of helping the working man. In a unanimous vote at a general membership meeting on January 11, 1940, the Local passed a resolution urging Tracy and John L. Lewis to end their differences. When Tracy rejected the request, the membership, under Van Arsdale's guidance, passed a resolution to petition other IBEW locals to demand reconciliation of the rival labor organizations. This did not sit well with Tracy and he would retaliate in years to come.

Meanwhile, the war in Europe was growing, and there was increasing speculation about whether the United States would remain neutral. The Local, following the lead of President Roosevelt, passed a resolution to keep the United States out of the war. Nevertheless, preparations for war were being made and jobs in the defense industry were developing rapidly.

Van Arsdale vigorously opposed U.S. involvement in the war. A speech he gave on June 1, 1940, reveals much about his thinking. The speech was given outside the Local's 25th Street headquarters as a plaque was unveiled honoring 1,400 members of the Local who had died in World War I. Mayor La Guardia led a contingent of notables at the event. The speech was also sprinkled with biblical and religious references, which hinted at his strong Judeo-Christian beliefs of brotherhood. Van Arsdale said in part: "We could not be gathered here at a more appropriate time than the present—for today many countries of the world are again at war, men are busily engaged in slaughtering each other. All members of the human race which unfortunately on occasion revert to the law of the jungle and on each occasion prove that man can outdo the beast in their mad combat to draw the life's blood from one another."

Van Arsdale said the United States cannot feel safe because oceans separate it from combatants or likely foes:

> We must concentrate on making the government defense program a success, but the workers of this country must make it known that we will not be drawn into any foreign conflicts, that not a drop of American boys' blood will be spilt on foreign soil.
>
> We must steadfastly refuse on any issue or for any reason that now exists or may develop in the future to leave America for the purpose of murdering other mothers' sons or being butchered and murdered ourselves.

There would be no threat to our security at this time had the ten to 14 million workers who have been denied employment for the past ten years been employed creating the necessary national defense.

He spoke of the strength of the Local in weathering the attacks of the Justice Department and the manufacturers in the Allen Bradley case and declared that strength came from the members solidarity and brotherhood. "We have followed the teachings of Christ—Love Thy Neighbor. . . . Labor today must make those in power realize that we are going to follow another teaching of Christ: 'Thou Shalt Not Kill.' That even on threat of imprisonment or death itself we will not go to foreign lands to kill other human beings."

Nevertheless, Van Arsdale said Americans must be ready to fight if the war came to these shores. It is telling that Van Arsdale larded his remarks with religious references and political tenets. He chose to make a major statement. It can thus be argued that the speech said much about Van Arsdale, including the aforementioned religious foundations of his philosophies and his dismay at the folly of violence at the expense of constructive activities that would help, not hurt, people.

But Van Arsdale also showed that if the battle came to him, in the form of the intransigence and belligerence of others, he would fight as he always did on such occasions. And this was shown in two strikes that would be among the most severe and violent in the Local's history.

The union battled on two fronts. The first strike, against the giant Leviton Manufacturing Company of Brooklyn, began on August 28, 1940. Leviton had long fought efforts to unionize its 1,900 workers, and had established, for example, a company pension plan to secure worker loyalty. Its owner, Isadore Leviton, considered himself a benevolent ruler of a family of workers (figuratively, but also literally, by hiring several members of one family)—and did not welcome outsiders who told him what he could dispense and how.

Local 3 struck for a $16 minimum wage, a forty-hour week, and a $4 increase for those earning above the minimum. Howell Broach was appointed as strike leader. The Local launched mass picketing outside the Leviton gates in Greenpoint and this led to a turbulent riot in September 1940. The strike and boycott of Leviton products was to last for six months. Leviton ignored all efforts at arbitration. Entreaties to settle by Mayor La Guardia, Eleanor Roosevelt, and Mrs. Henry Morgenthau, wife of the secretary of the treasury, were of no avail.

In an NLRB election, the union won with a vote of 1,299 for representation and a mere 70 against. But it was not until the War Labor Board stepped into the picture that the dispute was finally resolved. Local 3 was designated as the sole bargaining agent and wage increases of 10 to 25 percent were granted. The strike cost Local 3 an estimated $250,000 with workers getting

$7 a week in strike benefits. However, that cost was later defrayed by the IBEW. It is estimated that the dispute cost Leviton more than $2 million.

Van Arsdale had high praise for Broach. He was reportedly "painstaking" in his job, acting like "an older brother" to the picketers who came to him daily with their problems.[9] Van Arsdale also told the members: "You are the men who, through all kinds of weather and turmoil were out there on the picket line doing your bit. When I think of what you accomplished, I am more than ever proud to be a member of Local 3."[10] Picketers might also remember Van Arsdale showing up even in the early morning to lend his support to those who manned the gates in the cold and the dark. It was a common practice for Van Arsdale who endured all that his members did and worked the hardest of all. One consequence of the Leviton dispute was a falling-out between Broach and Van Arsdale, the results of which, a few years later, would be dire.

As Van Arsdale told an interviewer:

> [One] other thing that happened during this strike was the bad effect it was having on Broach. Broach would call me and say he had to talk to me because it was terribly important, and then he would outline some things to me I was not aware of.
>
> But I could see that a lot of these things would have brought back a lot of the division in the Local. Broach was a fellow that could hate people. And I think I learned from that. I think I learned that when you hate somebody you do yourself more damage than you do to the guy you hate. He did not feel anything, though. So, it reached the point that all of our people were discussing all these different things and looked like we were on the way back to where we started.
>
> [Van Arsdale said he had reminded Broach of the terms of employment when he was made educational director of the Local.]
>
> You remember when you first came with us, . . . I said we do not receive very much salary here, but we all work together and we enjoy our work. If you think you could adjust yourself [after having been the IBEW president] . . . we would be glad to have you with us.
>
> So with the Leviton strike, we had all cut our pay down. And the men were assessing themselves to finance the [strikers] to the extent they were. There was a meeting every week of the strikers. I was in court defending myself against unfair charges [stemming from the concurrent Triangle Cable strike] and I would go [to the Leviton picket line] in the night.
>
> Mr. Broach would take a nap every afternoon. So when it was over, I said, "I think Harry [Howell] that you remember our early conversation and it does not seem that you have adjusted yourself. I think it is better that you go your way so we wo not have a lot of friction that we've been able to get along without."[11]

Broach left in an apparent huff, nursing a grudge that would emerge at the 1946 San Francisco convention. But that was in the future. In 1943, Van Arsdale had his hands full with the Leviton and Triangle disputes. (The latter had led to another indictment and a short stay in jail.) In August 1940, just before the Leviton strike, Local 3 members struck Bishop Wire and Cable, Columbia Cable and Electric, Circle Wire and Cable, Eastern Tool and Tube, and Triangle Conduit and Cable, as the exploited workers attempted to get a larger share of the huge defense profits the companies were enjoying. The strike was another financial strain for the Local. Union coffers were again drained by the payment of $10 per week to 1,500 strikers. Mayor La Guardia succeeded in gaining a settlement through arbitration, but the head of Triangle was a lone holdout.

A huge picket line was organized outside Triangle's Queens headquarters, and nothing could move in or out except for shipments earmarked for defense needs. But even that concession was not enough to impress Triangle's arrogant owner, Jack McAuliffe, of the union's willingness to negotiate an orderly, reasonable settlement. He hired strikebreakers and tried to shove them through the picket lines with the aid of security guards and the New York Police Department. In the fighting that ensued, many strikers were beaten by the police. One striker, Carl Roth, died as a result of violence, but it was Van Arsdale and other Local 3 leaders who were ordered arrested by Queens District Attorney Charles P. Sullivan.

Van Arsdale and sixteen others were indicted in December 1940, after the conclusion of the strike, in connection with the rioting. A. Lincoln Bush, president of the New York Electrical Contractors Association appeared as a character witness for Van Arsdale at the trial. Despite all evidence and arguments to the contrary, Van Arsdale was convicted and sentenced to one to three years in jail.

The jury was so confused by the case that it ordered him imprisoned on a count that had not even been in the indictment—inciting a riot. Van Arsdale appealed and both the trial and sentence were overturned by the New York State Court of Appeals in 1943.

In reporting the verdict, the *Electrical Union World* compared the scene to "a Hecht and MacArthur Hollywood scenario." The paper quoted what it termed "a seasoned newspaperman" as saying it was "the most cock-eyed scene I have ever seen in a courtroom."

Van Arsdale, the paper reported, "sat back in his chair, smiling with evident satisfaction." In a newspaper interview shortly afterward, Van Arsdale commented:

> We do not believe in violence. We've always preached against it. We feel that whatever progress we make will be through organization and intelli-

gent action. . . . The fact that violence occurred does not mean that we believe in it or approve of it or started it. Yes, stones were thrown at the Triangle plant, but I believe they were thrown because of provocation by armed guards, police and strike breakers. There was a lot of resentment because many strikers were beaten by the police and had to be treated in the hospitals. The police records themselves will give you a pretty good idea of what the strikers were subjected to.

Then, of course, they were sore because Jack McAuliffe, president of Triangle, refused to let the Mayor arbitrate the controversy. We struck five conduit and cable companies at the same time and the other four were settled with the Mayor's help, without disorder of any kind.

[As for the trial, it] should have been clear to everybody, if only from the testimony of the strikebreakers, that the whole thing was concocted by Triangle. I attributed the entire case to the influence of Jack McAuliffe in Queens County. . . . I think it is regrettable that violence has occurred in a number of the strikes [against defense-oriented plants] throughout the country. But anybody knows that a great deal of that violence is provoked by the employers and if in some instances the workers themselves have gone to excess that is understandable.

You have men in these situations who for years have been denied the opportunity of union membership and who are employed in mass production industries in which men are not given the same consideration machines get. That's why there's violence sometimes when they feel their oats.

The fact that thousands of decent American workmen are willing to fight against great odds in their efforts to win a better life is the best guaranty that America will never be crushed by any foreign or domestic dictator.

Van Arsdale had spent a week in jail between his conviction and sentencing, and, as might be expected, said he had used that time to best advantage. "The first thing I did was throw myself on the bed and I woke up 15 hours later. The rest of the time I spent in some good solitary reflection and serious thinking that I did not have time for before. One thing I learned there was that many of the men in that jail are there because they could not find jobs. . . . Despite the international situation, I think the most serious problem facing America is unemployment."[12]

An aspect of the Triangle strike that, years later, was to give Van Arsdale amusement was that his Triangle nemesis McAuliffe was chairman of the greens committee of the Pomonok Country Club in Queens. The club was also a meeting place for the conservative Queens politicians who were McAuliffe's cronies. McAuliffe had even hired some of the caddies at the club as strikebreakers.

Local 3 men had also picketed the club as an adjunct to their Triangle strike activities. They had no idea that one day the site would be home to many of their members and encompass their headquarters. (Electchester Housing, inexpensive cooperative apartments offered to Local 3 members, as well as the Electrical Industry headquarters were built there.)

Van Arsdale was to lead Local 3 in another major strike before the onset of World War II. This one was against Consolidated Edison, which sought to use its own nonunion men for installations at its new huge Waterside Plant (First Avenue and 39th Street in Manhattan). It was Van Arsdale's contention that Local 3 had a long-standing understanding—a "gentlemen's agreement" —with Con Ed that only Local 3 men would install all electrical equipment in new plants.[13]

He and his officers had tried for eighteen months to win agreement from Con Ed on that point and when the company continued to resist, he pulled all of the 8,000 men of the A Division employed at construction sites throughout the city off the job, in effect instigating a general strike by the largest unit of the Local.

The Building and Construction Trades Council (BCTC), whose other member unions had similar "gentlemen's agreements," also saw Con Ed's obstinacy as a threat. BCTC President Thomas Murray said: "This is a vital problem which effects the work opportunities of every member of the BCTC. Complete unity of all the representatives of the Council is necessary for its welfare and existence. I urge unanimous support of the demands of Local 3."[14]

The Council formed a committee, headed by Murray, to try to achieve a settlement. If that failed, the Council would call a general citywide strike by 250,000 AFL building trades workers, the first such strike in the history of the BCTC.

Local 3 also dramatized its power by blacking out New York's "Great White Way"—in and around Times Square—for thirty minutes. Local 3 members took advantage of the phenomenon to hand out thousands of leaflets to theatergoers who may have been—and now literally were—in the dark about the issues.

Under pressure from the National Defense Mediation Board and the urging of the AFL, which had adopted a national defense no-strike policy, Van Arsdale accepted a plan that sent the men back to work pending a ruling from the National Defense Mediation Board. It ruled against the Local in September. It would be one of the few times that Local 3 was not entirely successful in attaining its strike goals, but then the action was overwhelmed by defense—soon to become war—needs.

It was during this period of both legal and labor strife that Van Arsdale sought to dispel any doubt that he had the total support of his membership. As noted earlier, he resigned several weeks before the scheduled election of the other officers of the local at the end of their two-year terms. He himself was not up for reelection because two years remained of his four-year term.[15]

A statement dated June 13, accompanying his letter of resignation, reveals much of what was troubling him at the time. Because it was so insightful, it is presented here only slightly abridged:

> Organized labor is passing through a very critical period. Only those in labor who are blinded by their personal ease and comfort believe that the American Labor Movement is impregnable to the attacks of the powerful interests that would weaken and destroy it.
>
> During the last seven years, the Congress of the United States, under the leadership of Franklin D. Roosevelt, has passed more liberal labor legislation than during any other period. Unfortunately, organized labor and its leaders have not taken advantage of this legislation. They have failed to organize the millions of unorganized workers in industry. They have failed to concentrate their efforts in the low-wage areas and they have failed to curb the inhuman practices of unscrupulous employers who conduct their businesses under such conditions.
>
> The damage caused by the mistakes, the inefficiency, the inability, the inertia and selfishness, while serious in itself, is insignificant compared to the tragic indifference to the welfare of millions of rank and file workers displayed by the division in organized labor which still exists.
>
> Organized labor has had to fight a long, hard battle to be recognized as having a definite place under our present system of government.
>
> During this difficult period, one of labor's greatest assets has been the support and sympathy of the public because of the fact it was widely recognized that labor was the underdog.
>
> Since favorable labor legislation has been enacted, the powerful interests have spent millions of dollars in changing public opinion to the extent that it is now generally believed that organized labor exercises tremendous power and that the United States government is its active ally in crushing and preventing business from going forward.
>
> Nation-wide adverse publicity has been given the fact that some men in powerful labor organizations are not elected by the workers or have not been regularly elected by them.
>
> Organized labor is a great force in our country and has made it possible for organized and unorganized workers to have a better standard of life. The accomplishments of organized labor are something of which every citizen may well be proud and every active trade unionist particularly so, for they have helped make this possible.
>
> However, those who have the power to mold public opinion are not

willing to let labor stand or fall on its record of accomplishments as against its comparatively few mistakes and shortcomings.

They have successfully conducted a campaign to discredit organized labor in the eyes of the public because of the mistakes of a few apparently insignificant individuals, whom it is charged, have betrayed the trust and confidence which the men they represent have extended to them.

It must be remembered that on each occasion that an officer of a labor union accepts graft or is corrupted, it is because he has yielded to the temptations of the employers. The employer who gives a bribe is as guilty as a union representative who accepts it. Both are a menace.

A concerted effort has been made to discredit Local Union No. 3 and we have been the target of every conceivable method of attack engineered by the National Electrical Manufacturers' Association, the General Electric Company, the Westinghouse Electric and Manufacturing Company and other powerful monopolies, Walter Gordon Merritt, non-union employers, their henchmen and stooges and labor haters, large and small. . . .

Here followed already familiar reports of the Dewey and Arnold investigations.

Some of the serious problems with which labor is faced are:

The fact that organized labor has failed to take full advantage of the opportunities of the liberal labor legislation which should have made possible complete unionization of the workers of this nation.

The campaign of adverse publicity directed against organized labor and subsidized and encouraged by powerful and anti-union interests.

The anti-union crusade directed against labor by Thurman W. Arnold, Assistant Attorney General.

The lack of extensive trade union education among the millions of organized workers.

The fact that 10 to 14 million workers have been unemployed during the past ten years and millions of others employed on a part-time basis.

The fact that the eight-year campaign of the American Federation of Labor to establish the thirty-hour week in industry has not yet brought about this necessary social adjustment which [would] solve the problem of employment for many of the millions now unemployed.

The fact that the leaders of the A.F. of L. and the C.I.O. have not shown the statesmanship necessary to bring about a settlement of A.F. of L.-C.I.O. differences.

Each of the above situations is serious in itself and because they exist there is a danger that many or all of labor's rights will be lost because of the hysteria caused by the European war.

The Defense Program to a large extent has been placed in the hands of two industrialists who have received their training in monopoly-controlled industries, the past history of which has shown them to be strongly opposed to workmen exercising their right to organize [into] bona fide trade unions.

The present crisis affords an opportunity to Organized Labor to prove its value to our government and to the people of this country by playing an important part in making possible the necessary national defenses and in training the members of organized labor so that they would be in a position to defend our country against the invasion of any foreign nation or group of nations.

However, the methods of modern warfare breed dictatorships and make it necessary for countries to accept the domination of dictators or the use of dictatorial methods. Powerful labor movements in many foreign nations have ceased to exist. We must guard against the possibility of this occurring in the United States.[16]

It was an extraordinary document addressed not only in intent to the membership, but to AFL President William Green, CIO President John L. Lewis, and IBEW President Daniel Tracy, among others. It was also a statement meant to be read on a national level by a labor leader who knew that he was a power not just in New York but also within organized labor.

The squabbling between the rival AFL and CIO also angered him. He likened the rivalry to two brothers fighting with each other while besieged in a house that had been set afire by the encircling, savage enemy. Van Arsdale chided organized labor's national leadership for not taking advantage of opportunities offered by a sympathetic White House and Congress, making it plain that he would do differently if he were in charge. He was not seeking national office, but the thought must have crossed his mind and certainly others would have urged him to do so.

This shows Van Arsdale's strong practicality and his ability to focus on getting the job done. It was always the good of the working man and woman involved, not the aggrandizement of leadership.

By the same token he was critical, by implication, of the willingness of leaders like Lewis to afford themselves of luxuries while doing union business. There was also criticism within the IBEW, particularly from Broach, that Tracy preferred riding in limousines and politicking to dealing with his administrative chores.[17] Van Arsdale, who lived frugally and took little for himself, expected others to do the same while doing labor's work.

His impatience with union internal politics—when they got in the way of progress—is also implicit in the letter in references to the actions, apparently taken in pique, against Local 3 and Van Arsdale by President Tracy.

Van Arsdale, who was scrupulous in his stewardship of the local and business dealings, was obviously sensitive to press criticisms of labor, as directed not only against him, but also against others because they served to denigrate the cause—a cause that was almost holy to him.

The statement also indicates Van Arsdale's enmity to the government controls that hampered the rights of workers to bargain freely. Certainly, he and others in organized labor had felt the results of that in the WPA and the Defense Mediation Board, and more of the same was likely to come as war approached.

It was, as Van Arsdale put it, a critical period for labor, but war was to make him the father of invention.

7

America at War

With Europe at war, President Roosevelt ordered an immediate buildup of U.S. defenses. He set a production level of 50,000 planes a year and proposed huge increases in both the army and the navy. Congress obliged by appropriating $4 billion for a two-ocean navy. Roosevelt created the National Defense Advisory Commission (NDAC), whose seven members were led by the president of General Motors, W.S. Knudsen. The commission's mission was to mobilize all facets of the economy in support of the defense campaign. It was Knudsen whom Van Arsdale had in mind when he warned of anti-labor, monopoly-minded industrialists. Roosevelt sought to dispel labor's fears of harsh controls by appointing Sidney Hillman, president of the CIO's Amalgamated Clothing Workers Union, to head the commission's Labor Division.

IBEW President Tracy was appointed assistant secretary of labor in charge of military and war-related construction. Tracy was also responsible for certifying labor disputes for the National Defense Mediation Board. In addition, he would be one of the architects of the AFL's "no-strike" policy that was implemented after the United States entered the war in December.

Tracy was also called upon to use his contacts and political skills to persuade unions to put aside many of their hard-won contractual gains in order to aid war production. He helped to fashion voluntary wage stabilization programs and became the chairman of the Wage Adjustment Board, which mediated conflicts between construction unions and government purchasing units. Tracy did try to hold firm for the eight-hour day and union wage levels, but argued for a lessening of overtime rates when shifts lengthened.

The labor picture, however, was being disrupted by the national draft. On

September 16, 1940, Selective Service began, which resulted in a growing shortage of workers—while, at the same time, President Roosevelt called for round-the-clock, seven-day-a-week industry operation. The AFL and the CIO supported this as a way to combat unemployment and increase wages if the forty-hour week was maintained. Joseph S. McDonagh, secretary general of the AFL's Metal Trades Department suggested that the week could be extended even to forty-eight-hours for six days with time-and-a-half pay for overtime.

Meanwhile, Van Arsdale scored a victory in Congress successfully lobbying for a minimum wage and hour law for the portable lampshade industry. But Van Arsdale also did all he could to aid the defense effort. He made the Local's school building and equipment available for defense-related training. He urged the members: "You have the opportunity to help your country, your union and yourself. ENROLL NOW."[1]

Nevertheless, he kept a wary eye on anti-labor forces, and how they might attempt to clothe anti-labor sentiments in patriotic garb. The nation's press, overwhelmingly on the side of the employer, overplayed minor strikes and alleged communist influence of unions whereas industry price-gouging went largely unreported. Union newspapers were often tiny and lonely voices shouting against the wind generated by the Hearsts, Gannetts, McCormicks, McClures, and Newhouses in their newspaper chains.

Electrical Union World was one of those that strove to tell the other side. By 1941, it had increased its number of pages and included reports from labor news syndicates. Its April 7 issue told of the dire situation of migrant workers seeking defense-related work. An editorial in the same issue was critical of the misuse of "cooling-off" periods as a way of stalling righteous union demands. Yet another editorial warned of the dangers of communists attempting to take advantage of the defense effort to instigate self-serving strikes.

Van Arsdale was to have a little war of his own. *Life* magazine, caught up in the wave of anti-union sentiment, printed an article in its October 27, 1941, issue entitled "AFL Ditches a Racketeer but It Cannot Ditch Its Critics." The article referred to the ouster from the AFL of George E. Browne, president of the International Alliance of Theatrical Stage Employees. Browne and his aide, Willie Bioff, were on trial on extortion charges in New York. *Life* also praised the rabid, reactionary columnist Westbrook Pegler, who blared forth anti-union rantings in the Hearst newspaper chain.[2] Among the photos of alleged union racketeers was one of Van Arsdale, referring to his conviction in the 1933 shooting in New York, with a caption stating that he had shot two men. Van Arsdale sued for $200,000 in damages.

Meanwhile, Van Arsdale led a successful battle at the 1941 IBEW convention in St. Louis to have future conventions held every two years. The IBEW leadership opposed this, seeking a four-year cycle of conventions. Van Arsdale's stand was in keeping with his philosophy that union leadership be held accountable to the rank and file by being forced to achieve positive results in a shorter period of time or being removed more quickly if they did not satisfy the needs of the membership. His victory also helped to strengthen his position as a power in the International.

Van Arsdale, who had long deplored the interfamily bloodletting between the AFL and the CIO as counterproductive and inimical to the growth of the labor movement, provided the IBEW and AFL with an example of union peacemaking.

He entered into a precedent-setting agreement with Local 1224 of the United Electrical, Radio, and Machine Workers of the CIO to end jurisdictional disputes in the industry of manufacturing and distribution of electrical supplies, lamps, and fixtures in New York City. Both unions agreed they would attempt to obtain equal wage scales in all plants organized by each other. They also agreed not to attempt to organize a plant that the other was seeking to organize. A similar agreement was signed between Local 3 and the CIO's Local 65 of the United Retail, Wholesale, and Department Store Employees Union.

The mainstream press chose to ignore the significance of Van Arsdale's actions and instead continued to pillory unions as using strikes in defiance of the defense effort. Their diatribes were deflated by a report of the Office of Production Management (OPM), which showed that "the actual time lost to the defense program [due to the actions] of the American Federation of Labor during the critical five-month period ending October 31 [1941] was exactly 30 seconds per day—10½ minutes per month—two hours per year of man work."[3]

The controversy was overwhelmed by the bombing of Pearl Harbor by the Japanese on December 7 and the entry of the United States into World War II. Local 3 pledged "all out" aid to the war effort and Van Arsdale led the way, including by participating in a clandestine meeting with President Roosevelt and helping in a super-secret project under the English Channel. Armand D'Angelo, a former union official who later became chairman of the Joint Industry Board (JIB) and the city's Commissioner of the Department of Water Supply, Gas, and Electricity, told of this and other aspects of Van Arsdale's strong patriotism in an interview. "We worked more hours during the war at straight time to build the battleships in the [Brooklyn] navy yard . . . to try to get the work in here with the assurance of the President. And there's an interesting story, you know, the time he was called down to the White House and they got him in through one of the back doors to meet with FDR [to help with the planning for] the building of the pipe cable underneath the English Channel . . . and so many things, very strong patriotic things."[4]

One of these other things was having Local 3 work with the city's air-raid warden unit to demonstrate—this time with official sanction—how Times Square and the Great White Way could be quickly blacked out so it would not serve as a beacon for enemy bombers. D'Angelo related that newspaper columnist (later television impresario) Ed Sullivan was named air-raid warden of the Great White Way and worked with him and with industry representatives, including the Artcraft Strauss (Sign) Company and General Advertising to be able to black out Broadway. "And what we did on our own time was to tie together the circuits of the signs," he said. "It was a gigantic job. We had a hundred men do that in a month. But then we could black out Broadway in two minutes."[5]

The most significant decision was Van Arsdale's agreement to suspend the six-hour day on national defense jobs for the duration of the war, allowing for workdays of seven or eight hours. Nevertheless, the work situation in the city was not good for building industry workers. Defense contracts were relatively few in comparison to other areas and Van Arsdale urged his men to seek jobs elsewhere. *Electrical Union World* began to run features listing out of town jobs. For instance, the Christmas issue, just eighteen days after Pearl Harbor, told of jobs in Pearl Harbor, Washington, DC, Birmingham (Alabama), Buffalo, Philadelphia, and Detroit.

At a mass membership meeting on June 16, Van Arsdale spoke of the present and the hoped-for future: "We are going through trying times," he said. "We have seen many firms go out of business because of the restriction of civilian production—and we will still experience more trying and difficult times. But if we all hold together, we will be prepared to face the future calmly and bravely and initiate the progressive programs we have in mind as soon as complete victory is achieved and the new world gets under way."[6]

One way to ensure Local 3's future was to have as many of its officers as possible in high places in industry and in agencies that affected the Local. To that end, business agent Howard McSpedon became president of the New York Building Trades and Construction Council, a post that Van Arsdale had held earlier. In the years to come, Local 3 officers were to take leading positions in other industry associations and in city and state departments, thus providing friends in high places for labor and the Local.

By 1943, the loss of jobs in New York and the depletion of the union roster because of men entering the armed forces meant lower dues revenues. To offset the losses in the union coffers, Van Arsdale and his officers took cuts in pay in November 1943. Van Arsdale's salary was reduced to $100 and his officers shaved $10 off their $100-a-week salaries.

While the officers were cutting their own salaries, the Roosevelt administration sought to keep wages from rising. FDR ordered that wages be frozen for the duration of the war, but—to make that measure more palatable—he allowed unions to negotiate for increased fringe benefits. Van Arsdale, who had already foreseen this eventuality, was ready for more benefit programs for his members.

Again, one of his primary areas of concern was the elderly worker (the image of his father no doubt an influence). He pushed through a provision that exempted workers older than 60 from paying dues if they had been members in good standing for fifteen years or more and had performed five years of continuous service. Pension payments were subsequently raised from $40 a month to $50 a month and disabled workers were now eligible for a full pension as well. The increases were to be paid by a 10 percent assessment on all wages above $80 per week. Van Arsdale also achieved another major innovation by securing the agreement of the employers to collect the assessments.

Up to this time, the Joint Employment Committee (JEC) had been the apparatus for many such joint ventures and it was the logical unit to handle the administration of the newly formed Pension Fund. But as its duties increased, it was felt that the JEC had to change and in spring 1943, the JEC became the Joint Industry Board of the Electrical Industry (JIB), which would administer all collective bargaining agreements, make surveys and studies of the industry, arbitrate disputes, operate pension plans, and study the possibilities of establishing an apprentice system and the classification of the employees in the industry. Its first meeting was held on March 30, 1943, with A. Lincoln Bush, Louis Freund, E.A. Kahn, Walter Knapp, Julius Hoffman, Louis D. Kennedy, David Davidson, Louis Lidsky, S.J. O'Brien, and Denis J. Crimmins as employer representatives and Van Arsdale, Bert Kirkman, Hugh Morgan, Jeremiah P. Sullivan, Nat Bedsole, Howard McSpedon, Gerald J. Duffy, Nat Chadwick, Albert Jansen, and Fred Hansen representing the Local.

Bush was elected chairman, with O'Brien as vice chairman, and Crimmins was named secretary-treasurer. Van Arsdale was referred to as the founder of the JIB, but it should be noted that neither he nor any other union representative was named as an officer. The philosophy was to let management stand in the forefront and take bows to cement cooperation. It would not be until 1965 that the first union representative was named JIB chairman.

Max Kamin, a confidante of Van Arsdale, described the working atmosphere within the JIB:

The relationship was good all the time with the union trying to get the best for its men and the contractors trying to get the best on a contract. . . . And Van was faithful and so were the contractors. . . . And Van's policy for all the time was he always asked for a day's work for a day's pay. That's what we would get, what we were entitled to and we had to give the employer what [he] was entitled to. . . . And the men got indoctrinated with that. They knew they could not horse around. And if they did, they got laid off or something like that. The organization was run on good faith, you know what I mean? On both [making] an agreement and following through.[7]

George Schuck, Jr. tells of Van Arsdale's practice of riding with a business agent along his route just to keep a personal eye on things.

When he was riding, if he saw a Welsbach truck parked by a driveway, he would tell [his driver] to stop and find out what the man was doing. "Check and see if he had a heart attack," he would say. But he was adamant in holding to the position that if the man was being paid an hourly wage he should do what he was there to do. If you have the contractors' understanding that you are looking after their best interest, they are much more willing to negotiate benefits for [their employees].[8]

Robert Reade, a former Local 3 recording secretary, also tells of the times that Van Arsdale rode with him.

When I was the night foreman he rode with me twice a week, usually two or three o'clock in the morning. He would spend several hours with me. And we would ride all over Brooklyn and Queens. And sometimes he would make me take a ride up through the Bronx, even though that wasn't my jurisdiction . . . and he would be checking the street lights when we went through. And in those days, he had his own car, but he'd rather ride with the foremen . . . and make sure that he was keeping you on the ball. And he checked on us and made sure we were doing the job. And we had better do the job or we would have to answer to him.[9]

Former labor editor Austin Perlow, of the *Long Island Press*, added to this view.

Well, I know one of the big problems in the construction trades in New York City has been this constant battle against the union cry of more, more, more . . . [but] I think it has been worth it to the industry. And the industry realizes it is strike free. It's a union they can talk to. It's a union they can reason with. It's a union where management is contributing as much to the worker's welfare as the union itself.

I mean they prefer it that way. They know the people they are dealing with. They know their thinking. They know they can talk to them. That they can understand each other. Sure, it's expensive, but they know out of a Local 3 electrician, they are going to get a day's work because if they don't, in the old days, Harry Van Arsdale would go up to a guy and take his book away from him. "You are gold-bricking on the job, you son of a bitch. We don't want you around here! Out!" A man is getting damn good wages and damn good fringe benefits and he is taken care of by the union and he is taken care of by the Joint Board, he's got nothing to worry about.

Harry Van Arsdale wanted that man to give a good day's work for what he was getting. And he would go around from job to job and inspect. And there was no gold-bricking. He wouldn't stand for it.[10]

In an article in the *Reader's Digest*, an unidentified contractor was quoted as giving this answer to a question about how he could afford paying high wages to Local 3 men. "'See this cement floor,' the contractor answered, kneeling down. 'Several years ago, if you wanted to hack a channel and lay a wire in it, you'd do it like this.' He struck at the floor with an imaginary mallet and chisel. 'Took four hours,' he continued and then began to drill with an invisible drill. 'Takes only 20 minutes. We get an honest union. No payoffs and honest work. No loafing. You don't know what that means to a contractor.'" The same article quoted Van Arsdale as telling his local members: "You produce more and I'll get you more." He also told a boss: "From now on, you decide how many men a job needs—not the union." Goldbrickers were hauled up on union charges and told: "What do you want to do, loaf or earn more? We're bucking for a raise, but you are not helping us get it." He also told contractors: "We've got to find ways to get costs down."[11] And in that regard, union members were encouraged to think of ways to cut costs by thinking of time-saving devices or techniques.

All this was part of the Van Arsdale credo of honesty in his business dealings. He would give employers everything they paid for, but at the same time he meant to be sure that his members were treated well and fairly. He also dealt from a position of strength. Employers knew the power of the Local and Van Arsdale's willingness to use that power if necessary.

Van Arsdale became a master of persuasion. D'Angelo told how he used this talent in dealing with the contractors. "All the contractors didn't agree with everything he was trying to do, but he got around them to the point where if a man was hurt, he should get paid, and if a man doesn't get paid for a holiday, it's not a holiday for that man," he said. "So he developed a relationship with them where they came to trust his word."[12]

There were many who could attest to that. Efrem A. Kahn, president of the New York Electrical Contractors Association from 1945 to 1950 and a member of its board for twenty-five years, told of Van Arsdale's integrity: "Harry Van Arsdale never took a ten cent piece in his whole life. I know the man. I've known him for years and years and years. He never took it. I will tell you that I have had countless lunches with Harry Van Arsdale. He picked up a lunch check as often as I did. Maybe more than often. This is what this individual was. And I don't know any other union leaders that I could say that about."[13]

But as a general rule, Van Arsdale did not socialize with the contractors. "He didn't even have time to socialize with his members," D'Angelo said, "except if there were three meetings going on the same night, he was going to get to all three. That was his socializing."[14]

But there was another form of social relaxation, D'Angelo continued. "When we got through at night, 11 o'clock or midnight, whatever the hour, late all the time, he wouldn't go to bed, he'd first have his dinner, or something to eat and whoever was there at the meeting that we'd just left, he would invite a couple of the people to come with us lots of times."

But liquor was not an important part of this picture, D'Angelo said. In later years, Van Arsdale might drink an occasional old-fashion, but "at one time, he would drink nothing but a bottle of beer occasionally. He detested seeing men changed by alcohol."[15]

D'Angelo said he met daily with Van Arsdale and he reinforced what many others had said about Van Arsdale's seeming round-the-clock schedule and apparently inexhaustible energy. "We spent days together," he said. "Hours were nothing to us. Receiving a call from him, like at midnight, was not unusual, or 8 or 9 at night, not unusual; or early in the morning. 'Could you meet me?' 'Could you come to Hawaii?' Which I did, by the way. . . . I enjoyed all the years I ever worked with Harry Van Arsdale. I enjoyed them."[16]

Van Arsdale's management style was successful because of the esteem that he enjoyed. He overwhelmed his associates by the force of his personality and intellect. William Blain, a former financial secretary of Local 3 and a close aide to Van Arsdale, said:

> Harry truly believed that there wasn't anything that couldn't be done. . . . If you disagreed with him, he respected your opinion so long as you could justify your statement and back it up with documentation or some personal experience to show him that his thinking was not entirely correct. And yes, he would change his opinion, and yes, he would respect you for that. In fact, I think some of the people he respected the most were people who from time to time butt[ed] heads with him. One of the things that Harry didn't like were "yes" men. And of course the easy road to take with Harry was to yes him to death, but he wasn't so naive as to not be able to realize

what you were doing. He liked honesty, I think if you had to choose one word. [And] Harry would be the one who would come to you and tell you what he wanted. He would not send an emissary in his place. He would pick up the phone, no matter what time of the day or night it was, and tell you directly. He did not send a messenger.[17]

But Blain added that the exception to this was D'Angelo. If Van Arsdale transmitted his orders through D'Angelo, it was accepted as from Van Arsdale personally.[18] D'Angelo was one of the Van Arsdale brain trust along with Bert Kirkman, Howard McSpedon, and other key officers and Local officials. In 1944, they and the contractors achieved another milestone in the JIB. An agreement at the start of the new year set up the first major change in the pension plan since a hospitalization plan for Local 3 members had been included in it. Moreover, on March 15 of that year, the JIB assumed the responsibility for the assets, liabilities, and administration of the Pension and Hospitalization Plan of the Electrical Industry.

Members would be entitled to $15 per week starting with the second week of hospitalization through a ten-week period. The plan was also renamed the Joint Pension and Hospitalization Plan and the combination of welfare benefits and hospitalization fees was another milestone in labor–management pacts. The hospitalization benefits were extended in 1945 to members' wives, followed in 1946 by a death and pension premium benefit.

But 1946 was also the year of the IBEW convention in San Francisco, which was to have painful repercussions for Van Arsdale for years to come.

The convention was explosive because of the rivalry between the incumbent IBEW president, Edward J. Brown, and his challenger, former IBEW President Daniel Tracy, whose service in the Roosevelt administration had ended. Van Arsdale opposed Tracy, whom he felt had not been a good president nor one who had shown great friendship to Local 3. Moreover, Tracy was also supported by Howell Broach, which did not endear him to Van Arsdale. However, Van Arsdale was never a man to let personal feelings get in the way of whatever was best for his members. It was Tracy himself, not Broach, who was the deciding factor. Van Arsdale's son, Thomas, gave this insight into his father's character and methods. "His foremost objective was to further the well-being of the organization and the trade union movement. He had a lot of associates he did not favor, but he set his personal thinking aside and worked with that person as long as that person was willing to work to achieve the objective."[19]

The campaigning by both camps got ugly with political dirty tricks and name-calling. Spies were planted in each camp and poison-pen letters were circulated while Brown and Tracy hurled bitter barbs at each other.[20] Broach's campaign tactics allegedly went so far as paying taxi drivers not to service the Local 3 delegates who were deliberately placed in an out of the way hotel.[21]

At the end of the nine-day convention, Tracy was victorious by a slim margin: 80,928 to 77,428, with most of his support coming from southern members whereas Brown carried the northeastern districts. Van Arsdale was removed from the Executive Council and Broach was placed on it.

Whatever personal hurts he may have felt, Van Arsdale remained a pragmatic leader. In his papers, Tracy tells of a conversation he had with Scott Milne, the new international secretary, in which Milne quotes Van Arsdale as saying he would accept being frozen out of the IBEW inner circle but "that he did not want the international interfering in any way with Local 3."[22] Thomas Van Arsdale believed his father "showed character when he stayed with his commitment to Brown when others walked away and made new alliances."[23] Harry Van Arsdale was "disappointed" at the outcome of the election, but "went on to concentrate on building a stronger organization and doing great things, such as pioneering benefits programs in New York. . . . The defeat of Brown was a key point in time and circumstances. If Brown had won that election, it is very possible that the next president to follow Brown would have been Harry Van Arsdale, but the defeat of Brown [signaled] a purge of all those who had supported Brown. . . . But Harry always played down division and always looked forward never dwelling on the past."[24]

But the past would always come back to bite Van Arsdale in the ensuing years. Knowing that he was a marked man, he took some preemptive steps. "Harry took a leave of absence as business manager in 1948, probably as a strategy knowing that they were going to come after him in the purge," Thomas related. "John J. Kapp filled in for him as acting business manager. During that period, Harry worked primarily on benefit programs, particularly the death benefits society. But then Kapp had a heart attack and 18 months later Harry came back and took over the leadership again of Local 3."[25]

The International dropped the "other shoe" in October 1949, when Tracy revived the old monopoly charges against Van Arsdale (the core of the Allen Bradley case) and accused Van Arsdale of substituting the IBEW label with the Local 3 label on manufactured items. He further charged that Van Arsdale did not follow proper procedures in submitting Local 3's contracts to the International for approval.

Van Arsdale fought back, claiming that the International leadership was trying to muzzle and railroad its opponents. One headline in the *New York Daily News* was: "Electric Union Defies AFL Try at Discipline." Van Arsdale was quoted as saying that the IBEW sought to "put a stooge" in his place as a way of having clear sailing at the 1950 convention. Moreover, the members of the Local had been incensed at Tracy's and Broach's maneuvers and were vocal in their warnings to them not to interfere with the Local, said Thomas Van Arsdale.[26]

Thus, more than 2,500 members held a mass meeting November 10, 1949, and voted to support Van Arsdale to defy Tracy and his order to remove the Local 3 labels. Local President Jeremiah Sullivan declared: "Go back into the history of trade unions and study our organization. I say it is outstanding in the United States, if not in the world. We have obtained bigger and better benefits for our members since 1934 and we are proud of these gains. We have protected one and all in this organization and where does it all come from—from one man in this organization and let's not kid about who I mean—from our Business Manager Harry Van Arsdale Jr." His words were met with a roar of approval from the assemblage, and speaker after speaker rose to praise Van Arsdale and damn his enemies.

In gratitude, Van Arsdale told the throng: "I want to thank each and every one of you for your support because as I have said before there are times when things are discouraging. I think that no man could have a better reward than to do a good job for a trade union. Some men set out in the labor movement with very high ideals and they get off the track because of discouragement and obstacles and start thinking of furthering their personal ambitions. I'll take the memory of this vote of confidence tonight to my grave."[27]

It was speculated by some that if Van Arsdale were to be suspended or expelled, and an attempt made to place Local 3 in receivership, the members would have opted to leave the IBEW and become an independent union.

The counterattack weakened Tracy's drive. Tracy had no choice but to arrange for hearings before an impartial referee, Professor Douglas B. Maggs of Duke University. The hearings lasted from January 10, 1949, to February 28, 1950, and in a compromise arrangement, Van Arsdale pleaded guilty, and, as a penalty, was barred from holding union office for three years. The penalty was suspended by Tracy, an indication of the strength of Local 3.

In the years immediately following the fateful 1946 convention, Local 3 and Van Arsdale had a reputation of being aloof from the International, but that was a misinterpretation of the policy of avoiding anything that might be construed as political. The other side of the coin was that other delegates to subsequent conventions viewed the New York Local contingent almost as foreign emissaries. "There was a general trend in the IBEW, that if you were from New York you were something different. Everybody else had this in common—they were not from New York," Thomas Van Arsdale said.[28]

The 1946 convention did set New York apart. The convention established one more unit of membership—the BA. Members with that designation had the same voting rights as the A group members and paid the same per capita rates. The difference was that A members were entitled to death and pension benefits for which they paid an additional sum. The significance of this, according to some observers, was that this structure was created by Local 3 and was another sign of the influence it wielded in the International. In fact, the Local was operating as a virtually autonomous body by the end of the 1940s. It was this power and the awe with which many viewed Van Arsdale, because of his innovations and achievements, that fueled political vendettas against him. And although Van Arsdale would vigorously defend himself against attacks, more often giving more than he got, it can be conjectured that he was grieved to do so because such actions diverted attention from other goals that would more directly aid the membership. Moreover, it may be justly said that he preferred to stay within his own "castle" in New York and let the other barons battle to be king within the International. As a powerful member of the court, he would still wield tremendous influence, but because of his avowed lack of interest in wearing the crown, he would avoid having daggers drawn against him.

With the growing singularity of the union, and with the grudging recognition and respect of its power, Van Arsdale would enter the 1950s with an unfettered agenda in the area of benefits, education, civil rights, housing, and welfare that would lay the foundation for the golden age of the Local and also provide an example for others in organized labor to follow.

8

The Working Man and Woman

Learning and Compassion

At the heart of Van Arsdale's achievements in providing a vast array of benefits for his members was his love for the rank and file: the ordinary people. He agreed with Lincoln: "Common-looking people are the best in the world: that is the reason the Lord makes so many of them."[1] Van Arsdale could not do enough for them. It was his calling, his mission, the reason he worked practically round the clock.

Irving Stern, director of organization of the Amalgamated Meat Cutters and Retail Food Store Employees Union (Local 342), knew Van Arsdale well, and spoke of Harry's love for the worker.

> Harry's heroes were rank and filers. Harry talked about this rank and filer who participated in a strike of his own union or some other union or a rank and filer who helped in the development of building projects. And he would always remember people, of the early '30s and '40s who were loyal to him. He remained loyal to them for decades after.
>
> They were part of his group. And wherever he met them, or wherever he met their families or children, Harry had his hand out to greet them. Harry introduced everybody to everybody else. If there were people he knew and you were with them, you had to meet everybody on that line. It was almost like a constant receiving line. If you went to a bowling alley in Electchester, Harry would introduce you to all the children, all the mothers, to everybody, because he believed people ought to shake hands and ought to know each other.

And he felt the heart of the union were the rank and file. He used them in everything that the union was involved in that he tried to build. Within the union itself he would have various clubs. It was all a matter of getting the rank and file involved.[2]

Saul Lasher, secretary of the Metal Trades Council of New York, spoke about the Van Arsdale's proletarianism in the story of a walk he took with him after a meeting.

We left the Waldorf Astoria. We walked to 53rd Street and Lexington Avenue. By the time I got Harry downstairs into the subway, he had a contingent of thirty, forty people—union people—following him and he used to have the meetings with them right in the subway station.

I'm talking about shop stewards or just workers. They would say "Hello, Harry" not Mr. Van Arsdale . . . and he would stay and talk to them. He had the patience of a saint. The respect that was due this man. He never went into a taxi! I don't remember seeing him going in a taxicab. He'd sooner walk. And I asked him, "Why do you walk?" He says, "I always meet people from the union and they always stop to ask, 'How are you doing, brother?'" . . . and that's something that very few people have the ability to do . . . that's where he came alive and that's how he was. Mayors called him, governors called him and if they didn't respect him they wouldn't have bothered him. . . .

That's the way it is. . . . He was the hardest working. He never had anybody doing anything he couldn't do twice as good and that's saying a lot for a man. . . . Money meant nothing to Harry. Politicians meant nothing to Harry. The only thing Harry lived for was the labor movement and the worker, "the little guy at the bottom," that's what he called him.[3]

Van Arsdale had an infinitely creative mind and his curiosity about and affinity with people in all walks of life fed that creativity, said D. Bert Haring, a contractor, member of the Joint Industry Board of the Electrical Industry and a close friend of Van Arsdale.

He was a creative person who could attract a variety of people including other creative people, who would come to him from time to time with their thoughts. And he was almost of boundless energy and could coalesce and meet with different groups at different times on different subjects. So that he was moving almost like a chap who plays four-wall handball, intellectually. I mean I think the fact that he had . . . the capacity, after he had brought the level of the electricians up to such a high level. And he didn't quit, he kept going. He reached out to [workers in other fields]. He was boundless in that process. . . . The man had the basic element that it was a much broader base than just electricians, it was society at large. He gained the respect of the electrical employers that he negotiated with. I mean he could punch them out intellectually with ease. I mean he was far superior in fact, content, agility, in verbal communication. His day-to-day intimate contact with people in charge . . . he couldn't be dominated by the employer.

He was far and above most of the employers. When he did meet one of quality, he embraced them. I mean he certainly was looking for his equal at all times. I think that is the positive aspect. He wasn't looking to dominate people, he was looking to find his equal. He was not afraid of a new idea.

I'd be with him and he'd go over and he'd start to chat with someone. I'd say to myself, "Why is he bothering with that person?" I mean he'd be talking to the waiter at some affairs. And sincerely. You know he wasn't conning him. He wasn't looking for a bigger cut of steak or something. He was just interested in the person.[4]

The breadth and depth of Van Arsdale's affinity and identification with the rank and file was also shown in the constant stream of letters he received from them. They wrote as they would not to a brother in the union, but to a brother in their family. And he became part of their family; if not a brother, then a father, or a father confessor. They told him of their troubles or of the events of their daily lives and looked forward to his letters of reply, which— despite his jammed scheduled—would come, often filled with advice and reports of actions he had taken on their behalf.

Van Arsdale kept much of this correspondence in his private files. A typical indication of his loyalty to friends and good union members is shown in letters he wrote to Charles Mangano, who had been arrested several times while walking the picket line in the Triangle strike. Mangano had been turned down for enlistment in the army during World War II because of his police record. He wrote to President Roosevelt asking that he be allowed to serve. He also asked Van Arsdale for help in allowing him to enlist. Mangano was subsequently accepted into the army, presumably because of Van Arsdale's intervention.

Mangano had also written that he and other electricians had been demoted in their engineering unit because of grade regulations. Van Arsdale replied: "Sometimes in life it seems that those who try the most have the hardest road to travel. I know you will not allow this to discourage you. Keep trying and I know you will soon receive another promotion. The old saying is, 'they can't keep a good man down.'" (Apparently "they" could not: Mangano eventually rose to the rank of master sergeant.)

Another correspondent was Jacob Solomon of Parish, New York. Van Arsdale expressed concern over a compensation case involving Solomon and said he would attempt to contact the chairman of the State Industrial Commission to look into the matter.

John J. Mullin of Brooklyn, a pensioner, said he enjoyed fishing during his retirement. Van Arsdale's reply was jocular, but also revealed his strong work ethic when it came to active union officers. "I read your letter to Fred Hansen and he told me he would get in touch with you," Van Arsdale wrote. "If he tries to go fishing with you, be sure it's not on a weekday as he would probably be fired. Tell him he can go only on Sunday or any night between 12 midnight and 8 A.M. I hope that you will continue to enjoy yourself for many years. When you consider how many years it was necessary for you to work to make a livelihood, you should be entitled to take it easy."

The letters show that Van Arsdale was a "people person" and it was for those like Mangano, Mullen, and Solomon, that he initiated his programs, one of the most beneficial, visible, and ongoing was Electchester.

As World War II ended, civilian needs once more demanded attention and housing was paramount. There had been a building hiatus during the war years because of the diversion of work and materials to the military effort. But soldiers were returning, new marriages were beginning, and a host of children had been born during the war.

Van Arsdale and the JIB attempted to ease the problem. In 1946, Local 3 and the Electrical Contractors Association signed a no-strike, no-lockout agreement, which was to be in effect during the housing shortage. It was agreed that the men and women of the "A" construction division of the Local would work seven hours a day at a rate of $2 an hour—they would not return to the prewar six-hour day. Moreover, the union agreed to use high-speed tools and recently developed techniques to hasten the construction of new housing.

Van Arsdale was mindful of the housing project that the Amalgamated Clothing Workers had built on Manhattan's Lower East Side in 1926. He reasoned that Local 3 could and should have such a project of its own. On March 7, 1949, Van Arsdale called an 8 A.M. meeting of the members of the Local, and proposed that Local 3 build its own project that would provide not only housing but also more jobs.

After getting advice from Abraham Kazan, who had spearheaded the Amalgamated project, Van Arsdale formed a committee and met with State Housing Commissioner Herman T. Stichman and other officials of the State Division of Housing to see what tax exemptions and financial help might be available.

Stichman and his aides said that a long-term tax exemption would be available if the Local sponsored a nonprofit cooperative. The project would also have to be open to the general public as well as to Local 3 members. It was also advised that an initial investment of $1 million would be needed, ahead of mortgage commitments. The state would help—largely with technical advice to shepherd the project through the reefs of bureaucracy and the shoals of financing.

Van Arsdale asked the members of the JIB to provide the seed money but they turned him down. However, he sold them on the idea, and they suggested taking the seed money from the union pension funds under JIB control, but Van Arsdale showed that the pension fund was not large enough. After much discussion, the local and the employers agreed on the following formula: $250,000 from the pension fund, $200,000 from the JIB, $300,000 from contractors' subscriptions, and $250,000 to be raised by the Local membership. Actually, $300,000 was raised by the members through sponsors notes, paying 4.5 percent interest. These notes would be redeemable in three years unless the individual amount was used by a member as a down payment for an apartment in the cooperative. The cooperative was expected to be ready for occupancy in three years.[5]

The JIB chairman, Efrem A. Kahn, helped to make the project attractive to contractors by pointing out to the Board that funds would be protected by the government. Rentals could be held low and thus create demand.[6]

Arnold Beichman, a former editor of the *Electrical Union World*, had this comment: "It was Local 3 that pushed it through. The Board couldn't have cared less. . . . It was Harry's idea from the beginning. . . ."[7] Beichman also said that Kazan had advised Van Arsdale to encourage members to make as large a down payment on each apartment as possible so as to lower monthly charges. "Then, if you have a Depression or anything like that, you won't have to foreclose," he pointed out.[8]

Harold Webster, a former JIB chairman and former president of the National Electrical Contractors Association, in referring to Electchester, said: "Everything that is here originated because of him, absolutely. No question about it. Of course, he had a lot of help. When Pomonok was a golf course and when he first decided it would be desirable to have a housing project, he brought it up before the members of the Joint Board and everybody pitched in and helped. But he absolutely started it and he was a hard worker in making sure that we jumped the hurdles and there were plenty of hurdles."

Van Arsdale, however, never claimed sole credit for Electchester or, for that matter, any other of his innovations. The JIB took the kudos. His philosophy of teamwork was outlined in a 1975 interview. He was referring in this instance to his work with his Local officers, but his words would apply to anything he initiated.

> We have a team and they [would] rather talk about a captain of a team [i.e., in giving him credit]. But when I think back on the contributions, it would be counterfeit to take credit for a lot of other people's thinking, contribu-

tions and effort. And that's the way it must go on because if you have an organization where there is only one person [who leads and takes credit] and that person becomes corrupt in their thinking or delinquent in any direction, that would be a difficult and bad situation, one you really have to guard against. . . . A fellow plays on a team he gets his reward as being part of a team. He [doesn't] care whether somebody else knows about it. He knows the role he has played.[9]

The First Housing Company, a reference to the innovative aspects of the joint venture, was formed on April 25, 1949, operating under the New York State Limited Dividend Housing Law. Its mission was to purchase the land needed and then build and maintain the housing. A few weeks later, the company bought the 103-acre Pomonok Country Club (as mentioned previously, where Triangle CEO McAuliffe had golfed, and which had been picketed during the Triangle strike). Stichman held a news conference announcing the $20 million project. The *New York Times*, in an editorial, declared in part:

The 2,000 apartment housing project . . . represents an original and interesting development, not only in housing but also in labor relations. It is an example that bears watching and emulation by other union-employer groups; it promises a price for ownership or rental that seems startlingly low by today's standards; since a union is involved in the sponsorship and the building trades unions are also cooperating; it may provide a yardstick as to what self-interest in fast and economical construction can mean in the cost of housing. We at the *New York Times* . . . congratulate Local Union No. 3 of the International Brotherhood of Electrical Workers and employer associations affiliated with the Joint Industry Board of the Electrical Industry on seizing an opportunity to do some helpful pioneering.[10]

The Local held a contest among its members to name the project. The winner was George Klein who lived in Parkchester, a Metropolitan Life Insurance complex in the Bronx. His choice may not have been terribly imaginative, but it was deemed eminently suitable and ear catching: Electchester. Klein was awarded a $100 savings bond.

Construction of the first group of 383 apartments was started in 1950. Price per room was $475 with average monthly carrying charges per room of about $26. Apartments ranged from 3½ to 5½ rooms.

Van Arsdale ran into a problem in trying to induce his membership to leave their homes in the city and move to Flushing, which many felt was too out of the way. There were also complaints that the costs were too high. Lance Van Arsdale, Harry's cousin, reported that Van Arsdale got Lance's mother and father to leave their Brooklyn home and go to one of the first

apartments available in Electchester as a way of priming the pump and providing an example for others to follow. "Their apartment was the model
apartment which was used to show prospective tenants what life could be
like in Electchester," Lance said. "My mother made herself available at all
hours when anybody wanted to see the apartment."[11]

The sponsors' notes took care of much of the financial burden, and, in
1952, this was supplemented by a $5 weekly payroll deduction plan, which,
at the end of sixty weeks, would give a subscriber the $300 needed to fi-
nance the apartment. Some members also volunteered their free construction
labor and contractors contributed some materials without charge. Van Arsdale
spoke about that: "[Members] came Saturdays and Sundays and connected
up or did all the work in connection with the electric ranges. And the Brooklyn club wired one building on weekends and the Bronx club wired another
building. And there are fellows around who will tell you that this is the building
that the Bronx club wired. This is the building that the Staten Island club
worked on. It was very cooperative, but we had to be very careful not to
overdo that. You know, a guy that does electrical work all week, doesn't get
much thrill doing it for nothing, you know, on Saturday or Sunday."[12]

Van Arsdale took personal pride in Electchester. For instance, he would
climb down into excavations to help with tree plantings, or, while strolling
with a friend, interrupt a conversation to pick up papers from the sidewalk
and deposit them in waste baskets.[13]

Brian McLaughlin, another close aide of Van Arsdale (who went on to
become president of the New York City Central Labor Council in later years),
also had this insight into Van Arsdale's proprietary interest in Electchester
and the example he set for others:

> Electchester had committees to run the every day activities of the housing,
> for instance, the Presidents, the Board of Directors, whatever. They ran the
> housing. They managed the employees. They ordered the materials. They
> did the maintenance. They made financial decisions and considerations.
> They did the politics with whichever political entities were involved. Who
> were those people? Some of them weren't electricians. Why did they do it?
> What inspired somebody who was a school teacher or a taxi driver or a
> plumber or a lawyer—it wasn't just Local 3 people who lived in
> Electchester—to dedicate their time? It's because Harry's attitude and ac-
> tions were contagious. For example, it'd be eleven o'clock at night and
> Harry would be walking out of the First Housing office. He would, like,
> amaze people that here he would be coming out of the First Housing office
> at that hour of the night. Or on a Saturday morning he'd be going into the
> housing office. People respected that so much that somebody of his stature
> could be involved with those kinds of relatively trivial day to day things.

But that was the secret to his success. There were so many other people, other than electricians, who were a part of that success. Harry reached well beyond the membership of Local 3 and many of them played a very important role. You know? People who gave time in the Credit Union or with the Auxiliary Police or with the Little Leagues or with the Scout troops—all because of the example of Harry.[14]

Hy Greenblatt tells another story of how Van Arsdale attempted to get others to work as he did. Van Arsdale wanted residents to aid in cleaning their own buildings as a way to save money, Greenblatt said.

Every building had a porter [which was] Harry's idea of being a little frugal. We'd only have three porters for the five buildings and we'd relieve them of their duty of washing the halls and we the cooperators would wash our own halls. Well, that didn't sit too well with everybody, but it worked out fine. There were six people on every floor, each would have a week. My wife and I would sweep and mop the floor, just your landing, and if everybody did theirs the porter didn't have to do it so he could do other things and we could save the salaries of two porters throughout the course of the year. And when we kicked off the campaign, when we opened the first building, Harry Van Arsdale and Hy Greenblatt swept and mopped six floors. We started at the top. I had the broom and he had the mop. He used to keep old clothes in my office. He'd come in the office, put on his old clothes, and we started on the top. I swept and he mopped. And by accident as I swept the floor my broom would knock on the door so that the member could come out and see Harry Van Arsdale mopping the floor. And needless to say after that the program became successful. If Harry Van Arsdale could mop the floor so could we mop the floor. . . . [So] how you get this loyalty, there's my answer: doing it.

[Whatever the dirty job, somebody has to do it, even Van Arsdale.] We had a clogged up sewer. Harry said to me "Get a crew of fellows together. We'll never get the City department to clear that up. We're going to do it ourselves. I'll meet you Saturday morning at 8 o'clock. Have a ladder, buckets, we're going to go down in that sewer and clean it up. Arrange for a couple of fellows." So I got in touch with a couple of guys and we got that sewer top off. I was a little, skinny guy. We got the ladder down there and I was ready to go down. But you know who went down? Harry Van Arsdale was in that sewer shoveling muck into the bucket we were bringing up.[15]

Under Van Arsdale's stewardship, in subsequent years, a shopping center, a community center, and a Public School were built. In 1964, the Electric Industry Center at Electchester was also built. It contained, among other things, a 1,200 seat auditorium, a 48-lane bowling alley, the Joint Boards, fully equipped, modern dental and medical units, a cafeteria, and a bar.

Within Electchester there are numerous playgrounds and a full program of community events including picnics, art shows, parades, scouting activities, field trips, and senior citizen clubs. In short, the entire complex has become a comfortable, middle-class world unto itself, fulfilling Van Arsdale's vision as a workers' warm sanctuary, a just reward for a life of honest labor.

As a sign of appreciation for him, Jewel Avenue, which runs in front of the Electric Industry Center, was renamed Harry Van Arsdale Jr. Avenue on August 19, 1988. "Residents of Electchester wanted to perpetuate the name of Harry Van Arsdale Jr. Because he was the one individual responsible for the building of Electchester," said McLaughlin.[16]

Van Arsdale also explored the possibility of building a retirement village for Local members in Florida because so many retirees went there. But the idea never got out of the planning stage because the cost was prohibitive, said Hy Greenblatt. Thought was also given to building a rehabilitation center for disabled workers on land adjacent to Electchester, but that too had to be scrapped because of the cost.[17]

Nevertheless, Van Arsdale, continued to flesh out his plan for an enlightened worker able to better enjoy the fruits of his labor. "The union which negotiates a contract only is not a union," he said. "It must go further and try to improve the life and welfare of its members in many other ways too. Of course, the contract helps in that direction, but it's not enough."[18]

On another occasion, he said: "A union is not just wages and hours. It's brotherhood. It's brotherhood. It's the worker who visits you when you are sick. It's the vehicle for a better life. It's a classroom." William Blain, retired Local 3 financial secretary, added: "Speaking from an elected officer's point of view, I had heard Harry make a statement that he made over and over many times. And he always stressed that an officer of the union had but one job, and that was to serve the members, and to serve the membership, and that was the only job that individual really had, everything else became a secondary item. So if you're looking for a particular legacy from the standpoint of working in the labor movement, and furthering the aims and goals of unionism, that would have to be it."

Van Arsdale, Blain continued, always felt that a person representing working people should be on the same level as the people that he represented. Blain pointed out that Van Arsdale practiced what he preached by living in an apartment in Electchester.[19]

Van Arsdale's sense and practice of fraternity, his self-sacrifice, and his communal philosophies were in the best traditions of worker societies and guilds since their inception. But Van Arsdale's genius and legacy is that he carried them further than anyone else had done before. For example, the year 1949 saw his successful negotiation of paid vacations for the Local's construction workers—an innovation at the time—followed by paid holidays.

Another example of union brotherhood, with one member helping the other, was the establishment of a loan fund to aid lower income members of the manufacturing and supply divisions in paying for their apartments. Every member in the manufacturing and supply divisions contributed $2 a week into the fund for fifty weeks. Applicants for apartments in the Fourth Housing unit, a complex of five buildings set aside for the lower income members, could then borrow the necessary down payment (usually $1,800–2,200) for their flat. A deduction of $10 a week was made from their paychecks until the loan was repaid.

By February 1954, 1,171 families had moved in. That same year, the Local and the employers negotiated an annuity plan to further cushion the lives of members. Its aim was to provide additional funds for death benefits and supplemental pay during times of unemployment, sickness, or injury. In time, this also became a valuable savings mechanism for the members, bolstering the peace of mind for those living in or out of Electchester.

Local 3 members became eligible for the plan on the first day of work for a contracted employer. Employers contributed an agreed-upon sum into the plan, which was then invested. The sum in the account would be distributed to the worker participant or his or her beneficiary on retirement, disability, leaving the industry, or death. There was also an additional death benefit. Benefits could be paid in the form of a joint and survivor annuity, single life annuity, fixed monthly payments, or a lump sum, depending on the choices made by a participant, his or her spouse, or beneficiary. From its inception through March 31, 2000, the annuity plan for the Electrical Industry received $1,139,361,393 from employer contributors and paid out $500,270,158 to electrician members and beneficiaries. The annuity framework would serve as a model for the rest of the nation to emulate.

The ensuing years saw new benefits as well as expansions of those already achieved. Medical and dental departments for the members were established, as well as a loan fund (to borrow for a house, car, or other needs without interest). A tool and work-clothes allowance, and disability and optical insurance benefits were created. The benefit amounts were to grow. The cooperation between the Local and the employers within the JIB drew this observation from the Honorable Frank Barbaro, a chairman of the New York State Assembly Labor Committee: "There need not be the class struggle between management and labor. That is the driving force of the Joint Industry Board."[20]

"I loved and admired all my life what Harry Van Arsdale has done for organized labor," said William McSpedon. "Five hundred years from now we'll read about him being one of the greatest—and I say that without hesitation —one of the greatest labor leaders that the world has ever known, for what he has accomplished in his life span."[21]

Van Arsdale was to make more unique and pioneering contributions in the field of education. To Van Arsdale, education was the key to making the best use of leisure time. Where did this affinity for education come from? The Reverend Philip Carey had this insight: "It came from his own lack of education. He would do anything to promote tuition and scholarships. In this vein, despite his apparent much higher than average intelligence (by the measuring stick of seeing overall patterns and making accurate deductions from them) Van Arsdale never lost the [vernacular and accents] of the street and a rough and ready appearance."

Bertram Powers, president of Local 6 of the Typographical Union, described him:

> Harry Van Arsdale comes on as a medium height person, inclined to be stocky, powerful-looking man and a very gritty kind of a guy—a no-nonsense guy—with a heavy, heavy New York accent which would throw people off-guard because you would think, if you listened to Harry's voice, you'd say you were talking to a longshoreman or a Teamster or somebody, that didn't have much schooling, probably wasn't very bright. But Harry was very bright, very hard-working, very industrious, and did his homework and was completely dedicated to the labor movement.[22]

Van Arsdale began to implement his educational blueprint for his members by the gradual establishment of college scholarships, a program of lectures, libraries, and retirement enrichment, and, eventually, the establishment of the Educational and Cultural Trust Fund of the Electrical Industry.

One of his first steps was the enlargement of the reading room in the Local's 25th Street headquarters into a full-scale library in 1947. The following year, an annual scholarship program was created to provide tuition for the children of Local 3 members to attend college. The first scholarship was named after Reverend William J. Kelley, chairman of the State Labor Relations Board, who conducted Local 3's general election of officers in November 1948. In 1950, a contract was negotiated in which the JIB funded two more scholarships at Columbia College and the Columbia Graduate School of Engineering. Columbia University President Grayson L. Kirk called it "a pioneering step in higher education of the best kind."[23]

The scholarship program received worldwide recognition through the Voice of America. The *Electrical Union World* noted in the March 1, 1951, issue: "Even listeners in the Iron Curtain countries—Russia, Poland, Hungary and the other countries under Stalin's dictatorship—have by now heard about the achievements of a trade union in a democratic country." Local 3's international reputation was enhanced by visits of foreign unionists. A Turkish delegation toured Electchester and the Local headquarters during a stopover en route to the AFL-CIO convention in San Francisco in 1951. The Federation had chosen Local 3 for the tour as an example of what U.S. unionism could do. "There is nothing like it anywhere," the Turkish spokesman said.[24] Another idea was germinating in Van Arsdale's head: Bayberry Land. The idea was for a rest and convalescent home for Local 3 members. Van Arsdale had a number of conversations about this with Efrem Kahn, and it was Kahn who introduced the idea in a board meeting on September 8, 1948.[25] Almost exactly a year later, a board committee, including Van Arsdale and board member Harry F. Fischbach,[26] found a suitable site—a 314-acre estate, which had belonged to Charles Sabin, on Great Peconic Bay in Southampton, Long Island, known as Bayberry Land. The land was purchased from his widow, Mrs. Dwight Davis, for a mere $131,250.

The prospect of sharing their posh, exclusive enclave with union workers horrified the socialites and millionaires who had made the Hamptons synonymous at that time with "old money" and the Social Register. Cholly Knickerbocker, a columnist writing for Hearst's *New York Journal-American*, was aghast at the thought of the invasion of blue-collar peasants with dirty fingernails into the land of the aristocrats.

In his column of January 11, 1950, Knickerbocker wrote: "This is some switch: The AFL is now invading Southampton, L.I., one of Society's favorite summer playgrounds. . . . That means next summer we will have laborers rubbing elbows with Dukes, Biddles, Vanderbilts and other social grandees. And, since the union will undoubtedly outnumber the Social Registerites, I think the only thing left for them to do is for them to organize a society union and buy a playground of their own. Very soon it will be that if you don't organize, you won't even be able to play."[27]

As Van Arsdale put it: "They didn't want common labor rubbing elbows with Princes and people like that."[28] Van Arsdale went on to say that a local newspaper that had characterized Local 3 as communist was apparently confusing it with another union, observing.

> There had been a union and there still is a union known as the United Electrical and Radio Workers. And it was acknowledged by all people that that Union was under Communist domination. A lot of the members [of that union] I asked, how could you ever allow that to occur? They said, "Well, those fellows work so hard for us. Our members thought it would be a mistake not to let them continue to work so hard for us." And, of course, I said, did it ever occur to you maybe they weren't working so hard for you?

You know, there's such a thing as being a Trade Unionist and there's such a thing as having interest to go beyond and attempting to use the trade union organization for things for which it's not established.

Well, there's different opinions. But the thing was the newspaper in Southampton had a big headline, "Communists Come To Southampton." And then the story followed up, these members of the Electrical Union were invading, you know, the millionaire retreats.

And nothing could have been farther from the truth. But that didn't have any detrimental effect on what we had to do.

Oscar Schneidenbach, was hired as resident director. He would also serve as a hospital administrator. He and his wife moved into the forlorn manor house, which apparently had been neglected and was badly in need of repair, on June 1, 1951. "We were practically camping indoors," he said. But several months later they had it in shape.

Van Arsdale related that Schneidenbach helped win acceptance for the union among the townspeople by taking an active part in community affairs, even becoming president of the Southampton Rotary Club.[29]

Van Arsdale also had high praise for the blue-blooded wife of a member who wrote a blistering letter of reply to Knickerbocker. "Her answer to him is a masterpiece," he said. The irate wife was Mrs. Elizabeth Li Volsi, whose husband Peter was in the sign division of Local 3. Her maiden name was Wright and she was a Wellesley College graduate, daughter of a concert pianist, a descendant of Revolutionary War General Horatio Gates and related to President John Tyler and U.S. Supreme Court Justice John B. Rector. She wrote in part:

I resent the slur you put upon some 30,000 union members and their families. . . . In my opinion . . . your statements make strange reading in a representative American paper. At a time when one hears cries on all sides for individual equality regardless of race, color or creed, your attempt to pit the "Registerites" against a special working class in this democratic America seems untimely, incompatible and in questionable taste. [She went on to praise the admirable qualities of her husband, other union members, and the Local, singling out Electchester as a proud achievement.] Instead of emulating some registerites by spending their monies in patronizing bistros or going to the Met not to enjoy good music, but to enable their older women to pose for cheesecake photos in an adjacent cocktail bar, the so-called "laborers" are dedicating their hard-earned dollars to the alleviation of the housing shortage and to the maintenance of a higher morale for their families through the provision of comfortable and healthful homes.[30]

Fischbach said he did not recall any opposition among the townspeople to Bayberry complex. "First of all, they're by themselves," he said. "It's isolated. They don't interfere with anybody in town."[31]

The complex functioned strictly as a rest home for about five years, caring for 672 patients who stayed for an average two weeks. Thomas A. Murray, president of the New York State Federation of Labor, said: "Bayberry Land is one of the finest achievements I have ever seen by organized labor."[32]

Nevertheless, it was felt that the site was underutilized. One reason was that the patients were without their families and it was a long trip from their city homes. But Van Arsdale thought of utilizing Bayberry Land for educational purposes and he introduced the idea into the 1956 contract talks with the employers. As he explained it:

> We found that when a man is ill for a protracted time in a hospital, he many times is anxious to get back to his family. And, by the same token, the family is very anxious to have him back. So, we were largely limited to the fellow who was either a widower, or who came from a very large family so that his wife wouldn't be alone and the children wouldn't be alone. . . . And we got the idea . . . that we would be better off to make use of it as an educational center with facilities for the convalescing members. And for the students, it also came in handy for a man who has been unemployed for a long time so that he can pick up the equivalent of a day's pay.[33]

An educational committee was formed. Van Arsdale thought it would be valuable to teach his members how to think. "Nobody in this union has cracked a book since television appeared," he told Murray Kempton, a columnist for the *New York Post*.[34] Van Arsdale consulted with Harry Carman, a former dean of Columbia University, who suggested a course to accomplish what Van Arsdale envisioned. Shortly thereafter, a course was offered called "Critical Thinking in Human Relations." A wide range of subjects was listed including semantics, logic, history, and psychology. Local 3 members who were college graduates aided the instruction staff by becoming discussion leaders. These men later became the core of the Local's Futurian Society. Workers who attended the courses received a stipend, as per the bargaining agreement, to offset any loss of pay while at Bayberry. This set the precedent for the payment in 1961 of the equivalent of jury duty pay to members who took courses on good citizenship. Members had to take the courses before reporting to jury duty because "We want our members to have a basic understanding of civic and municipal affairs," Van Arsdale said.

Of the Bayberry courses, John Goodale, one of the early instructors, said: "I believe that one of the strongest features of the Bayberry program is the residential character of the week. The same twenty-eight hours of classroom exposure could be given in the city, going to sessions one night a week for ten weeks, but I am sure that the effect would be quite different. The experience of a group living together for a week engenders a camaraderie that would not develop in periodic meetings spread out in time. Much of the learning experience that goes on in the program does not occur in the classroom. It happens in the dining room or in the library in an evening discussion with other members of the group or during walks along the beach."[35]

The courses were a reflection of the Van Arsdale philosophy and were a source of astonishment for William Michelson, who had been president of Local 2–3 of the United Store Workers of the Retail, Wholesale, and Department Store Union. He had also been a pioneer battler within the CIO progressive battalions and had a narrow view of the cultural breadth of the craft unionist leaders in the AFL.

> In the field of education, Harry was continuously an advocate of the broadest kind of education for his rank and file. [Van Arsdale's program for apprentices included not only instruction in technical matters but also] involved broad liberal arts skills, discussions of politics and economics, etc. And that was a shock to me because I never expected this kind of personality and this kind of vision, this kind of total involvement in terms of a broad scope of the trade union movement in an AF of L official.
>
> The interesting thing about this is that his advocacy of this broad rank and file participation and education was totally devoid of any political overtones. Those of us who came from a milieu were—we were socialists or communists . . . and we were terribly involved in international politics, etc. Harry came with a kind of pristine purity on this question. All that he knew was that the labor movement was the road to building better lives for his members and better lives meant not only higher wages and better pensions and severance pay, but opportunities to learn, to travel, to participate, to undertake responsibilities. And, as a result, I met through Harry a great number of rank and filers in the electrical union who were wholly involved in various community apparatuses that Harry set up and for whom the electrical workers union was literally a way of life, and a non-political way of life, a pure trade union devotion and trade union dedication.
>
> And there was a whole host of these active rank and filers in education, in community activity, in Boy Scouts, in Bayberry, in education and so on.
>
> [It was] an organizational apparatus that existed nowhere else in the labor movement. It didn't exist in the old Jewish socialist unions like the Amalgamated. It didn't exist in the ILGWU [International Ladies Garment Workers Union]. It didn't exist in the left unions to any of the extent that I found it in Harry's union. And that attracted me to him.
>
> [Moreover] the strange phenomena about Van Arsdale's organization

capacity and his vision as a trade unionist is highlighted by the fact that he had no political ideology. The ideas of developing this extensive rank and file activities was not a product of his correlated political activity. He didn't have aspirations for the working class. He didn't talk about socialism. He didn't talk about anything else except immediate economic improvements. He talked extensively about minimum wages and talked extensively about organization. And he had an inherent genius really for understanding that the strength of his union really rested with—and that his position in the labor movement really rested very firmly upon—his unassailable position as the leader of Local 3.[36]

Van Arsdale saw aiding his members economically through vocational proficiency as another boon of education. Van Arsdale believed that an educated labor man would be more on a par with the college-educated management figures he might meet across a negotiating table. Irving Stern of the Amalgamated Meat Cutters and Retail Food Store Union said:

Education . . . everybody had to be educated. Everybody had to be trained. I guess in retrospect that was the thing I respected the most, because I believed in training and education. And I was so impressed with what they were doing in this field. The fact that they had enough faith in the rank and filers and a belief that rank and filers could learn, that rank and filers could be trained, that rank and filers could achieve the knowledge and the insights to give leadership.

And that was a constant comment. He said: "You see these leaders of industry? They're trained. They're sent to college. We have to do the same with people in labor. We have to train them. How are we going to lead? How are we going to compete? How are we going to achieve our goals unless we give these people that kind of education?" And he believed in every sense of the word. He believed in training people.[37]

Since its inception, Bayberry has been the site of a wide spectrum of seminars open to members and their wives and even to IBEW representatives from other states, Canada, and delegates of the electrical industry in Great Britain.

But the convalescent mission of Bayberry was hardly ignored. In 1969, Bayberry's convalescent facilities were expanded to include single-story residential structures, a new administration building, and a recreation center. The buildings were named in honor of the pioneer members of the Pension Committee. The name "Harry Van Arsdale" was not among them, in keeping with Van Arsdale's desire not to take credit for his works but to share the credit with others.

The camp was enlarged in 1972 to include facilities for the children of members, disadvantaged kids, and Boy Scouts, illustrating Van Arsdale's lifelong interest in helping the young. At Van Arsdale's instigation, Camp Integrity was created with the mission of not only providing youngsters with summer fun but also imparting ethical values of honor. "We've had some experiences that were very rewarding," Van Arsdale said. "You hear some employers talk about what a wild bunch of kids they got and the things they resorted to and how in a short period of time they were so proud because they learned how to conduct themselves so differently. So we feel that a lot of these youngsters might have gone in a direction that might otherwise been different [if they had not had the experience of the camp]."[38]

Van Arsdale had a particular interest in the Boy Scouts and the Local sponsored its first troop in 1954. Many more were to come. Because of his work with the Scouts, Van Arsdale was named official liaison of organized labor with the Scouts. He also served as vice chairman of the organizing committee of the Manhattan Boy Scout Council and was a member of its executive board, and he received the Silver Beaver and Good Scout awards from the National Council of the Boy Scouts of America.

When Van Arsdale was appointed to the Executive Board of the Manhattan Council, he said: "I think that is a leading force today in molding our boys and young men for their future responsibilities. We cannot take the importance of this movement too seriously and I strongly and sincerely urge everyone to give their wholehearted support to Scouting in every way.

"For my part, I expect to do everything in my power to set a record in the number of new Scout units organized in Manhattan, for I believe that Scouting should be available to every boy in our city."[39]

Van Arsdale consistently advocated offering educational opportunities to youth—opportunities he did not have when he was young. Again, you will not find Van Arsdale's name on any of the scholarships he fostered for his members, their children, or other deserving youths. The establishment of scholarships was another aspect of the astonishing array of welfare, education, and pension benefits developed by Van Arsdale in the 1950s and 1960s.

In 1951, every contractor whose business earned at least $1 million annually agreed to finance additional scholarships for the combined arts and technical courses at Columbia University and its graduate engineering school. Van Arsdale, speaking of how the number of scholarships was enlarged, said:

> We always try to involve our employers in any of our activities. We used to have ten runner-ups to ten selected students and from one of that ten was the winner. And here were the employers and we are all participating and someone would say, "Gee, aren't they ten fine young men?" (We didn't

have girls at first, you know.) And invariably, even the meanest employer would say, "Oh, they are great. They are fine looking, a credit to their parents." And then, you would suggest well, isn't it a shame that of these ten youngsters we are only able to give one of them a scholarship? And the employers would say, "Yes, it seems a shame to have these ten youngsters and they are all holding their breath as to who is going to win out of the ten." And then everybody . . . in the circle agreed what a wonderful thing it would be if we had a scholarship for each of them.

And then they were asked, well, if we could develop an idea that would be fair and equitable to every employer would you support an idea to have a scholarship for all those who had the qualifications? And we were not negotiating here. We were just having a conversation. Negotiations cost money, but a conversation doesn't cost money. Invariably, they are all decent men. They all said, "Oh yes, I'd support anything providing it was equitable and providing the cost of it wasn't prohibitive and all of that." . . . So to make a long story short, a suggestion was made that if every employer who did a million dollars worth of business—not profit, business—would make a scholarship available and the union suggested that the scholarship would be in the name of that employer or whomever he designated.[40]

Young women were brought into the fold the following year when the daughters of members received scholarships at Barnard College. In subsequent years, the scholarship program was further expanded to encompass a spectrum of universities and additional courses of study including dentistry, teaching, business administration, and social work.

The Local, in conjunction with the New York City Public Library system, established in 1952 what amounted to mini-branch libraries at each plant where at least 100 members were employed. In addition, because television was becoming more and more popular in 1952, classes in television techniques were organized by the Local. Moreover, the first of many weekend conferences to come was organized that same year for Local members at the Cornell School of Labor and Industrial Relations. The initial topic was social security and developments in labor unions. This was later expanded to a complete curriculum in labor relations, citizenship, and industrial practices and conflict resolution.

The growing number of Spanish-speaking members in the Local occasioned free English classes in 1953. In the years that followed, the Local sponsored courses in public speaking for Latino members. The courses were offered at Cornell University under the aegis of the Local's Santiago Iglesias Educational Society.

Van Arsdale also wanted his members to have at least a high school equivalency diploma, and, in August 1958, he arranged with the New York City

Board of Education to give general education diploma refresher classes at the union headquarters. This was followed by classes for officers and business representatives on world affairs at union headquarters in April 1959.

Van Arsdale also recorded public service announcements for television and radio as part of the New York City Labor Department's campaign to combat illiteracy. "He was a great supporter of that particular literacy program," said James McFadden, then New York City Labor Commissioner.[41]

Van Arsdale also initiated a training course in industrial electronics within the Local and the JIB in 1962, and, in 1963, as always with his eye on the needs of the aged, Van Arsdale prevailed on the Education Committee of the JIB to begin work on a program of preretirement training so senior members could get the most out of their pension and benefit programs.

Increased technical, union, and vocational skills were offered a few months later through courses in job techniques and shop steward training, as well as classes on self-improvement and leisure time use. The following year a course in atomic radiation was created in recognition of the growing use of nuclear power plants in the electrical industry.

New Year's Day 1964 saw the birth of the JIB's Educational and Cultural Trust Fund. It was an expansion of the Father Kelley and company scholarships and was financed by employer contributions. Within a few years, the fund made significant contributions to a number of prominent cultural, African-American, and Latino organizations, and the Boy Scouts. But greater milestones in education lay ahead as Van Arsdale pressed for the formation of a labor college. He was also instrumental in the establishment of the Robert F. Wagner Labor Archives at New York University.

When the Local moved its center of operations to the Electrical Industry Center in Queens, the old headquarters, which had been the site of so many in-house classes for members, was reborn as Empire State College—the Labor College of the State University of New York—the first accredited labor college in the United States. The impetus for the college had come not only from Harry Van Arsdale but also from the union members who had attended nondegree labor courses at Cornell University. However, the road to establishing the college was arduous because of Cornell's initial ambivalence toward the project. "They felt we were not educated enough academically to meet their standards," said Dr. Harry Kelber, former director of the Educational and Cultural Fund of the Electrical Industry.[42]

Van Arsdale mobilized all his forces in seeking to establish the college. He appealed to Governor Rockefeller and in a seven-page memo, he wrote in part:

> Serious working adults who are concerned with the complex problems of our society are responding eagerly to an opportunity to study in a Labor

College. It will be the only institution of higher learning in the metropolitan area to offer an undergraduate degree in industrial and labor relations. . . . Cornell's two-year, non-degree program, has demonstrated that a substantial number of labor leaders, despite their heavy work schedules, are capable of serious and sustained academic study if the courses are interesting and useful, and if the school administration takes into account their special needs and problems. The two-year program has approximately three-hundred students who come from more than one-hundred and ten local unions, and representing virtually every industry in the Metropolitan area. A substantial majority of the students are in decision-making positions and one-third of them are black, Puerto Rican or from other minorities.[43]

Subsequently, with significant help from Governor Nelson Rockefeller and through a diligent and vigorous campaign by students and labor leaders, Van Arsdale pushed the project through. He also mobilized the rank and file of labor from a number of unions, to support the project. Bernard Rosenberg, a Local 3 business agent, wrote in his dissertation:

In order to remove any possible cause for further delay, Van Arsdale, with the assistance of his son, Thomas, then the Business Manager of Local 3, arranged with that union to make available a seven-story building located at 130 East 25th Street at Lexington Avenue, which had been the former headquarters of Local Union 3 before it had moved to its present location adjoining the Electchester housing development in Queens. The seven-story building, which was owned by the Electrical Workers Benefit Society, whose director was Thomas Van Arsdale, had 18,000 square feet of usable space. Because it had been used to upgrade the skills of Local 3 members, its rooms were easily adaptable for classrooms, a student lounge, an auditorium, and offices for faculty and staff. Van Arsdale felt that the building could accommodate students of the proposed Associate Degree Program and of the two-year Labor-Liberal Arts Program.

At the initiative of Van Arsdale, the Electrical Workers Benefit Society's president, Edward J. Cleary, who was also president of Local Union 3, proposed to lend the building to Cornell for one dollar a year in order to house the new program. At the same time, Mister Van Arsdale asked this writer [Rosenberg] to undertake the task of converting the structure into a college building at little cost to the union.

This was no mean task. Volunteers were recruited, committees were formed, and the work of putting a college building into place was begun. Volunteers came from the Carpenters, Painters, Laborers, and Electrical Workers unions, as well as from a number of others. The Volunteers were joined by retirees who came to participate in the: "labor of love." One volunteer retiree Al Albanese, from District Council 9 of the Painters Union—organized a team of volunteers who painted the entire building at no cost and every painter had to have their handiwork personally approved by Albanese.[44]

After Van Arsdale's death in 1986, President James Hall of the Empire State College Council proposed that the Center for Labor Studies of Empire State College be named after Van Arsdale. The proposal was made in a resolution by Hall to members of the College Council. The resolution read:

WHEREAS, Harry Van Arsdale Jr. dedicated his life from the age of 15 first to the causes of his fellow electricians, leading Local 3 of the International Brotherhood of Electrical Workers to a preeminence in progressive unionism and,

WHEREAS Harry Van Arsdale Jr. gave exemplary leadership to the New York City labor movement through his chairmanship of the Central Labor Council from 1957 to 1985, showing responsible and enlightened political leadership in civic affairs and numerous union negotiations supporting the cause of workers in the New York City area and,

WHEREAS Harry Van Arsdale Jr. provided extraordinary sensitivity to education as the primary vehicle for broadening the experience and realizing the intellectual potential of workers and,

WHEREAS Harry Van Arsdale Jr. was a key supporter in the creation of the Center for Labor Studies, Empire State College, and lent his support, advice, and counsel from its inception and initiated the innovative apprenticeship educational [Associate Degree] program of IBEW Local 3 and,

WHEREAS, on the 24th of April, 1986, request was made by Dr. Frank Goldsmith, Dean of the Empire State College Center for Labor Studies, after consultation with the faculty and staff of said Center, that the Council of Empire State College consider the recommendation that the name for the Center for Labor Studies be changed to The Harry Van Arsdale Jr. School of Labor Studies, Empire State College, State University of New York.

THEREFORE BE IT RESOLVED that in recognition of the enormous contribution that he has made to unionists, the cause of the poor and minority groups, and the education of workers, the name of the Center for Labor Studies, Empire State College be *THE HARRY VAN ARSDALE JR. SCHOOL OF LABOR STUDIES, EMPIRE STATE COLLEGE, STATE UNIVERSITY OF NEW YORK.* [Italics in original.]

Thus, the Harry Van Arsdale School of Labor Studies was born, offering degree programs not only in Labor Studies but also in Cultural Studies, Social Theory, Social Structure and Change, and Historical Studies. Members of almost every union in New York City have attended, and its graduates include a host of labor leaders.

Van Arsdale threw the doors of education open to those of all races just as he opened the books of membership in the union to them, broadening the ranks of apprentices. But Van Arsdale would not accept an honorary degree for himself. Apparently he so revered education, that he refused to demean it by not working for the degree, an extension, perhaps, of his credo of an honest day's work for an honest day's pay. He turned the honor down in a letter to Dr. Clifton Wharton, Jr., chancellor of the State University of New York, February 23, 1981, saying that although he was "greatly honored" to be considered for an honorary degree, "because of a long-standing policy, I am reluctant and cannot accept." A second attempt was made in later years to get him to accept, but again he turned it down, said Bernard Rosenberg. "I asked Harry as to why he did not want to accept that honor. He told me that he had to drop out of high school, so how could he be awarded an honorary degree."[45]

Dr. Harry Kelber felt that Van Arsdale could have been a professor.

> But my feeling is here's a man who had little time for education yet was brilliant. I think this often happens with people who are self-educated and who are in positions of influence. He realized the importance of education. He was a self-educated man. [I believe he felt] that he had missed so much in his life that he wanted others [to have what he missed]. I think he could have been a top professor. He was a brilliant man. And his brilliance was detected at an early age as well. He was capable of abstract thinking and inductive reasoning. He could see situations and come to generalized conclusions. He had no formal readings in sociology and psychology, but in terms of psychology he had insights into people that were just tremendous, absolutely.
>
> He was an avid reader. And not only a reader [but an incisive speaker]. I always attended so many educational meetings with him. He would get up and talk for 45 minutes off the cuff on all current events and making analyses of situations and so on. He had to have read this material. And he would collect material. And he would pick out points that he would want to emphasize. One of his things was that he could make the same speech a dozen different places. He had certain formulations that would seize him and he would be so infatuated with them that he would repeat them. But if you attended four or five different meetings along with him you'd hear him say a lot of the same things. But at the same time he was very fluent about that. And he could field difficult questions, often questions about the union that might be embarrassing to others.[46]

Historically, Local 3 had been a father-son union: fathers passing down knowledge to their sons who worked as their apprentices and who, through their fathers, became members of the union. Because most of the early electricians were drawn from Northern Europe, the membership within the construction division, the top craft level in the Local, was totally white and remained so during periods of sporadic employment. In 1955, Van Arsdale opened up the construction division to everyone when he notified all divisions in the Local that all members in good standing could register their sons for apprenticeship in the construction division as long as they were high school graduates and were between the ages of 18 and 21.

Van Arsdale also realized that African Americans and Latinos needed their own bases of power within the Local in order to help make their voices heard. Many study trips were taken to Puerto Rico to see labor conditions firsthand. The plight of Latino and African-American minorities was of particular interest to Van Arsdale. To give a helping hand to Puerto Ricans and other Latinos and to bring them more securely into the Local 3 fold, portions of the *Electrical Union World* were printed in Spanish in a number of issues.

Van Arsdale focused on the injustices done to African-American and Puerto Rican workers, many of whom were entering the Local in the lampshade division. Studies were made, conferences were held, and, in August 1957, Van Arsdale was appointed by Mayor Wagner to a ten-man Committee on the Exploitation of Workers to end the injustices done to African-American and Puerto Rican workers by racketeers. The gangsters would pose as trade unionists, engineer "sweetheart" contracts, and impose inordinate dues. Bringing other city unions into the campaign, Van Arsdale stated that inequities of low wages and exploitative, crooked unions and bosses were "no longer a human problem. It has become so bad it is now a community problem." He added: "It is the duty of every decent human being to want to see an end to the frightful conditions brought about by unscrupulous employers with the help of unsavory scoundrels posing as trade unionists. No one can correct this condition, whether it is 30 or 300 workers—except the workers themselves. If they stand together, if they will not work another day under a filthy, dirty contract, that will terminate such a contract."[47]

Again, using his own Local as an example of responsible, humane unionism, Van Arsdale recommended that Local 3 consider whether a union member making less than $50 a week or $1.25 an hour should pay dues. "If we condemn the boss for paying low wages, why should we take part of that worker's low wage?"[48] Local members came through and voted in October to relinquish the dues. Local 3 went after substandard conditions and wages in the lamp and lampshade industry and won salary and benefit gains for the workers, mostly Puerto Rican, after a seven-day strike, which ended January 22, 1958.

Continuing his campaign to aid minority members of Local 3, in 1958, Van Arsdale helped organize the Santiago Iglesias Educational Society for Puerto Rican members. In 1960 he aided in the creation of the Lewis Howard Latimer Progressive Association, named after an African-American associate of Thomas Alva Edison. Financial contributions were also made to African-American and Latino organizations.

Paul Sanchez, an officer in the regional office of the AFL-CIO and a former member of Local 3, worked with Van Arsdale on Puerto Rican matters within the Local and told how Van Arsdale aided the Latino community. After the merger of the AFL and CIO, Van Arsdale convinced George Meany of the need for more Spanish-speaking officers in the Federation. Meany then appointed a Latino to head a group dealing with complaints from minorities. During a study tour of Puerto Rico, Van Arsdale saw a picture of Santiago Iglesias, founder of the Puerto Rican labor movement. Sanchez continued:

> When he asked who the man was and they told him Harry knew something about him because Meany had told him about Santiago Iglesias. When we flew back to New York Harry called me and he asked me about my impression about the meeting and about Santiago Iglesias and did I learn anything more about Santiago Iglesias. I gave him my impressions, you know, and he suggested that once we come back to New York we should try to form some sort of an organization to help Puerto Ricans in the mainland, and that perhaps we wanted to name it after Santiago Iglesias. So that's how Santiago Iglesias Educational Society started. Now I had the honor of being the first president of the Society. And I remember that there was a lot of talk about closed doors for minorities in terms of jobs in the Local. One day Harry called me, and he also called the president of the Latimer Association, which was another organization representing Blacks within our organization. And he told us that he wanted at least 250 candidates. Now I'm talking about back in 1959. I'm not talking about the other day, I'm talking about 1959. And he wanted those candidates for apprentices. [So] I know that doors were open for our Puerto Rican people and the Spanish-speaking people and also for Blacks.[49]

Sanchez also tells a story that further illustrates Van Arsdale's dedication to helping people of all races and nationalities who were in need.

> I remember one case and this happened about 1959 where this man told Harry some personal problem that he had and Harry decided he was going to do something to help this man. On a very cold, snowy Sunday, Harry walked I would say about a mile from Chambers Street to the East Side Drive where this man lived. Harry went to this man's house to inform him

that on next Monday he was going to work in a better job where he was going to make more money so that he could help his family resolve the problems. And this man Harry Van Arsdale, a man of his stature, his position, walked all that distance to go up and inform that man of what happened and that he was going to help him. And I know that story so well because I was that man, I was that person. He didn't have to prove it to me, but he showed his sincerity, what he wanted to do for people. And from there on I did not abandon that man anymore.[50]

In 1962, the gates opened even wider when Van Arsdale pushed for the five-hour work day and promised the industry that 1,000 new apprentices would be enrolled to meet any labor shortage entailed by the shorter day. The addition of apprentices had a twofold purpose: one was to make the proposed five-hour day more attractive to employers and the second was to allow for the hiring and union admission of more minority group members. The five-hour day meant that the sixth and seventh hours needed to fill out the shift would be paid at overtime rates. Mediator Theodore Kheel explained: "Harry recognized that the employers could not afford this increase in the rates unless they got off-setting benefits. What he did for them was to increase the ratio of apprentices to journeymen. . . . [This relieved having to pay a journeyman working at a premium rate from doing work that could be done by an apprentice paid at a lower rate, such as picking up supplies and other "go-fer" activities] so, it's advantageous for the employers to have more apprentices."[51]

Recruitment drives were held within the National Association for the Advancement of Colored People (NAACP), the Urban League, other African-American organizations, and Puerto Rican and other Latino groups for prospective candidates. The recruitment drive was greatly aided in 1966 by a new state law in which the open recruitment program was enlarged and strengthened. A fourteen-member joint Apprentice Committee was established, half from the Local and half from the JIB, and it provided monitors, including members of the Iglesias and Latimer societies, to administer the apprenticeship examinations.

Van Arsdale would fight a never-ending battle for racial equality and justice. His early, consistent interest in racial equality was shown by his previously discussed denunciation in 1938 of what was reported to be "a very contemptible attempt on the part of some individuals who formed groups of members [and fomented] a whispering campaign of racial prejudice and hatred among our members."[52] Union veteran Joe Jacobson says of Van Arsdale: "To him it made no difference what your religion was, what the color of your skin was. Nothing. As long as you were a good union man, that was all he was interested in."[53]

Meanwhile, the membership continued to gain increases in wages and benefits during this period. Vacation allowances were raised, serious injury benefits and disability insurance were increased, and the annuity plan and death benefit schedules were initiated. Everything continuously improved with each contract within the various divisions, each negotiated by committees and the officers attached to the various divisions, but all also under the close supervision of Van Arsdale.

Although Van Arsdale was doing all this for so many people, he himself lived an almost Spartan life. He took a salary of $175 a week in 1956, earning a little more than his Local brothers. Until he moved into an apartment at Electchester, his home was the house he had built with his father in Ozone Park and his small hotel room in Manhattan. Irving Stern visited him in Electchester and told of Van Arsdale's lifestyle:

> He lived in Electchester. [His apartment was] very simply furnished. Certainly, not in keeping with the status and prestige and, one might say, the eminence that Harry achieved in the movement and in this community. Harry would use the subway to get into the city. He would travel about the city by bus. He didn't own a car. He lived simply. We'd go to dinner after meetings. I wasn't beyond using an organization credit card for dinner and I'd say, "I'm going to have some veal. How about you?" And invariably, he would eat spaghetti. That was Harry. Yes, a drink or two occasionally after the meeting, either at the Gramercy Park Hotel or various other restaurants. Harry lived simply, dressed simply. No car and no big shot was Harry. And I respected him for that and admired him because he stayed that way all his life.[54]

There is a famous photo of Van Arsdale riding on the back of Arnold Beichman's motor scooter as a way of traveling quickly from one meeting to another. He didn't care about appearances. It was just the best way to beat New York traffic.

As he established this pioneering path of pensions and benefits, Van Arsdale and his union leadership also dealt with the day-in/day-out business of the union: organizing, grievances, and strikes. In the 1950s and 1960s, Van Arsdale's life took another turn as he became more and more active in the politics of the city and the state.

Harry Van Arsdale Jr. advocating a thirty-hour workweek in the 1930s.

Part of a delegation of American trade unionists to visit the Soviet Union for May Day celebrations in 1937. (Van Arsdale is sitting third from the left.)

Unveiling of a memorial plaque in May 1940 honoring Local 3's members who served during World War I. *Left to right:* Harry Van Arsdale Jr., business manager; Bert Kirkman, president of Local Union No. 3; Mayor Fiorello H. LaGuardia, Joseph Burkhardt, First District Commander of the American Legion, and Gerald Duffy, Chairman.

Back row, left to right: Harry Van Arsdale, Sr., Harry Van Arsdale, III, Harry Van Arsdale Jr., and Thomas Van Arsdale, with Bert Kirkman and Fred Hanson in front.

Addressing a crowd at the old union headquarters at 23rd Street and Lexington Avenue in 1946.

In support of health care for the aged through Social Security, President John F. Kennedy addressed a rally at the New York City Center in 1960. With him are Harry Van Arsdale Jr. and Gerald J. Ryan, president of Uniformed Fireman's Association Local 94.

As guest of honor, Reverend Martin Luther King Jr. was with Harry Van Arsdale Jr. at the first meeting of the Brotherhood Party at the Hotel Commodore in New York City, October 1961.

Harry Van Arsdale Jr. helped organize the low-paid taxi drivers in New York City in 1962. After many unsuccessful organizing efforts by other labor unions, Harry brought his experience and influence to the situation and brought it to a successful conclusion.

Harry Van Arsdale Jr. and IBEW President Daniel W. Tracy with a scale model of Electchester.

Harry Van Arsdale Jr. being transported between meetings by Arnold Beichman in November 1962.

Heavy downpour of rain did not prevent Governor Nelson A. Rockefeller and Senator Jacob K. Javits from visiting Electchester on November 3, 1962.

The Equal Opportunity Day Award for 1963 was presented to Harry Van Arsdale Jr. by (*left*) Whitney M. Young Executive Director, National Urban League. Also present was A. Philip Randoph (*center*), President of the Sleeping Car Porters Union.

Senator Robert Kennedy and Harry Van Ardale Jr. campaigning in Electchester.

Harry Van Arsdale Jr. with President Lyndon B. Johnson in the White House.

His Eminence Francis Cardinal Cooke and Harry Van Arsdale Jr. at Labor Day Mass in 1973.

From left to right: Harry Van Arsdale Jr., David Rockefeller, and Thomas Van Arsdale in September 1983 at Bayberry Land.

Harry Van Arsdale Jr. with Cardinal O'Connor at New York City's 1984 Labor Day Parade.

Harry Van Arsdale Jr. with former Supreme Court Justice Arthur Goldberg.

9

"Mister Labor"

When words failed to win agreements, Van Arsdale reluctantly but decisively used action as the practical solution. As Bertram Powers of the Typographical Union put it: "I think he had an aversion to strikes, didn't like strikes, and certainly could never be called strike-happy or quick on the trigger for strikes. But not that he was afraid of [using] strikes, he just, I guess, felt that a strike was a failure, something had failed at the collective bargaining process that you had to have a strike."[1] So, while harmony and progress walked hand in hand in the Joint Industry Board (JIB) in the late 1940s and early 1950s, there were strikes in other divisions of Local 3.

Perhaps the most notable strike, in terms of length and publicity, was the thirteen-week walkout against the Holmes Electric Protective Company, a subsidiary of New York Telephone. It began in September 1949 after an arbitration effort by Mayor William O'Dwyer failed. Van Arsdale told the cheering strikers at a meeting: "You have swept the Holmes officials off their feet. They didn't think you'd stand solidly together, but you showed them." Ironically, his words were printed in the same issue of *Electrical Union World* (September 1) as a letter from President Truman lauding the JIB and the Local for twenty-five years of labor peace.

Most contracts were negotiated peaceably during this period, but there were notable exceptions, for example, the Ketay Manufacturing Company, which Van Arsdale accused of subjecting its 1,000 workers "to exploitation as bad as anything experienced in years gone by." On June 1, 1953, at the

122

end of a twenty-three day strike, Local 3 members won significant wage and benefit increases. In May 1954, Circle Wire and Cable was struck. The walkout lasted sixteen weeks and ended with a pay increase and a guarantee of an hour and a half overtime for each day lost during the strike. Jumping ahead, the U.S. government became the target of mass picketing in February 1956 after a nonunion contractor was awarded a contract for a job at the New York Post Office in Manhattan. Five thousand Local 3 men took to the streets in protest and the contractor was forced to go union.

This period saw Van Arsdale's political stature blossom as he became a familiar figure at prestigious functions around the city and began to gather a host of awards. When Robert Wagner became mayor in 1954, he relied increasingly on Van Arsdale, who had been instrumental in swinging labor support to him, to mediate labor disputes and to be his overall labor troubleshooter. (Wagner also appointed Armand D'Angelo, assistant business manager of Local 3, deputy commissioner of the Department of Water Supply, Gas, and Electricity, a post in which he would be greatly able to further the cause of Local 3.) In October 1954, Wagner appointed Van Arsdale to a three-person panel to help mediate the dispute between the International Brotherhood of Teamsters and 3,000 trucking companies. In 1956, Van Arsdale was named to be part of a three-member "citizens' committee" to help settle a strike against Macy's called by Local 1-S of the Retail, Wholesale, and Department Store Union.

Years later Wagner said one of the things that drew him to Van Arsdale and that made him prime mediator material was his ability to get along with labor leaders of every stripe.

> It's interesting that one labor leader who seemed to be able to get along with both sides here was Harry. He was accepted. He was in the Building Trades and in an important union—the electrical workers. And there was Marty Lacey who was with the Teamsters . . . and he was also friendly with [David] Dubinsky. Dubinsky liked him and later on, he with Dubinsky helped to create the Teacher's Union.
>
> The thing that impressed me about Harry, as I began to know him, was his devotion to his union. That was his life. . . . He had great social vision which sometimes you didn't quite realize until you knew him because he was a rough and ready fellow in many ways. . . .
>
> When I was mayor, I knew him well. He had supported me and I had supported him on strikes and things like that. But when I first went into Gracie Mansion and I was mayor I'd get a call from Harry at night, perhaps 11:30, and he'd say, "Can I come over and see you?" Well, the first time he did that I said, "God, there must be something. The person must be falling apart. The city must be falling" . . . and he'd come over and he'd

met some fellow in his travels, some poor fellow that needed help—was getting a raw deal from one of the [city] departments, welfare or whatever it was, and could I help. I said to myself, "This man really cares about people. He really worries about them and will go out of his way to help and he don't care what time of the day or night it was." It was in his character. And he had a fabulous, a wonderful character. You'd ask him to be at meetings [and] Harry was there if it was a good cause.[2]

Wagner and other mayors dealt extensively with Van Arsdale after he became president of the Central Trades and Labor Council of Greater New York on November 19, 1957, and particularly after it merged with the New York City CIO Council in February 1959 to form the New York City Central Labor Council (CLC).

Van Arsdale's personal power greatly expanded when he assumed the presidency of the CLC as it allowed him to become a prime shaper of labor relations and actions in the city. It gave him a forum and a platform from which to launch his programs to improve the lot of workers citywide, and to have greater influence on national (and even international) labor trends. In other words, having established Local 3 as a model union, he sought greater challenges and wider goals (while at the same time taking care of business at the Local).

Labor lawyer and mediator Theodore Kheel observed:

Harry's successes were primarily and understandably in matters that were directly related to trade unionism. He knew the labor movement. He also was aware of how politics impact on the labor movement. He was aware of how social issues impact on the labor movement. He thoroughly understood the times in which he was living.

Harry was a unifier. He sought to bring people together, but his aim at all times was to help the working man. That was his overwhelming objective. Now, he was also interested in people who were poor, who were downtrodden, who were deprived, but that was ancillary, or conjunctive with his primary overwhelming interest in the working man. He was a trade unionist first, last, and always. And that is reflected in his novel approach to the racial problems in his union.

It was revealed by his heroic effort to organize the taxicab industry. It was reflected in his activities in politics supporting individuals with whom he could do business and getting things from them in exchange—most notably Nelson Rockefeller. The relationship there was very close and very productive, very important for the trade union movement.

He understood the limitations of the Central Labor Council, because it has no power to order or command. It only has the power to persuade, and therefore it needed somebody with Harry's skills to know how to use a symbolic position to achieve concrete results.

And Harry took this instrument, a delicate instrument, like a Stradivarius violin, and he played it as a master violinist, and he got things out of the violin that was the Central Labor Council and for the affiliated members that nobody else that I can possibly think of could possibly have accomplished.[3]

To return to the Central Trades Labor Council (CTLC) for a moment, Van Arsdale had been a member of the CTLC executive board under Martin Lacey, who had been president of the CTLC since 1945. Lacey was also president of the Teamsters Joint Council-AFL and was a partner with Van Arsdale in battling the influence of racketeer-dominated unions, a particular thorn. Van Arsdale was a member of a committee on the exploitation of Latinos who were victimized because of their difficulty in understanding English. At a convention of the Association of Catholic Trade Unionists in New York on July 5, 1957, Van Arsdale chastised unions that collected dues and assessments from workers earning only the minimum wage. He said justice was due those workers who have endured "every possible abuse."[4] Van Arsdale had established the principle in his own union of not collecting dues from such workers unless he had secured higher wages for them and he carried this philosophy forward in the CTLC.

Shortly after that convention, Lacey became ill and died. Van Arsdale was named to replace him and one of his first actions was to endorse legislation (sponsored by U.S. Senator Irving M. Ives of New York) to combat racketeering elements in unions and solidify democratic practices in them.

He returned to this theme on September 12, 1957, when he called on every member of Local 3 to stand behind George Meany in the battle against union racketeers then under the glare of the McClennan Committee in the U.S. Senate, which was focusing on such racketeering. "He's fighting your battle," Van Arsdale said. "The labor movement is tied together. Those who do something bad hurt the whole movement. Are you going to just give George Meany lip service? Or are you going to stand with him actively for decent unionism? A line has been drawn between the forces of evil and the forces of good in the labor movement. Which side do you stand on?"[5]

Van Arsdale, scrupulously honest in dealings in his own union, detested racketeering and winced every time the press exploited that issue. "He did not want to read anything bad about unions and corruption," his wife Madeline said. "He felt it was a reflection on everybody else. He would be embarrassed when other unions were not doing what he felt was the right thing."[6] (Because of the many sour personal experiences he had with the press, Van Arsdale was wary of it—one reason he was reluctant to speak to a reporter about his own career. He doubted that the press would ever tell an objective, evenhanded story about labor. "The people who spend the largest amount on advertising would not want the true story told," he said.[7])

In June 1958 Van Arsdale launched a campaign for the four-hour work day. It was time, he said, for labor to "work up a new set of values" pointing out that "there are going to be hundreds of thousands of workers made permanently unemployed by automation and other new developments unless we get our workers employed and the country ready for a four-hour day."[8] With his leadership and with that proposal, the CTLC became a major force. (It would not be until 1962 that any union acted on it, and—no surprise—the union that did was Local 3 of the IBEW.)

The proposal galvanized the council. Thomas Donahue, then an officer of Local 32B of the Service Employees International Union (later to serve as president of the AFL-CIO), said: "The Central Labor Council of those years . . . was a kind of old fashioned organization which dealt with constituency problems. But it didn't really have a leadership role in the city at all. And when Harry came in he changed all that and made it an activist organization . . . and energized the entire labor movement in the city, pulled it together, got people working together, laid out targets and campaigns and issues that he was going to be interested in. . . . He involved the Central Labor Council in everything that was possible in the city."[9]

Van Arsdale, with his hybrid union of craft and industrial workers, was one of the first to advocate merging the AFL craft unions with the CIO industrial units. He was a prime mover—nationally and locally—in bringing about the marriage: "There's been too much division in the labor movement," he said.[10] He included the Teamsters, which had been ousted from the AFL because of corrupt elements, in this statement. Van Arsdale certainly had no love for corruption but felt that a clean and policed Teamsters would add to the strength, through numbers, of a national labor organization.

The merger of the city units of the AFL and the CIO was announced February 4, 1959, bringing together some 600 local unions with more than 1 million members. Van Arsdale was named as president of the new New York City Central Labor Council, AFL-CIO. Matthew Guinan, the Transport Workers Union secretary-treasurer, was named the first vice president; CIO Council secretary-treasurer, Morris Iushewitz, became secretary of the new group; and James C. Quinn, secretary-treasurer of the old AFL Council, became treasurer of the CLC.

At his first meeting as president, Van Arsdale began to remake the Central Labor Council into his own image: he set out to model the CLC after Local 3, implementing—as much as possible—the programs and structures he had fashioned in Local 3. Thus, he created committees dealing with the exploitation of minorities, community services, housing, civil rights, education, civil service, political education, and the shorter workweek.

In his remarks to the group, he focused on the need for more public housing as a way to solve the problem facing people "who may be drastically affected by the demolishing of large residential areas by the city to make way for new roadways, housing projects and other developments. Hundreds of thousands of families may be uprooted and forced to pay higher rents than they can afford for new apartments or move 30 or 50 miles from the city to lower rental areas."

Turning to civil rights, he told the Council members: "Laws protecting civil rights should be obeyed and the rights and dignity of the human being should be recognized and respected. There is too much hypocrisy on civil rights and the labor movement must not be a party to that hypocrisy."

He also called on the Council to have union members take a more active part in political organizations. "We must develop an active political role on the district level and seek among our members, people who can be developed into leadership in their own election districts."

In addition, he called on the Council members to meet with law enforcement or other agencies to combat union racketeering; urged the establishment of a system to alert union members to all strikes in the city; and urged that labor representatives speak in public schools to tell labor's story and counter anti-union propaganda by employer groups in the various media. He summed up: "If we continue to work together we will see a united labor movement in this city which we have long hoped for."[11]

Van Arsdale also backed up the sentiments of his council proposals in other forums. At a pension luncheon in June 1959, he urged unions to develop their own candidates for public office to ensure a voice in lawmaking bodies. At the same time, he criticized "fair weather friends of labor" in high political office who say they are friends of labor, but who fail to help labor at critical times.

He also used the same platform once more to plead for the cause of more public housing. He indicated that he had been appointed to a task force on middle-income housing organized by Governor Nelson Rockefeller, and said he hoped that the program would provide funding for thousands of housing units around the state.

Rockefeller had long known of Van Arsdale's interest in housing. It was on September 20, 1957, that he and Van Arsdale shared the same rostrum at the unveiling and presentation of a memorial to Fiorello H. La Guardia at the La Guardia Houses on the Lower East Side. Van Arsdale said that La Guardia "knew that the real strength of a nation is its people. . . .

It is very important for all citizens and the little people particularly to insist that housing be made available for the very reason that sitting here you can just look around and you can walk a few blocks in any direction and see housing [in which] in the year 1957 no human being should be expected or required to live in the United States.

[Referring to the La Guardia houses, Van Arsdale continued:] La Guardia knew what this kind of housing would mean in America and to its little people. He, as much as any man, knew that this kind of housing would be a challenge to poor health caused by slums, a challenge to the causes of early deaths of babies and others, born in hovels without sufficient light and air and decent surroundings. He knew that this kind of housing would be an inspiration to people to live in a different and better kind of life than if they had been condemned by circumstances to continue their lives in vermin infested and filthy surroundings.[12]

Van Arsdale's interests were many and various, and so were the interests of the Council. Van Arsdale and the Council called for the establishment of a national council of the unemployed with its members recruited from both union and nonunion ranks. The group would not be affiliated with the AFL-CIO, but would operate independently. Members would be enrolled when they applied for unemployment insurance.

William Michelson, of the Retail, Wholesale, and Department Store Union, commented on the control that Van Arsdale exercised over the Council through his energy, force of personality, and political skills:

I want to emphasize because the question comes up continuously about the role of the Central Labor Council. The Central Labor Council was Harry Van Arsdale. In its personality, in its activity, and in its program. The meetings of the Central Labor Council which took place once a month on Thursday were unqualified bores. Nothing happened at those meetings. Where the Central Labor Council was active in a program, it was active through the intervention of Harry—through Harry's personal capacity to call up local unions and insist and hold them to account. . . .

Harry was a tireless worker. My life, for all the years that I was in the Council is marked by Harry calling me at two o'clock or four o'clock in the morning and that kind of thing. . . . The Council was lucky that it had as a spokesman someone like Harry. What would happen is that Harry's technique of mobilizing unions was to call them to account, call the leadership of the unions to account. He would call up a union leader and say "can you bring some people here? Make sure you do." And the next time he saw him or her he would say, "Did you do it?" or "Why didn't you do it?" or "Where were you?" And because he was tireless and demanded everything of himself and because he was continuously on call, nobody could say no to Harry. If you needed Harry to come to a meeting to make a speech, Harry was there.

Therefore, he built up on a personal basis, an enormous, inexhaustible supply both of goodwill and of credit checks that he called on time after time after time.

So it is not necessarily negative to say of the Central Labor Council that it was Harry Van Arsdale. If Harry Van Arsdale was not there, the Central Labor Council could not exist as a viable force. It would exist in form only, but with no influence."[13]

Van Arsdale gave another overview of the work of the Council in remarks made some years later before a Cooper Union Forum. In a sense, it was a progress report on the committees he had established. It also illustrated once more his deep commitment to the disadvantaged and exploited worker.

Among the very active committees of the New York City Central Labor Council is a committee on community services. It indicates that one of labor's goals is to make a contribution in whatever way they can to the rest of the community. We have a committee on civil rights, very active committee, which indicates that labor recognizes that there is still considerable ignorance in our ranks as well as in other places, that we are still victims of habits and customs which we should've shed years ago or which we would've been better off if we never possessed.

And this committee is working among all of the affiliates to do an educational job to stamp out what we consider ignorance of a type that is bad for us and bad for our community and bad for our country, an ignorance that deprives some of our citizens because of their color or their national origin, of their human rights.

We have an educational committee which indicates that one of the goals is that they aspire to have a better understanding of things of which they are not thoroughly familiar.

We have a committee to end exploitation, which has been in existence for some time, which recommended that the City of New York should have a Committee on Exploitation which has [now] been established for some time [and] which includes representatives of the various religions, representatives of the Commerce and Industry Association which represents the employers of this city, representatives of all the social agencies, representatives of the National Association for the Advancement of Colored People and the Urban League, the Puerto Rican Labor Office, every segment of the community that would want to give some of their time and effort to put an end to the exploitation that exists in this city, of workers, the largest percentage of whom are Americans recently arrived in our city from other sections of our country: the South, where they didn't have an opportunity for a fuller education; Americans from the islands of Puerto Rico that've have come here and are subjected to every kind of exploitation.

The exploitation of the slumlord who overcharges them for sub-standard places to live; the exploitation of the shylock; the exploitation of the certain types of businesses that sell these people trinkets and other things on an installment basis, and then proceed to levy garnishees against their salaries, even to the extent that some cases that we've had where someone appeared and told the housewife, who didn't know much about the English language, that her husband had ordered something and that she should sign a slip, and she signed the slip and later that would be sold to people who handle these matters and then a garnishee would be placed against people who hadn't received any goods whatsoever.

The type of exploitation that exists as a result of an unscrupulous employer dealing with a racketeer union, entering into phony contracts and then proceeding to exploit the worker. Exploitation in some instances from well-meaning unions who have neglected certain of their members. Now, there has been some improvement in this, but nowheres near sufficient; this is not just the responsibility of organized labor, this is the responsibility of every segment of decent citizens in our city and in our community. It's everybody's responsibility to see that no human being is unfairly and unjustly taken advantage of, in the manner that these men and women are taken advantage of.

We have a committee on the shorter work week, unemployment and automation that has been functioning for some three years and three months. As a result of what we have learned, we have urged, requested, circulated every central labor council in the country and every affiliated union to establish a committee to make a study of automation and unemployment and whether or not there is a need for a shorter work week. Now, this is an indication of some of the problems with which the labor movement is undertaking to find solutions.

He went on to draw parallels between the programs established in the council and those he had set in place at Local 3, once more showing that his achievements within Local 3 were those he hoped would be copied by other locals and labor organizations around the nation.[14]

Brian McLaughlin, elected president of the New York Central Labor Council in June 1995, also touched on this latter point in his discussion of Van Arsdale's work with the Council.

Historically, across the country central labor councils were underfunded service organizations, even to this today although under [AFL-CIO President] John Sweeney we are now making the transition to change how Central Labor Councils are structured to have more resources for them to be able to operate, more staff, etc.

Harry had a Central Labor Council that had the lowest per capita [dues] in the country—five cents per member per month—while others were anywhere from 15 cents to 50 cents and he provided day in and day out inspiration, encouragement and support for organizing.

Years later, many organizations are just forming the kind of programs [within Local 3 and the CLC] that Harry envisioned.

[For instance], the Human Service arm of the Central Labor Council was an extension of what similarly we do in a strike, saving a worker's job, saving their opportunity to earn a living, keeping intact their family which might be jeopardized by some of their social problems.

These problems include alcoholism and drug addiction, and he added that the "cradle to grave" benefits that Harry achieved in Local 3 was "really much of what he inspired others to do in the Central Labor Council."[15]

Early in his CLC term, Van Arsdale was to embark on another major project that vividly illustrates his passion to organize all exploited workers. In this case, his mission was to help the beleaguered nonprofessional hospital workers, most of whom were African American or Puerto Rican. Van Arsdale had the Council throw its full weight on their behalf in a campaign by Local 1199 Retail Drug Employees Union to organize the nonprofessional workers in nonprofit hospitals: "These workers were being exploited and they [the Central Labor Council and its member unions] had a duty as trade unionists to help the exploited for we were once exploited too."[16]

But the organizing drive by Local 1199 had reached a critical juncture, as explained by its president, Leon Davis:

When we came to the point where we had signed up a considerable number of workers in the hospitals, management turned their backs on us. They wouldn't talk to us. They wouldn't meet with us. They wouldn't have conferences. They wouldn't have anything to do with the union. It was in that crucial situation that Harry was what I call the God-father of our union. If it were not for his help, in every possible way, 1199 could not have survived.

Hospital management was entrenched in the city politically. The trustees of the hospitals were the Who's Who in Wall Street. They were the rich and dominant group in our society in New York and generally speaking, the dominant group of people in every community where voluntary hospitals exist. . . .

Harry said our union was on the right track in organizing black and Spanish workers . . . he believed that workers rights ought to be for all workers regardless of who they are, where they are, what they do. . . .[17]

Moreover, according to Moe Foner, a publicist for Local 1199 during the strike and later the executive secretary of the Local, Van Arsdale saw the situation as a unifying force for labor in the city. "My feeling is that Harry, being very wise, saw this as an opportunity around which to unite the labor movement, the Central Labor Council, and this would be a way of doing it— to support a group of low-paid minority workers. . . . And when Harry saw the violence of the opposition—the Who's Who of America—acting toward their workers as if they were dirt . . . Harry became indignant. He said: 'Who do these guys think they are anyway?'"[18]

Even Van Arsdale, however, was uncertain at the outset about getting full labor support for a strike, Foner said. "He originally felt he could take this up to a strike with support, but he felt the labor movement would not really support a strike against the hospitals."

Many of the unions at that time were starting to get into the area of doing so well that their members were indifferent to the trade union movement as a struggling group of workers. Peter Brennan, at the time head of the New York Building and Construction Trades Council, said Van Arsdale faced the task of reeducating

> . . . a lot of people as to the real basis for trade unionism—seeking fair wages, a safe job, equal rights [and] all the things that a human being is entitled to. . . . It was tougher for union leaders to get their rank and file to rally around a cause. . . . There were a lot of leaders that believed in that, but what they had to have was a leader to come out and say "Let's get together. Let's start to move." And that is what Harry did.
>
> He got a number of the leaders of the different unions together, good people who wanted to do this and then they had to go back and they had to get their members to understand when they asked them to come out and participate in the struggle of a union who probably had lesser wages and probably were not as organized as long as they were, that you have to help them to get going.[19]

Van Arsdale felt that the hospital management might attempt to make a reasonable settlement when they saw that the workers were adamant in achieving their goals. Foner continued: "But he was getting more and more demoralized by the arrogant attitude of the hospital trustees. He told us: 'These guys are going to fight you to the last drop. This is an issue for them of their right to run their hospitals and I don't think we are going to be able to change that and I don't think that the labor movement is in a position to put its reputation on the line to engage in a long drawn out battle with them.' He was also unsure of whether the workers would support a strike. But Van Arsdale changed his mind when he spoke to the workers. He was not only moved, but he was enraged by what management was doing. He decided he was going to change that position and would work—he, the unions—to support them."

When hospital trustees refused to budge from their demands, a strike was called on May 8, 1959, at six private hospitals followed by a seventh hospital on June 5.[20] The hospitals would be represented in negotiations by the eighty-one member Greater New York Hospital Association. Any agreement would apply to all of the association's members.

Mayor Wagner entered the picture early to attempt to mediate and was reportedly told by Van Arsdale that if the workers failed to gain union recognition, it would deepen the impression that African Americans and Puerto Ricans were "an abused minority." He also told a reporter: "One of the main aims of the New York City AFL-CIO is to put an end to exploitation of minority groups and all workers."[21]

At an emergency meeting of the Council on May 16, Van Arsdale said all city unions had a "solemn obligation" to aid the strike. He called on his fellow labor leaders to exhort their union members to bring food—"cans of beans, sardines, anything you have around the house" to help feed the strikers and their families.

He also asked them to have their union members join picket lines and said that the following day would see the picket lines extended to construction sites under way at several of the struck hospitals. "No electrician will cross that picket line," he said. Other building trade unions might also honor the lines, he added, thus bringing the weight of Local 3 and the Building Trades Council to the battle lines.[22]

Moreover, Van Arsdale also induced Local 3 members of the Construction "A" Division to vote unanimously to assess themselves $1 a week for the benefit of the striking hospital workers. The Executive Board of the Local also voted an interest-free loan to Local 1199. In essence, Van Arsdale had fashioned his Local 3 members into a labor troubleshooting task force ready to fight in any labor hot spot.

Brian McLaughlin noted:

> When there was an action where workers were trying to form a union or to have workers have an opportunity to join a union, Harry had a well-educated membership in Local 3 who all were encouraged and inspired to help the less fortunate.
>
> One of the logos, in fact, on the Local 3 newspaper, was "Help the Less Fortunate." Of course, when we think of the Central Labor Council that I lead today, two of the three largest affiliates are the Teachers and the Hospital Workers, 1199, two unions and two different kinds of struggles, one in the public sector and the other in the private sector, that Harry's direct influ-

ence or political influence [strengthened by] the participation of Local 3 members or [and through] their direct participation on the street engaged in a struggle or an expression of solidarity which was the case of 1199.[23]

McLaughlin added that Van Arsdale had Local 3 overnight workers, such as night street lighting personnel, and other Local 3 members augment the early morning hours on picket lines of pharmaceutical and/or hospital workers seeking to form a union.

Leon Davis commented:

> One of the things he used to do is wake me up at two o'clock in the morning. Then he would come over on a motorcycle . . . driven by a member of his staff.[24] He used to sit on the front and he says "Leon, stay on the back. We're going to cover all the picket lines. . . ."
>
> We had about 30 picket lines going in the city. He used to go into the headquarters of the strikers, introduce himself, introduce me and encourage the workers to sit out and fight it out and he promised that he would help. He could give financial aid and [help in] other ways and he did. It was his encouragement that frankly brought a lot of other support from other unions in this city and state.
>
> We received a few hundred thousand dollars in financial support from other unions, like the ILG [International Ladies Garment Workers Union], and Amalgamated and so forth, many unions in the city, and that was a result of Harry Van Arsdale calling them and insisting that they provide the support, the financial support and other support that were to win the strike. . . .[25]

On May 26, 1959, Van Arsdale said "all union members should feel partly responsible, for which we all need to feel a little ashamed."[26]

> In a city in which unions have accomplished so much we find 30,000 working people being treated as serfs. These people have been subjected to a reign of terror and they are confused. Yet their greatest complaint is not their low wages, but rather the extremely poor treatment they have received from their employers over the years.
>
> These people are seeking the status of human beings. Among other things they want the right to belong to a union. But it is difficult to stand against the pressures being brought against them. We are being subjected to rule by injunctions and in one case an injunction was given by a judge who is actively participating in the management of one of the hospitals.
>
> There are Hungarian Freedom Fighters working in some of these hospitals because they are terrified that if they do not, they will be deported to Hungary. It is unbelievable that the people who manage these hospitals, people we have found on some occasions to be upstanding and de-

cent can be responsible for treating these employees the way they are being treated. . . .

Yet at one point in the strike, a false statement that a settlement had been reached was issued by these employers. They still have hopes that they can come up with some formula which will be a substitute for a union. These are powerful men and they asked us if we could find such a formula. We asked them how do you find a substitute for a man's religion, for his patriotism. We told them they gave us a very difficult task indeed in trying to find a substitute for a man's right to join a union.

We are determined to see to it that these kings of industry and finance are required to abdicate to give an opportunity and a chance to people who are willing to sacrifice and suffer to improve their station in life.

Taking another tack, Van Arsdale took on the whole issue of medical care for the masses. His comments are still pertinent and are another example of his ability to see far into the future and to present bold solutions for long-term problems. He spearheaded a motion within Local 3 recommending that the CLC establish a committee to study the possibility of having organized labor buy or build a hospital in each of New York's five boroughs to "give proper care at proper cost to all our citizens." The motion came after Van Arsdale criticized the high cost of hospital care at a membership meeting of Local 3 on June 11, 1959. "With the present cost of hospital care so high, one illness can wipe out a family's life savings," he said. "Many of our citizens who have been faced with exorbitant hospital bills and who are now well aware of the low wages paid to hospital workers [an average of $25 a week] are beginning to wonder why hospitals charge so much and where the money is going."[27]

When the strike by hospital workers was into its thirty-eighth day, Wagner again called both sides to City Hall in a mediation effort that went nearly round-the-clock. Finally, on the forty-second day, a tentative agreement was reached, but not without the threat by Van Arsdale to extend the walkout to an eighth hospital to end the "dilatory tactics" of management.[28]

On June 22, members of Local 1199 roared approval of the pact, ending the strike on its forty-sixth day, and lifted Leon J. Davis, Local 1199 president, and Van Arsdale to their shoulders and carried them in a triumphant parade.[29]

Although there was plenty to sing about, the pact did contain some sour notes. The agreement was described by union officials as a "partial victory." Davis said the agreement provided only "backdoor recognition" for his union, but predicted: "We'll be in the front door before long." The terms of the agreement that did not recognize the Local as bargaining agent, but allowed it to handle grievances and to organize workers. Other provisions included improvements in wages, hours, and benefits. The plan incorporated many of the proposals introduced weeks earlier by Theodore W. Kheel, arbitrator for the Transport Workers Union and the Transit Authority, but which management had rejected out of hand.

AFL-CIO Regional Director Michael Mann said the support of the labor movement for the strikers was "the finest display of unity" in the city's history. "The newly merged NYC Central Labor Council and a ten-man negotiating committee worked around-the-clock. All unions in the AFL-CIO —international and local—rallied behind the fight in behalf of these exploited workers," he continued. "The battle marked a resurgence of the union spirit in New York and the whole city is talking about it. The motto was 'These workers shall not be abandoned.' "[30]

But the idea of labor-operated hospitals and medical plans was not forgotten by Van Arsdale who introduced the ideas on September 20 at a biennial convention of the AFL-CIO. He told the convention that the CLC had set up a committee to consider building its own hospital chain and medical insurance system—in competition with Blue Cross and Blue Shield of New York— to "bring medicine closer to the people." In essence, it would be an extension of the programs he had already put into place in Local 3, which had become a laboratory for the plans Van Arsdale hoped could be established nationally.

He also told the convention delegates in San Francisco that even a labor-sponsored medical school could be established. "We have sweatshop standards in our hospitals," Van Arsdale said. "They underpay their staffs and underserve their patients. They make no accounting to the public. Yet, we are confronted with sky-rocketing costs that must be paid out of our welfare funds. Blue Cross has gone through the motions of providing community representation on its board, but it is a farce. Labor is outvoted 5 to 1. The program is under the control of big business and the hospital administrators. We intend to develop a program that will benefit all the people of the city." Van Arsdale's remarks made the front page of the *New York Times* the following day. (The United Hospital Fund and the Greater New York Hospital Association vehemently denied Van Arsdale's charges.)

As previously mentioned, the 1959 strike left unfinished business. Local 1199 did not receive official recognition as the bargaining agent for the non-professional hospital workers until 1962, when 1199 struck Beth-El Hospital. At the time, Van Arsdale was serving on a myriad of advisory boards, one including the Permanent Administrative Committee Advisory Board on New York City Hospitals. When the strike began, he, as a representative of the CLC, quit the Board to throw the full support of the CLC and Local 3 behind the hospitals workers once again. Local 3 members, including Van Arsdale, joined more than 1,000 other trade unionists in a picket line June 23 in front of the hospital. Shortly after Local 1199 struck Beth-El, the Manhattan Eye, Ear, and Throat Hospital was struck over demands for union recognition, a contract, and higher wages.

Van Arsdale induced Governor Rockefeller[31] to step in as a peacemaker, pointing out that minority leaders, including Malcolm X and A. Philip Randolph, saw the impasse as a volatile racial issue, inasmuch as the majority of the workers involved were African American or Latino.

According to Leon Davis, Van Arsdale called Rockefeller and said "I think you ought to pass a law [like] the Wagner Act in this state." So, after discussions in which Van Arsdale took part, Rockefeller sponsored legislation extending collective bargaining rights to Local 1199. The law was passed on April 24, 1963.

Thanks to Van Arsdale's help and the example of Local 1199, the way was cleared for the unionization of hospitals nationwide. It was also an inspiration and a blueprint for the organization of low-paid minority workers in other industries including hotels and nursing homes, and domestic workers, according to Peter Brennan. "It went on from there," he said.[32]

The hospital strikes accomplished what Van Arsdale had hoped they would. They had coalesced the city's labor force, energized the Central Labor Council and made it a power for the working man and woman in the city as a figurative extension of Van Arsdale himself. And that was only the beginning.

Van Arsdale's accomplishments, energy, and expertise garnered him a series of awards and also landed him on a number of panels and committees. A sampling shows that during this period he was appointed to New York City's Housing and Redevelopment Board; the Council of Long Island University; the Office of Coordinator of AFL-CIO State and Local Central Bodies; the Board of Trustees of Carnegie Hall Corporation; the labor member of New York City's Office of Collective Bargaining; the Board of Lincoln Center for the Performing Arts; the United Housing Foundation; the New York City Public Development Corporation; the United Fund of Greater New York; the New York State Mediation Board Labor Management Advisory Panel; the Mayor's Committee on Exploitation; the Executive Board of the Manhattan Council of Boy Scouts of America; and a committee to bring the 1964 World's Fair to New York City.

Concerning the fair, it is worth noting some comments Van Arsdale made extolling New York as "the capital of the free trade union movement" in a hearing (on October 23, 1959) in Washington before the Presidential Commission for a Location of a World's Fair site. His words also give further insight into how he viewed the nation, the city, and its people.

New York City to so much of the world is the earthly personification of what human freedom means. It is to our city that millions of people from every part of the world, free and unfree, have come and have tasted the joys of liberty and democratic pride.

Name a race, a culture, a creed, a nationality—it's all to be found in New York City: Indians, Arabs, Chinese, Turks, Hungarians, Armenians, Spaniards, Russians and they all live together respecting each other's right to privacy, the pursuit of happiness and the ambition to rise from the status of immigrant to American citizen.

It is in America that the foreign visitor sees this vast melting pot, a phenomenon which exists nowhere else on the face of the earth. I agree that New York City is not America, but it is in New York that a visitor can see and understand more quickly the secret that is America, that makes America the wonderful country it is.[33]

Of Van Arsdale's willingness to accept appointments to panels, Mayor Robert Wagner observed: "You know, he was always available to go on anything, which was terrific, on any committees. He not only lent his name to these committees [but] he was there. He was there and he participated and he played an important role which is a great tribute to him and an asset to the city."[34]

Van Arsdale, moreover, refused to take any payment for his work on committees even though it would be offered to him. Committee treasurers were often in a quandary because he would return their checks instead of cashing them. Hy Greenblatt, who had been executive secretary of the Joint Board of the Illumination Products Industry (also administrator of the Combined Pension Funds and second president of the Harry Van Arsdale Jr. Memorial Association), recalled that:

> Anytime he was appointed to any board or commissions, like Lincoln Center and things like that, he never accepted any [fees]. . . . In fact, he used to laugh. He said, "They called me and said, 'Do us a favor, please cash that check.' And I told them, 'Oh, no, I sent it back.' And they say, 'You're causing us more trouble by not cashing it.'" And he says, "Nope, nope. My feeling is this. If I could help my city, my state, my country, then it's my duty to do so."

Greenblatt added that Van Arsdale's sense of civic responsibility prevented him from trying to evade jury duty and that he once served for many months on a grand jury even though it must have put a severe crimp in his schedule. Moreover, he felt so strongly about that duty that he later instituted a class within the Local to prepare members to be better jurors. "It was our right to do so and our responsibility," Greenblatt continued. "And he took it very seriously."[35] Local members would be paid $15 by the Local in addition to the $6 given by the city or state, but the increased sum would be dependent on the member attending a course on city government one night a week for nine weeks. "We want our members to have some basic understanding of civic and municipal affairs which is why we're putting on these courses," Van Arsdale told the members at a regular meeting.[36]

In January 1960, Van Arsdale again made the entire nation take notice. In conjunction with the Joint Industry Board of the Electrical Industry, an unprecedented agreement was reached with Local 3 that the cost of labor increases would not be passed along to the public. The Local had won a 50-cent an hour wage increase, along with other benefits totaling $10.5 million, spread over two years. The employers agreed to absorb the higher costs in return for which Local members would achieve greater efficiency on the job and save money for the employer. As outlined by a report in the January 15 edition of *Electrical Union World*, the program would allow employers to "hold the line" on consumer prices through automation, "greater efficiencies in packaging and delivery of materials, broader education for members, greater use of power-driven tools, safety techniques and reduction of time-wasting periods." The development won national praise. Senator Jacob Javits of New York, in a telegram to Van Arsdale, congratulated the local and the employers for recognizing their "obligations and responsibilities not only to each other but to the entire American economy. The agreement is a long step forward in establishing dynamic and effective labor management relations." (In the same vein, the Central Labor Council, under Van Arsdale's lead called on the city's Transit Authority not to raise the 15-cent fare following contract gains by the Transport Workers Union.)

The (New York) *Daily News*, in an editorial of January 13, 1960, said the pact represented "a philosophy which it's to be hoped may spread throughout U.S. Organized Labor. If it does, we can hope to keep wages going up without further shrinking the dollar's buying power and without pricing more and more of our goods out of foreign markets. The new Local 3 contract is hereby recommended to the careful attention of union leaders and union members all over the United States."

The *Daily News* editorial, representing the conservative view of its owner, absolved the employers from having any responsibility in the matter of cost "pass-alongs," but a more balanced view was given in the March issue of the *New York State Industrial Bulletin* by writer Tom Brooks:

> Somehow over the last three decades, the 30,000 member IBEW local in New York City has evoked amazement consistently and admiration sometimes tinged with envy. And, management has confessed frequently to har-

boring the same mixed emotions as it watched Local 3 and its business manager operate.

"Frankly," says one electrical contractor, "we were worried when this year's negotiations came up. Costs have been skyrocketing in our industry and we think the public is sick of both rising wages and rising prices." But the industry sighed with relief when Mr. Van Arsdale pledged his union's support for a drive to reduce costs to compensate for the two-year $10.5 million wage and fringe package in the making.

"With anyone else but Harry Van Arsdale Jr.—and Local 3—it'd be just talk," says a contractor. "But we know that Local 3 will deliver on its promises."

To help the Local keep its promises, Van Arsdale initiated efficiency seminars that the members attended on their own time and that became part of the innovative fabric of education woven and pioneered by Van Arsdale.

It was all part of a philosophy noted in an earlier *Reader's Digest* article that described Local 3 as "a union whose members are taught that to get more, you must give more." The writer, Lester Velie, tells of a tour he was given by a Local 3 official of a work site. He wrote: "'Look at this automatic pipe-threader,' the union man said. 'Used to take a man an hour to thread a length of pipe by hand. Now look. The machine does the job, *untended*, in a few minutes.' He pointed to a winch like device pulling cable through a conduit. 'Used to take seven or eight strong men to pull wire by hand,' he said. 'Now one man and this machine can do it. One of our boys invented it when we put on a drive for ideas.'"[37] (The members vie for awards in submitting ideas.)

The public-spirited posture of the Local, under Van Arsdale's leadership, also caused it to contribute funds to worthy causes, for example, $10,000 to a campaign against juvenile delinquency waged in 1960 by the American Guild of Variety Artists. Members also joined in civil rights campaigns, such as April 30 when more than 400 Local 3 members picketed in front of an F.W. Woolworth store in Manhattan in support of the battle for equal rights by African Americans in the South. In October, Van Arsdale called for an end to "gradualism" and for immediate action to end racial discrimination. He spoke before 500 labor leaders at the CLC's first civil rights conference. He also urged the group to encourage union members to vote for Democratic presidential candidate John F. Kennedy in the upcoming elections.

Within Local 3, Van Arsdale's position was so solid that he continued to win reelection by overwhelming majorities. In 1960, he resigned his four-year job in order to run with his other Local officers in that year's biannual election. He did this in order, he said, to avoid additional expense for the union in having an election two years hence for the post of business manager. He and his slate were reelected. (The membership cast 20,099 ballots, which set a record.)

In January 1961, Van Arsdale and the Council moved to enlarge labor's base in the city by starting an intensive drive to organize all nonunion workers. It was also a part of his design to build a labor voting bloc to defeat laws that "shackle labor." Speaking at a special delegates meeting, he added: "These laws were not based on wisdom and were a menace to the state."

But labor's success was contingent on maintaining Mayor Wagner and other friends of labor in office. The CLC had joined Van Arsdale in endorsing Wagner's 1958 bid for the U.S. Senate. Van Arsdale and other AFL and CIO officials met with Democratic Party leaders and told them that "Wagner was the best possible candidate."[38] Van Arsdale also stated: "The reason we supported Robert Wagner was that we always felt he had a genuine interest, not a phony one, in the problems of the working people."[39] And 1961 was to see a major effort in the direction of keeping friends of labor in office—the formation of a new party. This would be in tandem with another great adventure—revival of the proposal for a four-hour day, which led to a secret FBI investigation of Van Arsdale.

10

United Federation of Teachers and the Brotherhood Party

The Central Labor Council (CLC) had shown its strength with the hospital strikes, but Van Arsdale thought of a more festive way of showing that unions meant to play an important role in the city's power structure. His idea was to revive the Labor Day Parade, which had not been held for twenty years.

The parade would, according to an editorial in *Electrical Union World* (July 15, 1959), "demonstrate most effectively that the spirit of unity still prevails as strong as ever among members of the American labor movement. It will prove that organized labor is undaunted in the face of a growing anti-labor trend characteristic of big business interests today." In 1959 Mayor Wagner proclaimed September 7, "City of New York Trade Union Day." In signing the proclamation, he said he was proud that New York was a "good union town."

Local 3 prepared for the event by renting the 107th Armory building on 65th Street, between Lexington and Park Avenues, as a recreation area for members and their families after the march down Fifth Avenue.

On the appointed day, an estimated 115,000 marchers, including more than 19,000 members of Local 3, walked down Fifth Avenue, which was lined with 400,000 spectators, in a spectacular show of labor strength. Van Arsdale was at the head of the parade as grand marshal. In its report on the parade, *Electrical Union World*, proclaimed: "It was more than a parade. It was the rebirth of a new militancy among union members."

Included in the parade were performers from fifteen Broadway shows, stepping along to show tunes, riding on show floats or vehicles, and dressed in all their theatrical finery. Among the dignitaries on the reviewing stand were Governor Rockefeller, Mayor Wagner, Francis Cardinal Spellman, Manhattan Borough President Hulan Jack, and New York State Industrial Commissioner Martin Catherwood.

According to Arnold Beichman, then editor of *Electrical Union World*, not everything went smoothly. He said that AFL-CIO President George Meany became extremely angry at Van Arsdale because of his plan to invite the Teamsters Union, which had been ousted from the AFL-CIO in a corruption scandal, to march in the parade. "It had reached the point where Meany would have removed him as president of the Central Labor Council," Beichman said.

"Meany blew up and he ordered Van Arsdale to bar the Teamsters from the parade. Van Arsdale was very unhappy about that because the New York Teamsters were headed by John O'Rourke who was a very decent guy," Beichman continued. "Van Arsdale was ready to resign."

Beichman said he contacted Meany, whom he got to know when he was a reporter with (the defunct newspaper) *PM*, and told him he was making a mistake in his treatment of Van Arsdale. Beichman said that, on his advice, Meany invited Van Arsdale to meet in Washington and the situation was resolved.[1]

In 1960, the parade was even bigger. AFL-CIO President George Meany, as Grand Marshall, led approximately 175,000 members down Fifth Avenue in a parade that included more than 200 floats and 150 bands. Almost the entire membership of Local 3—28,000 members—heeded Van Arsdale's call for a show of force.

Included in the parade were members of a labor organization with which Van Arsdale and the CLC were to be deeply involved that year: the American Federation of Teachers. Van Arsdale's efforts would be crucial in achieving collective bargaining status for teachers. That effort would also influence the organization of other white-collar and academic groups.

The Teachers Union, began as Local 5 of the American Federation of Teachers (AFT). The Local was expelled from the AFT because of its alleged communist taint, and was replaced by the noncommunist Teachers Guild, which became Local 2 of the AFT. The guild, under the leadership of Charles Cogen, and other teacher groups uniformly had little success dealing with the city's Board of Education, particularly with the right to bargain collectively. The teachers, as public employees, were regulated by New York State's Condon-Wadlin Act of 1947, the most restrictive provision of which was a ban on striking under pain of dismissal.

Nevertheless, the guild staged an unofficial job action at the beginning of the 1958–59 school year. The equally militant High School Teachers Association also struck for one month, closing the city's evening high schools and resulting in hefty salary increases.

The following spring, after Schools Superintendent Dr. John Theobald made an unsatisfactory salary adjustment proposal, the guild threatened a one-day strike, and sought the advice of Van Arsdale and the CLC. Van Arsdale and Council Secretary Morris Iushewitz met with Theobald on April 14, and an agreement was reached on salary increases, equalization of salary steps, and class sizes. The threat of a strike was removed.

To strengthen the position of the teachers, the guild knew that the teachers needed to present a solid front. Cogen wrote to Van Arsdale, saying in part: "You will recall that we have been most eager to work out a merger with other teacher organizations in New York City, particularly the High School Teachers [Association]. On the two or three occasions when we discussed this problem you were much interested and offered assistance. . . . We believe the time has come when you could help in a very definite way. We would like to discuss this matter with you. . . . [Your] experience in matters of this kind [and your] persuasive power and prestige as head of the New York City labor movement go a long way toward making this a success."[2]

Carl Megel, president of the AFT, also asked Van Arsdale to help, noting that: "This [merged] organization can make a great contribution to the cause of the American labor movement."[3] With Van Arsdale's help, in May 1960, the guild merged with the Committee for Action through Unity in May 1960 to form the United Federation of Teachers (UFT), Local 2, and became the most prominent among several groups that sought to speak for teachers in the city. "The formation of the UFT was the most important event in the history of teacher unionism in the United States and perhaps in the entire field of public employment," wrote historian Philip Taft.[4]

Still faced with a stubborn schools establishment, the UFT made plans for a strike on May 15, 1960. The Board of Education spiked the walkout by promising to hold a collective bargaining election, permit a dues check-off for the UFT, and grant sick leave to substitute teachers.

However, discussions dragged on and the UFT called a strike for November 7. Van Arsdale had misgivings: He and the other experienced labor leaders knew of the extreme vulnerability of the fledgling UFT. First, it represented only a relatively small portion of the city's teachers, with only 10,000 members out of more than 40,000 teachers. Other teacher groups opposed the strike and would cross any picket lines, thus severely weakening the UFT's bargaining position. And there was the Condon-Wadlin Act.

Even the most stalwart member could not be expected to hold out for long and any strike had a good chance of failing. It would, in effect, be the end of the UFT, and deal a severe blow to the whole movement of teacher, and even public, employee unionization in the city. Yet, in the face of all that, Cogen and his supporters wanted to go ahead with the walkout as the best way to enforce all their demands.

Mayor Wagner and the CLC attempted to try to mediate the dispute and head off a strike, but negotiations failed, and on November 7 an estimated 15,000 UFT teachers walked out in the first teachers' strike in the history of New York City. Van Arsdale said he and Iushewitz had tried as hard as they could to avert a strike and said the walkout was "extremely regrettable."[5]

The following day, after strong pressure from Van Arsdale, Iushewitz, and other Council veterans, the UFT called off the strike despite impassioned entreaties from a minority of diehards. The UFT agreed to work with mediators to try to iron out their differences with the Board of Education. The board, for its part, agreed not to reprimand the teachers who had walked out.

Van Arsdale contacted AFL-CIO President George Meany and asked him to bring his weight and prestige into the affair. Meany agreed and Van Arsdale got Mayor Wagner to invite him formally into the dispute. At Meany's recommendation, David Dubinsky, president of the International Ladies Garment Workers Union, Jacob Potofsky, president of the Amalgamated Clothing Workers of America (both of New York and both AFL-CIO vice presidents), and Van Arsdale were appointed as fact-finders. Van Arsdale said that the CLC was "pleased that this situation is about to be adjusted. . . . We pledge to the families of New York City that there will be no recurrence."[6]

On January 11, 1961, the fact-finders recommended that the board call for an election by the teachers of a collective bargaining agent and recommended improvements in working conditions, including pay increases for principals and additional sick leave for substitute teachers.

The recommendations represented a huge victory for the UFT in that they forced the Board of Education to accept the principle of collective bargaining for teachers as well as gave the UFT a great advantage in its quest to represent all the teachers in the system. The UFT was given inestimable help by Van Arsdale and the Council. Van Arsdale lobbied the other Council officers on behalf of the UFT and asked for contributions for their war chest in the campaign to be the collective bargaining designee. Local 3 loaned the UFT $50,000.[7]

"The UFT has been forced to launch a major election campaign with thousands of pieces of literature, newspaper advertising and mass telephoning in addition to all the other details which go into an effort of this kind," Van Arsdale stated. "We all know that such a campaign cannot be supported from dues income alone. In September, the UFT will be faced with the crucial campaign for bargaining agent. We must not let them go into this campaign weakened by financial malnutrition."[8] He also asked the affiliate leaders to launch information drives on behalf of the UFT with their members.

Van Arsdale, once again, called on the members of Local 3 to go to work on the UFT's behalf. Local 3 members delivered campaign literature to the some 700 schools in which the UFT was not represented. Van Arsdale himself devoted his remarkable energy to the cause, calling associates at all hours of the night. It was almost as if Van Arsdale was a UFT member, said Albert Shanker, former UFT president.

But despite all the support being given the UFT, the Board of Education again stalled on a meaningful collective bargaining election. When the board was wracked by a scandal—involving alleged mismanagement of funds and bribery—Governor Rockefeller called a special session of the state legislature, which replaced the Board of Education on September 21 with a new board, including Morris Iushewitz of the CLC. The fine hand of Harry Van Arsdale was apparent in this.

The new board set the date of a collective bargaining election for December 16, 1961. Van Arsdale and Cogen once more secured the aid of Meany, as well as Walter Reuther, United Auto Workers president. The UFT won by a substantial margin.

AFT President Megel thanked Van Arsdale. "Teachers throughout the nation have been looking at the successful completion of the UFT's struggle for hope and new inspiration. We gratefully acknowledge your wonderful help and assistance," he wrote.[9]

The value of Van Arsdale's relationship with Mayor Wagner and Governor Rockefeller in the matter cannot be overestimated. "When Harry first brought it to the attention of Mayor Wagner that New York City teachers needed collective bargaining rights, Wagner listened. . . . He knew that Harry was not selfish nor out for himself, but instead was genuinely concerned about the teachers' plight. He never spoke for himself or even for a friend, but always for a group of people. Mayor Wagner wouldn't listen to anyone simply as a favor, but he would listen if he knew the person was genuine and sincere. This was Harry," said Donald Menagh, attorney for the CLC.[10]

Wagner was a friend of labor, which was Van Arsdale's prime consideration for an officeholder. Van Arsdale cultivated the friendship of every high state and city official who might help labor. This included not only Mayor Wagner and Governor Rockefeller but also their predecessors—Mayors Fiorello La Guardia, William O'Dwyer, and Vincent R. Impellitteri, and Governor Averell Harriman.

With the exception of Rockefeller and a few other Republicans, the majority of those he relied on were Democrats. But party labels were meaningless. Van Arsdale was apolitical in the sense that his constituency was the working man and he would support any man regardless of party who helped the working man. If neither major party fielded such a candidate, he would help create a party that would.

"Harry supported candidates if they proved to be real friends of labor," said Peter J. Brennan, president of the Building and Construction Trades Council of Greater New York. "By that, I didn't mean just coming to a dinner and speaking or saying something nice about labor from the podium. They had to show it by, if they were in office, voting for bills if they were in the legislature or the city council, voting for bills that protected the worker's rights and protected the worker's benefits and so forth."[11]

Wagner's sympathy for labor earned him the 1960 Union Label Award of Merit. Previous winners included former New York Governor Averell Harriman and Monsignor John Boland, commissioner of the state Mediation Board. The choices reflected Van Arsdale's support.

Mayor Wagner and Governor Rockefeller were also the principal speakers at a convention of the Building Service Employees International Union in May in New York. "The cooperation of labor and management with each other and with government and the general public is essential to our future progress," Rockefeller said. He pointed out that at his request (and at the prodding of Van Arsdale as the spearhead of other labor leaders) the state legislature had passed the state's first minimum wage bill and increased unemployment insurance and workmen's compensation and disability benefits.

To try to keep legislators friendly to labor, Van Arsdale and the Council strove to build a strong labor voting bloc. They had organized a citywide drive in 1959 to have every union member registered to vote. At that time, Van Arsdale had lashed out at false friends in the legislatures who told of their friendship for labor but voted anti-labor. Again, he called for the development of candidates for office from within labor's ranks.[12]

Van Arsdale's attitude toward fickle politicians became even more sour with the difficulty Wagner was experiencing with Tammany Hall chief Carmine DeSapio and other leaders of the Democratic Party machine in securing their backing in the 1961 mayoral race. So Van Arsdale believed that this was the perfect time to show labor's strength at the voting booth by forming a new political party that would ensure Wagner a line on the ballot.

On April 15, 1961, the *New York Times* broke the story that a fifteen-man committee, including representatives of the Teamsters Union and the most influential members of the CLC, had been formed to consider the formation of the independent party that would compete in city, state, and federal elections. The focus, however, was clearly on the city elections.

The labor reporter of the *New York Times*, A.H. Raskin, quoted "a top unionist" as saying: "We feel a party, in which the vote of labor and like-minded people in the community can be counted, is long overdue. We are sick and tired of being taken for granted, of being handed candidates we have to take without consultation and of being ignored once the balloting is over."

Raskin reported that several other members of the committee clearly indicated that a third party was being contemplated and not just a labor party in a narrow sense. They gave Raskin to understand that the party would be "a rallying ground for members of minority groups and others who shared labor's basic objectives of civic improvement."

Raskin quoted another union leader as saying, "We are not against the Democrats, the Republicans, the Liberals or anybody else in a specific sense. What we are against is the notion that we are a bunch of idiots with no worthwhile ideas, whom the politicians can push around without worrying about the consequences."

Another, reported Raskin, said the group was "fed up with the Democrats' thinking that we have no place to go and the Republicans thinking we are a tail on the Democratic kite."

Van Arsdale was cautious in his comments, reflecting his reluctance to reveal plans for the party before it had the strength to strike out and withstand being struck. He said merely that the party was concerned with using political tools to achieve its long-standing goals "to organize the unorganized, promote higher living standards and build a better community."

A few weeks later it was announced that the new organization was to be called the Freedom Party, which Van Arsdale said was "going to pick and choose candidates based on their records toward labor."[13] In subsequent weeks, leaders said they hoped to make it into a statewide party. Van Arsdale said union members would be asked for $1 donations to support the party. Would the Freedom Party compete with the Liberal Party? The latter drew its support from the International Ladies Garment Workers Union and its president, David Dubinsky, and the United Hatters, Cap, and Millinery Workers, and its president, Alex Rose—both Council members who were keeping the new group at arm's length. But Rose, Liberal Party vice chairman, said: "Every effort to involve workers in independent political action is good for labor and good for the community as a whole."[14]

The party's name was officially changed to the Brotherhood Party because the name "Freedom Party" had been preempted by the Young Conservatives group. "Somebody arranged for a group of students to get together and they beat us, you know," Van Arsdale said. "They actually beat us to getting the name. They never used it, but they're certified as having the name. But we had an idea and we got some information that indicated that somebody [high] in the Democratic party engineered that. So that is why we had to move over to the Brotherhood."[15] Van Arsdale also announced that Wagner, to no one's surprise, would be the candidate of the Brotherhood Party on Line E in the mayoral elections. "Wagner is the best friend of labor in the city," Van Arsdale said.[16] Wagner, who had also won the endorsement of the Democratic and Liberal parties, obliged by fashioning his platform almost identically to that of the Brotherhood Party, calling for a rise in the minimum wage, a six-hour, five-day week, new programs to promote racial harmony, and more funding and programs for education, housing, health care, and child care.

Van Arsdale outlined what he hoped would be the wider scope of the party in a Council meeting on August 8, 1961. He called for an all-out campaign to train union members with "Ability, Character, and Experience"— ACE—to eventually fill important elected or appointed posts.

In order to organize the Brotherhood Party "politically as well as economically . . . block by block," Van Arsdale urged delegates to participate in the leadership training program to develop "dedicated leadership during challenging times." He also declared that the Brotherhood Party can make "an outstanding contribution to the community, state and nation."

Armand D'Angelo, who took unpaid leave from his position as commissioner of the Department of Water Supply, Gas, and Electricity to help with the organization of the party, also told the Council delegates that "what is good for the trade union movement is good for the nation and for all workers, organized or unorganized."[17]

The Brotherhood Party dominated the tone of the Labor Day Parade. The 1961 parade outdid its predecessors in size with an estimated 206,000 marchers, including 26,000 members of Local 3. U.S. Labor Secretary Arthur Goldberg called it "the greatest Labor Day parade of the labor movement in the nation. Wagner was the grand marshal. Among the many dignitaries on the reviewing stand were Governor Rockefeller, former President Harry S Truman, and Senator Jacob Javits.

Following the parade, an *Electrical Union World* editorial (September 15, 1961) declared: "This party is no toy for some ambitious politician nor is it going to be used by any hard-boiled bosses for their own enrichment. The Brotherhood Party is your party, if you work at it. Our job here is to make sure everybody is registered to vote. Then make sure everybody votes—and, we hope, for the candidates of the Brotherhood Party."

In the same issue, the *Electrical Union World* reprinted the "Inside Labor" column written by Victor Riesel (originally published in the *New York Mirror*, September 7, 1961), who described the Labor Day Parade marchers as "a political army . . . marching into tomorrow's history." He added:

"They could well rip the Democratic Party from its old moorings and even reshift power balances inside the Republican Party. . . . A national labor party could well have been born this Labor Day morning."

Riesel called the Brotherhood Party a "creation" of Van Arsdale.

> The Brotherhood Party is, in effect, the political decision of New York's "conservative" unions—those which once had been Republican, or had been part of the old Democratic city machine in eras gone by. . . . One leader told this newsman, "One day we will merge the Brotherhood and Liberal Parties, just as the AFL-CIO were merged." If this should come after they have shaken the powerful Tammany and other city machines—a chain reaction of independent political action will be set off in other states across the country.
>
> Remember this Labor Day parade.
>
> If the marchers can walk to the polls en masse as they walked together up Fifth Avenue here, political history was made by that walk in the sun.

Riesel's column was reprinted in full in the *Electrical Union World,* which had become the unofficial party organ of the Brotherhood Party. The column reprints were distributed by thousands of Local 3 members who had been enlisted in the campaign. They worked with other union members in each of the sixty-eight assembly district headquarters in the city to help the party, as telephone canvassers, envelope stuffers, or gofers. Thousands of Local 3 members succeeded in obtaining the more than 50,000 signatures necessary for nominating petitions.

Van Arsdale's philosophies about and hopes for the party were explained in the first meeting of the Brotherhood Party Advisory Committee October 5 at the Commodore Hotel. The speech also stated Van Arsdale's view of communism. The Brotherhood Party, he said, is "not a labor party as such. It is not a class party. . . ."

> The unique development of the American trade union movement is that it has not become a movement based on the false dogmas of the class struggle, identification of a working-class which must destroy by a class war what those who speak in its name cannot win by the ballot. We have seen what the so-called worker's state, the so-called dictatorship of the proletariat, the so-called class struggle means.
>
> We saw it when the workers of Hungary rose in 1956 against their betrayers. We saw it when the workers of East Germany revolted in June 1953 against their betrayers and we saw it last August when those same workers were imprisoned behind the Concrete Curtain.
>
> We affirm that there is no conflict between the aims and aspirations of working people and their families and all others who live in this city. All of us want New York to be a community of which we can be proud. All of us together can make it such a community.

Van Arsdale painted a wry portrait of cookie-cutter politicians in contrast to those who would or were put forward by the Brotherhood Party:

> I am afraid that too often in recent years the consent of the governed has meant little to our governors except in those moments of stress, known as elections, when there is a descent from Mount Olympus by gods with a debatable claim to infallibility and a ceaseless search for immortality. . . . The Age of the Huckster demands that we make vast and sweeping promises about a utopian future whether these promises are realizable or not. The Brotherhood Party, I'm afraid cannot conform to the requirement of the Age of the Huckster. It is the fault of our training as trade union leaders and officials. The one man you cannot fool—and if you want to remain a trade union official it is a lesson you learn early—is a worker. He knows a phony promise when he hears one.

On October 15, 1961, Van Arsdale told an audience of shop stewards representing major city unions that the Brotherhood party was not a "one-shot effort." . . . "Despite the inaccurate statements of the press, the Brotherhood Party is established on a permanent basis." He also stressed that the party welcomed members from all walks of life, not just working people.

A number of other labor luminaries also gave strong support. Theodore Kheel, coordinating Mayor Wagner's campaign, said he would vote on the Brotherhood Party line because "I believe that the Brotherhood Party will be a force for good in New York City." David Sullivan, president of the Building Service Employees Union said he was confident that the labor movement in the city would show the strength needed to make the party grow. Jay Rubin, president of the Hotel Trades Council, observed that a big vote on the Brotherhood Party line "will give notice to [politicians] that we are in business and that we have the will and the strength to fight."

An editorial in the September 15 *Electrical Union World* issue blistered attempts by communists to infiltrate the Brotherhood Party by their words of support. This was an apparent reply to an editorial in the communist publication, *The Daily Worker*, which hailed the party as "a new and important force" in American politics. This, in turn, had led City Comptroller Lawrence Gerosa, running as an independent in the mayoral race, to charge that the editorial was "proof of the pudding that Wagner will get the city in the red."

The *Electrical Union World* editorial lashed back:

> It's quite possible that knowing the distaste which workers have for Communists, it is a deliberate act to sabotage the Brotherhood Party by making it appear that the Communists are real-buddy-buddy with the free trade unions which formed the Brotherhood Party.

> Nobody, of course, is going to be fooled by this Communist trickery which is pretty ancient by now. We know that the Communist "party line," made in Moscow, today demands that the local Communist hacks should love the Brotherhood Party. Tomorrow, of course, the "party line" will change without notice and then they'll hate us. . . .
>
> There is no room now and there will be no room tomorrow for Communists and their stooges in the Brotherhood Party. In the Communist vocabulary, the word Brotherhood does not exist.

The involvement of Local 3 members in the campaign led to ugly allegations leveled by the Republican candidate, state Attorney General Louis Lefkowitz. He charged that Local 3 and other Council unions had coerced their members into contributing funds to the Brotherhood Party and that Local 3 had handed over a large contribution to party coffers. Armand D'Angelo came under personal attack when he was under investigation for alleged patronage dealings at the city Department of Water Supply, Gas, and Electricity. All of this was vehemently denied and the charges evaporated shortly after the election.

Wagner proved to be a big winner in the balloting, winning by a margin of 397,980 votes. The Brotherhood Party contributed a disappointing 58,556 votes to his tally, which was far below what it had hoped to contribute. Moreover, on the Brotherhood Party ticket Wagner ran behind his top running mates, Paul Screvane (City Council candidate) and Abraham Beame (comptroller candidate). However, the relatively poor showing was ascribed to Wagner's appearance on two other lines as well. The Liberal Party, backed by Dubinsky and Potofsky, provided 213,985 votes.[18]

Wagner's victory, despite the relatively small turnout by the Brotherhood Party, buoyed the party boosters. An editorial in the *Electrical Union World* of November 15 stated: "The campaign . . . stands out as a sterling·example of effective independent political action by the labor movement. The Brotherhood Party is here to stay—and it will grow. It will grow because the party's pioneers, the unsung heroes of the shops, are the people who are doing the 'leg-work.' This same spirit, this sense of dedication, to a cause which was pulled out of the sweat shops, will some day win a decisive voice for labor in our city, state and federal government." An article in the same issue announced that the party was here to stay and quoted Van Arsdale as saying, "We are in the political action program permanently," and pointed out the party was the only one on the ballot to get all its candidates elected.[19] Speaking to Local 3 officers at a dinner meeting, Van Arsdale said that if the party could double its vote tallies in the next four years, it would eventually have the backing of a majority of voters.

However, despite the optimistic words, the party began a slow fade into history. An attempt to secure a line on the ballot for the 1962 gubernatorial elections was unsuccessful. The CLC, however, endorsed a slate of candidates, two of whom raised some eyebrows. They were Representatives Adam Clayton Powell, Jr., a Harlem political leader, and Charles Buckley, head of the Democratic organization in the Bronx. In endorsing Buckley, Van Arsdale and the Council went against the wishes of Mayor Wagner who had denounced Buckley as a "political boss." Both Powell and Buckley had also opposed the renomination of Wagner in the 1961 primary election, and Buckley had been opposed by the Brotherhood Party. In an editorial, the *New York Times* noted the irony of the 1962 endorsement and asked icily: "Is this the stuff of which labor's drive to uplift New York politics is made?" To Van Arsdale, the uplift was to gain whatever political advantage might accrue to the working man. By the same token, the Council refused to endorse any candidate for statewide office. In eschewing its traditional Democratic-Liberal endorsement, the Council and Van Arsdale, by remaining neutral in statewide races, gave tacit support to Governor Rockefeller and Senator Javits who headed the Republican ticket.

Van Arsdale attributed the failure of the Brotherhood Party to lack of support from other unions: "If every local union had participated, it would have been an entirely different story." The party was also hurt in that it did not appear on the ballot in the Bronx because some misguided party workers had put a number of false names on party petitions, Van Arsdale said.[20]

In assessing the Brotherhood Party, Kheel said:

> The Brotherhood Party, whatever its antecedents, was a Harry Van Arsdale production. The name—it's strictly Harry—like Camp Integrity, or Camp Solidarity. . . . Brotherhood, he liked that. And as he surveyed the political situation in New York, the organization Democrats were very unappealing. The Republicans, obviously, were not appealing. The Liberal Party was not attractive from his point of view. And he thought he could put together a Brotherhood Party that would be a "brotherhood party." And he made a valiant effort, but it didn't go anywhere. It was not successful.
>
> The Brotherhood Party was run by the Central Labor Council [but] it was Harry Van Arsdale. And it was good, as far as it went, but it didn't go far enough. It didn't have an outreach beyond the labor movement. And it did have the support of Harry Van Arsdale and others in the labor movement. It sounded better on paper than it turned out to be. I'm not sure, in fact I am sure that it did not have universal support in the labor movement. It did not have the support of, at that time, the Liberal Party, the unions that supported the Liberal Party efforts. So, what can I say, it was a valiant effort by Harry, it was a magnificent concept.[21]

Kheel also said he believed the party was formed primarily for two reasons: to show Tammany Hall chief Carmine DeSapio and other Democratic party leaders that they could not take labor for granted, and to consolidate labor as a voting bloc.[22]

The consensus among those involved at the time was that the party had been formed for the primary purpose of giving Wagner an additional line on the ballot. And there was agreement with Kheel's view that the party gave notice to politicians that labor was a force to be reckoned with.[23]

The energy devoted to the party, however, would indicate that Van Arsdale had more than a transitory entity in mind or that it was formed just to give Wagner a line. Wagner would have been on the ballot through the Liberal Party or as an independent if he did not win the Democratic nomination—which he did. The Brotherhood Party was just icing on the ballot cake for him.

Van Arsdale had hoped the party would be there to stay as a real force to make the Democratic party toe the line on labor issues, but, pragmatic as he was, he realized that it would forever be a shadow as a political entity and stood no chance of ever, as some had suggested, merging with the Liberal Party to form a stronger voting bloc. The Liberal Party apparently felt it was strong enough on its own and did not need any help (or sharing of power).

The time, energy, and money involved in mounting succeeding campaigns would have been immense and would have provided little return. Thus, Van Arsdale had made his point, as Kheel noted, and labor's political clout would continue to be a "big stick" within available reach to Van Arsdale if he ever needed it, a lesson that would not be lost, he hoped, to politicians.

But while the political campaign was under way, Van Arsdale and the Local 3 construction division were locked in deep discussions with their employers for a new contract for the upcoming year. A key issue was the four-hour day.

As previously discussed, Van Arsdale introduced the idea in 1958. Van Arsdale presided over several meetings of the Council and a shorter workweek committee. At a June 21 meeting, the committee urged all local unions to incorporate a shorter workweek proposal in upcoming contract talks. It also called on all central and state labor bodies to secure congressional action that would "bring the fruits of automation" to workers and consumers as well as to businesses.

"This idea of negotiating a 6-cent raise this year and another 6-cent raise next year is all out of date," Van Arsdale said. "There are going to be hundreds of thousands of workers made permanently unemployed by automation and other new developments unless we get our members employed and the country ready for a four-hour day."[24] Moreover, Van Arsdale pointed out that the current eight-hour day was actually an eleven-hour day when travel to and from the job was factored in.

The proposal brought immediate outcries in the press. A (New York) *Daily News* editorial asked Van Arsdale: "Do you expect to pay the same wages as now to twice as many people and if so, where is industry going to get the money?" The *New York World-Telegram* said the idea "could be a blueprint for a lot of no-hour days."

But Van Arsdale had always been a champion of the shorter workweek. In 1940, the Local 3 delegation to the AFL convention in New Orleans erected a neon light display touting the thirty-hour week as the answer to unemployment. Local 3 delegates continued to argue for the shorter workweek at subsequent meetings of the IBEW, AFL, and Building Trades Council.[25]

Others had also proposed a shorter workweek over the years. During the Great Depression, AFL President William Green told a Senate Judiciary subcommittee that labor was prepared to use its "economic force" through widespread strikes if necessary to gain a five-day, thirty-hour week. Green said "mechanization" of industry was posing the threat of a "permanent standing army of unemployed."[26]

In an interview, Van Arsdale detailed the genesis and the value of the four-hour day, saying that he had been impressed by an article written by Howell Broach on the subject, which said: "What are we going to do against the ravages of unemployment? . . . Probably the best answer now is: The four-hour day. We may just as well make up our minds to this. So long as there is one man who seeks employment and cannot find it, the hours of labor are too long, as Gompers once said. . . . Economists claim that in four hours a day we could produce all we need and still provide luxuries for the rich."[27]

But Van Arsdale differed from others in that he called for shorter hours during times of full employment as a hedge against possible future unemployment during times of economic recession or depression. His concept of the shorter workweek and workday with its benefits was not only for more employment but specifically for more employment of the poorest workers—minorities. This was a recurring theme on Van Arsdale's agenda for several years.

At a 1959 Lincoln Anniversary dinner, he declared that "unemployment should be tackled like a dreaded disease and eliminated for all time." That year he led a 900-man delegation to Washington, DC, to a national AFL-CIO conference to "get America back to work. " He called for a National Council of the Unemployed to secure full employment. His words were underscored the following year when the nation's rate of unemployment in June reached 5.5 percent, the third highest level since World War II.

As 1960 neared an end, the CLC's Shorter Workweek Committee sponsored a day-long conference on how to deal with the growing number of

workers displaced due to automation. The committee, which had been initiated by Van Arsdale, issued a set of proposals including greater consultation
between unions and management on how to soften the impact of automation, more money for more complicated work, more money for increased
productivity, and retraining for alternate jobs. Van Arsdale warned that a
"harvest of shame" would exist in every shop in the nation if unions were not
on the scene to protect workers.[28]

In 1961, Van Arsdale began to focus on the shorter workday and shorter
workweek. At a February 9 general membership meeting of Local 3, he
called for an all-out effort: a national campaign to achieve shorter working
hours to counter mounting unemployment in the building trades industry.
He read an article to members from the February 6 issue of *U.S. News and
World Report* indicating that 16 percent of building trades workers were
unemployed nationwide.

"The fact is clear that before the November elections the true figures on
unemployment were suppressed and we were told we were enjoying great
prosperity," he said. "However, anyone familiar with the facts, particularly
in the labor movement, knew that this was false and that prosperity did not
exist for millions of workers and their families." He urged members to write
to their legislators to demand bills to establish a shorter workweek, also
health care for the aged, a higher minimum wage, and an effective civil
rights program.[29]

George Meany added his voice to the campaign with a strong demand
for a thirty-hour week in a speech before the Convention of Hotel Employees in Philadelphia in March. However, Meany bent under pressure from
the Kennedy administration and eased off that demand. In the face also of
continued high unemployment, he compromised and endorsed a thirty-five
hour week.

But there was no compromise for Van Arsdale. In 1962, he joined others
in leading a drive to hold a massive rally of thousands of unemployed workers in New York City to dramatize the need for a shorter workweek. Shortly
after Labor Day, Van Arsdale and Local 3 entered into negotiations with the
employers for the electrical industry's 1962 agreement. The talks began on
October 6, but soon ran aground on the Local's demand for a four-hour day
and a twenty-hour week. Other demands included raises in hourly pay, increased vacation time, and a wide spectrum of improved benefits.

In an interview, Van Arsdale spoke of the basis for demanding a four-
hour day.

> In order to focus attention, we decided that a union ought to make a fight
> for the four-hour day. Because Broach wrote an article—I think he got all

the ideas from someone that went before him, but I don't criticize him for that. . . . It was very impressive; it was one of the things that impressed me to no end. It was a very impressive position to take. So, the Central Labor Council discussed that we ought to have a union fight for the four-hour day. Now, what union will make a fight for the four-hour day? Well, it was decided we will send out a communication to every union in the Central Labor Council, that we would like you to consider whether you are in a position to make a fight for the four-hour day. And we are prepared to pledge our full support for whichever union will make a fight for the four-hour day. Well, the union that decided they would be willing to make the fight . . . was the Electricians Local 3. And I don't recall that they had competed against any other organizations. . . .

It was included that whatever union would take on that fight would have to pledge themselves that they would not sign or renew a contract unless they establish shorter hours than they previously had.

Now Local 3 had for many years a six-hour day. And the fact that Local 3 was taking on the fight for a four-hour day. . . . There was no way that we could have renewed our contract for six hours without going back on that part of the pledge that had been taken.[30]

On December 14, the Local membership overwhelmingly—by a 5,000 to 3 vote—endorsed a negotiating committee recommendation calling for a citywide strike deadline of midnight December 31 to enforce demands for the four-hour day.

Van Arsdale did not attend the membership meeting as he was proposing the shorter workweek to the AFL-CIO at its annual convention in Bal Harbour, Florida. In a speech before the delegates, Van Arsdale outlined the precedents for demanding a shorter workweek and then addressed positions taken by President Kennedy and his brother, Attorney General Robert Kennedy.

> There are some who are attempting to interpret our efforts as disloyalty to the President of the United States. A few days prior to last year's election, I had the honor in Madison Square Garden of standing alongside the President of the United States and the President of the IBEW, Gordon Freeman. We stood in silent prayer because Martin Luther King at that moment had been incarcerated because of his fight for freedom.
>
> We have complete faith in our president. We think that after three years of study we have a little better idea of what is necessary in our cities than his advisers may have advised him.
>
> Further, I would like to say that we had an occasion to have as our guest Robert Kennedy, the Attorney General of the United States. He outlined to our executive board the program he has undertaken. I would suggest that

those affiliates who have expressed themselves, get to know him better because we came from that meeting with the idea that he understood our problems.[31]

Just how well President Kennedy and his brother understood the problems of the working man was brought into question in light of a reputed action taken by the brothers in months to come. Suffice to say, it was a blow and a disappointment to Van Arsdale.

But Van Arsdale was, of course, a man used to blows and to battling back. The *New York Times* hurled an editorial thunderbolt from its Olympus on West 43rd Street, predicting that the idleness resulting from any strike would "help prepare union members for eventually carrying their pressure for a shorter workweek to its logical conclusion—a no-hour day and a no-day week." The *New York Times* said the shorter week would drive up building costs and argued also that the construction division men already enjoyed a six-hour-day and thirty-hour week. It cast doubt on Van Arsdale's promise to make his electricians go to school for four hours daily and avoid overtime pay. Moreover, Van Arsdale and the CLC "might apply their energies to wiping out sweatshops and to raising wages for the tens of thousands of Negroes and Puerto Ricans now employed in New York at only a few cents above the Federal minimum of $1.15 an hour. Labor will only lose public sympathy altogether if it should close ranks behind such exaggerated demands as those of Mr. Van Arsdale."[32]

Van Arsdale fired back with an eloquent letter (the *New York Times* printed it December 20) in which he scathingly pointed out that "with the utmost seriousness . . . the no-hour day and a no-day week has existed for some time in our society." He was referring to the unemployed. He also noted the underemployed and part-time workers also fell within the purview of the *New York Time*'s disapproving words because they worked a three- or a four-day week.

> Our union leadership didn't dream up the four-hour day while in a state of unaccountable euphoria. We had thought long about it, in terms of the present trends in employment and the future. . . . It is our deeply held conclusion that the shorter work week and the shortened work day is an answer to what has become America's endemic unemployment problem.
>
> It is an easy thing to laugh about the no-hour day and the no-day week, but working people must find it quite ironic to be told about the "Soviet industrial challenge" while they live on surplus food commodities, grudgingly bestowed relief payments and editorial pieties about a roseate future.
>
> We look at economic life a little more practically. There is nothing sacred in an eight-hour day or a four-hour day any more than there was

something sacred about the six-and-a-half-day week. We are not a group of revolutionary Jacobins seeking to remake America in some scandalous fashion, seeking to exterminate the profit system or to impose runaway inflation. . . . We are seeking a better America where the skills of American workers will not be allowed to rot because of unemployment or the triumphs of computer technology or the impersonal workings of the market place.

Van Arsdale answered the *New York Times*'s haughty advice for labor to devote its energies to helping African Americans and Latinos by pointing out that this was just what labor had been trying to do for many years. On the other hand, he continued, "it would be of tremendous help if *The Times* would seek to uncover why racketeer unions and sweetheart agreements are still given legal sanction in this state."

Meanwhile, negotiations ground on. A threatened injunction sought by the contractors against the possible strike was withdrawn. Mediation attempts by Mayor Wagner came to naught and Van Arsdale was forced to call Local 3 out on strike January 11, 1962.

Van Arsdale, however, was careful to keep the strike from affecting New Yorkers' lives. He saw to it that there would be no blackout of signs and streetlights. The building site of the 1964 World's Fair (to which Local 3 had contributed $100,000) and Lincoln Center were exempted. Local 3 members would also continue to be on the job at all major projects so that the strike would not cause 200,000 other building trades workers to lose work. This was in keeping with a pronouncement he made in September during a seminar in Garden City, New York on government's role in collective bargaining when he said that unions would be shortsighted if they negotiated a contract without consideration of the public interest.[33]

Nevertheless, five days after the strike started, contractors ordered a general shutdown of construction work in the city rather than continuing contingency operations in the absence of 9,000 electricians. The order affected 80 percent of New York's $1.3 billion-a-year construction industry.

The first crack in the wall erected by the contractors came January 16, when the Greater New York Electrical Contractors Association, representing 120 contractors, accepted the Local's proposal of a five-hour day. The following day, all the contractors followed suit and the strike ended eight days after it had begun. The pact also continued a pioneering provision to establish an educational trust fund for members and their families. It would be the first such fund ever established in a collective bargaining agreement. Employers would contribute 1 percent of their payrolls or about $700,000 to $1 million a year to the fund. "Men don't live by bread alone," Van Arsdale said.

The CLC lauded the achievement "as the first real reduction in the work-week in recent labor history" and a victory "which will have profound influence on national thinking on automation and full employment." The Local 3 members worked a seven-hour day, but the sixth and seventh hours were at overtime rates. The apprenticeship program was also enlarged to ensure that there would always be enough workers on a job. As noted previously, this was also an aid to increase minority employment.

It was the first union in the nation to win such a contract. The example of the electricians sparked the 6,000-member Local 2 of the United Association of the Plumbing and Pipe Fitting Industry to also press for a five-hour day. Seven local unions of the Bricklayers, Masons, and Plasterers International Union, representing 6,000 members, pressed demands for a six-hour day.

But Ted Kheel explained that the five-hour day was not as revolutionary as it appeared to be:

> They got the same money for five hours as they were getting for seven, plus, if they worked the extra two hours—so that this was a substantial wage increase. However, at that point in time, the other crafts were also getting substantial wage increases, and the basic question became what did the electrical workers get for the five hour plus one hour of mandatory overtime plus one hour of voluntary overtime for seven hours as compared to sheet-metal workers, the plumbers, the pipe-fitters, and so forth and so on.
>
> If you add it up, the components of the seven hours, straight time, overtime, mandatory time, voluntary time, and divide it by seven, the rates were all comparable, you see. So that with some qualification, the settlement, financial settlement, was equivalent to the settlements that the other unions were making. But what was different was the way they computed how much they got for seven hours of work, you see. However, there was this added cost, that was more in the case of the electrical workers than for the other crafts. And Harry was concerned about how the contractors could pay for that. What he proposed was to reduce the ratio of journeymen to apprentices, or apprentices to journeymen.[34]

And that, as previously mentioned, opened the gates wide to the employment of minority groups in the construction division of the union.

But President Kennedy was not happy with the five-hour day. At a news conference, he said that he "regretted" the winning of the five-hour day. Kennedy said the pact did not meet two criteria he favored: the maintenance of the forty-hour week and limiting wage costs. He referred to a campaign speech he made in 1960 to the United Steelworkers of America when it advocated shorter work hours to spread jobs. He said then that the forty-hour week "in view of the many obligations that we had upon us at home and abroad, represented the national goal at this time."[35] In private, however, the president was reportedly much harsher in his condemnation of the Local 3 contract.

His ire was such that he unleashed his brother Robert on Van Arsdale and Local 3. The Attorney General ordered an FBI investigation to determine if Van Arsdale and Local 3 had attempted to coerce any contractors into accepting the shorter workweek, according to Arnold Beichman, then editor of *Electrical Union World.*

"The contractors, however, refused to go along with this frame-up," said Beichman. He said he had been told of the investigation by a bitter Van Arsdale, who felt betrayed by the Kennedys to whom he had given such strong support. Van Arsdale had divulged this as they walked along Central Park West in Manhattan, Beichman continued. Van Arsdale felt so harried that he did not risk speaking of the matter in a room where his words might be secretly recorded, Beichman indicated. "It was pretty bad."[36]

Robert Kennedy's investigation of Van Arsdale occurred less than a year after President Kennedy's secretary of labor, Arthur Goldberg, presented the U.S. Labor Department's "Award of Merit" to Van Arsdale. In presenting the citation on June 6 at the Columbia University Club, Goldberg noted that it was the first time that the award had been given to anyone who was not a national labor leader.

Goldberg said the award was being given in recognition by the U.S. government "of the service performed by an outstanding leader of labor in the local community—where it counts—in the interest of the people as a whole. Van Arsdale was also given an autographed picture of President Kennedy as a sign of the president's personal esteem.[37]

Meanwhile, Van Arsdale continued to stress the need for a shorter workweek. On February 28, 1962, Van Arsdale spoke at the Cooper Union Forum on the "Goals of Labor," stating in part:

> Unemployment is a cancer in our country. As reluctant as we are to recommend going to war, we would seriously recommend that a war to the finish be declared on the cancer of unemployment and that war be continued until such time as we develop a full employment economy in our country. Now with the coming of our understanding of education, some—the members of the construction branch of [the electrical industry] . . . have attended some 10,900 courses, not counting some 2,800 courses in electronics which they've attended, not counting any of the courses attended by the apprentices, which is required of their training.

> We, until such time as unemployment is cured, we in our union would like to work four hours a day and encourage all of our members to study, to attend classes and study for four hours of the day.

Van Arsdale also alluded to the new space age and advancements made in science and said that the working man needs to be armed with education and knowledge to keep up in the modern world.

The gaining of the five-hour day catapulted Van Arsdale to increased national and international attention. Irwin Ross writing in the *Saturday Evening Post* (May 12, 1962) said, "After the strike was over Harry Van Arsdale Jr. emerged as a national figure. . . . His achievement was a major labor breakthrough, whatever one thought of its wisdom. *Fortune* magazine, in an article bemoaning Van Arsdale's achievement nevertheless noted: "Van Arsdale's victory is sure to echo in union halls and at negotiating tables for some time to come. And that is just what Van Arsdale had in mind when he called his members out on strike last January. 'The electricians bring light to the world,' he said. 'Why shouldn't we lead the way?'"

Labor reporter A.H. Raskin, in a March 11 Sunday *New York Times Magazine* article, wrote, in part:

> The repercussions of that settlement [five-hour day] have been world-wide. An AFL-CIO representative in Africa found Nairobi textile and railroad workers agog at Van Arsdale's accomplishment. Many of them earn less in a fortnight than the New York electricians do in an hour and forty-eight hours is a short week by their standards. "This Van Arsdale is like an astronaut going into space," one awed Kenyan declared. Swiss building trades workers, arguing with their own federation over the merits of a cut in the forty-five-hour week, made Van Arsdale their champion.[38]

But Raskin added that sentiment within the rest of organized labor in the United States was not entirely laudatory, a feeling fueled by jealousy and envy. According to Raskin, it was felt that "Van Arsdale had got so far ahead of the parade that he had turned the campaign for shorter hours into a joke."[39]

Raskin went on to say:

> In personal terms, the unhappiest heritage of the fight for the twenty-five-hour schedule in construction was the widespread suggestion that Van Arsdale was motivated by an itch to win national attention and thus move to the head of the line as a possible successor to Meany. . . .
>
> In a movement where vanity often towers over talent and backbiting is virtually universal, this suspicion was enough to cause the general chill in the reaction of national leaders to the Van Arsdale strike. Turning frosty

was easy enough since most of them never liked his go-it-alone ways much anyhow.

[Van Arsdale denied he was seeking to oust Meany, Raskin reported, adding that Van Arsdale told him he had enough to do in New York. He further quotes Van Arsdale as saying:]

We knew we would have to travel a lonely road. We knew we would have to go through the mud again, just as we did when we were building the union. It is a good thing too. You get unrealistic when everyone is treating you so nice.

More of our fellow unions ought to go through it awhile. Too many unions feel the size of their balance sheet is their strength, or the number of friendly gestures they get from politicians when everything is peaceful.[40]

11

Troubleshooting Here and Abroad

In 1962, at the age of 57, Van Arsdale was in his prime. He had transformed the post of president of the Central Labor Council (CLC) into a major player in the New York economic and political arena. He was not a "power broker" in the traditional sense of one who exploits his position of power into personal gain or patronage. Van Arsdale used his power base, the working people of New York, for their good, not his. His "gain" was with the knowledge that he had helped improve their lives. Van Arsdale also used his presidency as a pulpit. His innovations and achievements gained him national recognition and he used his position to speak out on social, political, and international issues. Following the example of George Meany and the AFL-CIO, Van Arsdale used the power of his "pulpit" in early 1962 to speak about international matters and the threat of communism to free labor. Moreover, his increasing visibility on numerous boards, committees, and panels gave him the ear of "movers and shakers" in finance, business, and government, and he used that opportunity to further the cause of his constituents. In short, he became a powerful friend of labor in the court of the moneyed mighty, in essence transforming the business, financial, and political associations of the city into an expanded Joint Industry Board (JIB). The mighty, like the contractors, knew he could be trusted to be fair and judicious as a lobbyist, negotiator, or arbitrator. And, if that made him a power broker, so be it.

As was his habit, Van Arsdale brought prominent leaders and celebrities to speak before his union colleagues. In March 1962, Omer Becu, general secretary of the International Confederation of Free Trade Unions, which claimed to represent 56 million workers around the world, addressed a luncheon meeting of the CLC. After the address, Van Arsdale brought him to Cooper Union College where Van Arsdale was scheduled to deliver a speech on the goals of labor. In introducing Becu to his audience, Van Arsdale explained that the International Confederation of Free Trade Unions, with which the AFL-CIO was affiliated, "came into existence to prevent the communist World Federation of Trade Unions from interfering with the development of free trade unions in various countries throughout the world."

He said that he had been so impressed with Becu's remarks before the Council that he had planned to have them reprinted and distributed in a pamphlet to union members. In his remarks to the Council, Becu warned that "the war against the free world by Moscow has primarily been a war directed against free trade unionism."[1]

Continuing in the international arena, Van Arsdale became chairman of the AFL-CIO Committee for the United Nations, which earned him a personal plaudit from President Kennedy who declared in part: "The desire to be free from exploitation, economically as well as politically, the desire for equality of opportunity, for education, medical care, an adequate diet, and a satisfying remunerative job, with safe and decent working conditions; and the desire for individual welfare and dignity, to become a person in the highest sense of the word—these are the aspirations we share with the people of the world. They weld us together in common brotherhood." On a personal note, Kennedy penned a postscript saying: "I think it is especially important to stimulate visits by labor leaders from Latin America to this country. Best, JK."[2]

Van Arsdale had first alluded to the U.N. Committee on April 26 of the previous year in a notable speech at the annual dinner of the Columbia University Seminars at the Columbia University Faculty Club. He said in part:

> During the thirties, there existed what has been called the "labor-liberal alliance." Historically, this was a significant event in America. This alliance had enormous influence on public opinion and helped make possible the growth and acceptance of trade unionism in America. I am not suggesting that the labor-liberal alliance was fashioned in a wholly altruistic spirit. We know that some of these intellectuals measured the quality of liberalism by its unswerving adherence to Communist doctrine and Soviet world ambitions. Nevertheless, organized labor learned a great deal from its friends and supporters in the universities, the foundations, in government, the churches and synagogues.

By the end of World War II, this alliance had crumbled. Today, with the exception of those intellectuals who specialize in labor-management relations, the intellectual force in America feels as alienated from the labor movement as the labor movement feels alienated from the intellectuals. However, I think the time has come to see if the breach between us can be repaired not in the name of doctrinaire philosophy or vague ethic but because this isolation, this sulking in our split-level tents, is a luxury we can no longer afford.

More and more the American labor movement must move closer to the true vocation of the intellectual. The American worker may not quite have a life in paradise, but it is a far cry, materially, from what it was three years ago [1958]. The American worker has substantially improved his economic status. Now it remains to be seen what can be done to relate the American worker to the future existence of not only our country but the free world as well.

Van Arsdale chided the intellectual elements for not showing stronger support for the hospital workers during their strike, even if they had not been formally asked. "We have moved a long way, however, from those days in the thirties when a struggle of this kind would have evoked an instantaneous offer of help and support from people like yourselves. . . . I say we need you and I tell you that you need us. I hope that this monologue will have some echo and reverberation in the days ahead."[3]

Members of the intelligentsia were regular speakers at meetings of the Council and Local 3, joining the stream of lawmakers and officials who were in a position to help the working man were Labor Secretary Arthur Goldberg, Senator Robert Kennedy (despite the reported investigation he had launched against Van Arsdale) and New York state Governor Nelson Rockefeller. Rockefeller got a standing ovation from Local 3 members when he appeared at a general meeting on October 11, 1962. He told a capacity audience of construction division members that he appreciated the "unstinting cooperation and assistance" of Van Arsdale and other labor leaders in the state. Van Arsdale returned the compliment by telling the group that Rockefeller "supports our efforts for full employment" and that his sympathies for the working man would not be forgotten.[4] In November, Governor Rockefeller, Senator Javits, and other state officials toured Electchester.

Javits had also been a speaker at a special meeting for union leaders and rank and file members that was held at the Americana Hotel on October 24, 1962. He called for management and labor in the United States "to win decisively the economic struggle against communism." Javits also praised the "labor statesmanship" of Local 3, adding that it is "one of the greatest assets labor can have for itself and one of the greatest assets it can confer on the country." Van Arsdale described the Republican legislator "as one of the most outstanding Senators from any of the 50 states and a man who has advised us and guided us on many occasions."[5]

As the year came to a close, Van Arsdale used his position as leader of one of the largest central labor council's in the nation to speak out again on the national issue of unemployment, an issue with which he was becoming identified.

Speaking at the City Club in Rochester, Van Arsdale bemoaned the difficulty recent college and high school graduates were experiencing in finding jobs. He said again that a shorter workweek was the most decisive way to provide jobs for 1 million unemployed young people. He said no nation or corporation would or should "tolerate such waste of the talents of one million young men and women who, in their formative years after receiving their education, are idle."[6]

Van Arsdale's basic role, however, as the steward of labor in the city, came into play with the strike and lockout involving the city's nine major newspapers, which employed 20,000 persons, that began on December 8, 1962, and continued until April 1, 1963. The papers involved were: the *New York Times*, the *New York Herald-Tribune*, the *New York Mirror*, the *Daily News*, the *New York Post*, the *New York Journal-American*, the *New York World Telegram and Sun*, the *Long Island Press*, and the *Long Island Star-Journal*. On the eve of the strike deadline, Van Arsdale asked Mayor Wagner to do everything possible to avert the walkout. Wagner called in federal mediators.

The strike and lockout had its genesis in a seven-day strike conducted by Local 3 of the American Newspaper Guild against the *Daily News*. Other newspaper unions, including members of Local 3 IBEW, honored their picket lines.

Van Arsdale moved to secure the help of U.S. Labor Secretary Willard Wirtz in an attempt to mediate a settlement between the *Daily News* and the Guild. Van Arsdale foresaw the possibility that in December, when other union contracts came due, the other publishers might retaliate against the unions with a lockout. Wirtz helped to quiet the *Daily News*/Guild dispute, but the publishers insisted that the contract package given to the Guild set the pattern for the other newspaper unions.

The president of Local 6 of the Typographical Workers Union, Bertram Powers, resisted and struck the *Herald-Tribune*, the *Post* and the *Mirror*. The other members of the Publishers Association closed their doors in December, despite all of Van Arsdale's and Wirtz's efforts. The newspaper unions quickly formed a Unity Committee, and Powers was named chairman.

On January 10, Local 3 IBEW contributed $10,000 to the Unity Committee strike fund. In a talk before the membership of Local 3 on January 10,

Powers said the strike, in effect, had begun twelve years before: "It began when the Publishers Association members banded together and decided they would no longer negotiate with the printing unions or other unions whose members are employed at their plants. As a substitute for bargaining, they started negotiating with a single union and upon reaching an agreement with that union, would publicly announce that a pattern had been established. They would seek to impose that pattern on each of the other nine unions and were successful with that technique."

Van Arsdale and other CLC leaders showed their support for the strikers by joining in a mass demonstration and picket line in front of the *New York Times* on January 15, 1963.

Powers related the role played by Van Arsdale and Local 6's strategy in negotiations:

> The first time I met him was when he asked me to come to his office and talk about the strike. In fact, even before the strike occurred we were meeting because it was obvious we were going to have a strike.
>
> The reason for that strike in the papers was that the publishers had developed a pattern of negotiating with ten unions, and to their advantage they would take the ten unions and agree upon one of them as being the weakest or the most opportunistic, reach a settlement with that union, and then there would appear a story in the *New York Times* saying the publisher reached agreement with X union, and always the line would be, "it is expected that this settlement will be a pattern for the industry."
>
> Then they would proceed to make it a pattern by negotiating with a second, a third, reserving to the end Typo No. 6 [Typographical Workers Union]. By the time we would get there, when they would seriously bargain with us, the pattern would be well established and we wouldn't be able to change it. The reason that we couldn't change it would be that we would not get support from the ones that had settled for X, if we were looking for X plus Y. It would be an embarrassment for them to support us for Y, because they already agreed to X. So we would be left alone, and being alone, one union out of ten, and striking, would make us vulnerable to be replaced by strike-breakers while the other nine would cross our picket line.
>
> This 1962 strike was not an automation issue, the issue was an attempt by Typo to break the publisher tactic of bargaining by pattern bargaining, which really was to deny us collective bargaining. The table was set when we got there and we got what they had agreed to in the other unions. . . .
>
> I made up my mind then I was going to break that pattern. And I began to set my goals for that purpose, to reassert Typo as the leader in the negotiations. Rather than being last we would be first. And the way to do that

was for me to tell the other unions that we were not going to accept pattern bargaining, and that if they would, we wouldn't, and we would strike rather than accept an inadequate settlement. If they got a big settlement, fine, but if they didn't get one that satisfied us, we were telling them in advance we were going to strike.

When the strike began, the other unions weren't very happy about the strike happening. Some were allied with us, some were not. The ones who were more supportive were the Photoengravers and the Mailers, because the Mailers were in the same international union. Also the Machinists and the Electricians. They were higher paid and although very small in numbers, they were with us. The ones who were most opposed to the strike were the drivers, and the pressmen, the Guild being so-so, some being for, some against, but it was that kind of a situation—divided about half and half.

Harry Van Arsdale reached out and called me to meet with him, and we had a series of meetings discussing our viewpoints about strikes and no-strikes, even before the strike began because it was apparent that we were on a collision course with the publishers.

But once it started, there was a strong back-to-work movement by those other unions, being the ones that were not supportive. They wanted a settlement, for a lot of reasons. Harry's role was to keep them together, to keep the unions, the unity committee, from breaking up. And he was very helpful in that regard.

There was an effort on the part of the publishers to get the other unions to put pressure on our union to settle for less than we felt we had to have. But they—and these unions would always say, "Well, we don't want that, but if Powers gets it, we have to have it." Like shorter hours—I said we have to have shorter hours. They didn't want shorter hours, but if I got it, they had to have it. So that was a drag on me to get the shorter hours, and they were constantly putting pressure on me to drop that demand. Well the publishers managed somehow to get the other unions in on my bargaining as observers. Right? They were not welcome, but it was just a ploy to put more pressure on us. So Harry said to me—he said, "Now, Boit, you have to take them on a bus trip. Do you know what a bus trip is?" I said, "No, Harry, tell me what a bus trip is." He said, "You know that sightseeing bus at Times Square? That bus leaves 42nd Street and Broadway at the appointed hour and the tourists all get on the bus and the bus driver points out things of interest, and it goes down to the Battery; then it turns around, and [the only thing] he shows you is Broadway and it always ends up at 42nd Street and Broadway. And that's what you have to do with these people." So that's what I did. I took them on a bus trip. And when they got all through, they didn't know any more than when they started. Forever more, that's a word in our negotiations. In Typo, we say, when the publishers are bothering us—we'll say, "We'll take them on a bus trip."[7]

* * *

Harry had a headquarters building on, I think, 23rd Street, 23rd or 25th, on Lexington Avenue. And he would call me and say "I want to see you over here Bert." "Boit" he called me, B-O-I-T, and he'd say "meet me at seven o'clock," and he'd be signing checks or doing something to do with his work, and talking. We would sit, he and I, just the two of us, 'til like ten o'clock or twelve o'clock.

And we'd talk about all kinds of things—he'd do most of the talking, sometimes he'd let me talk, but mostly he would be talking. He would let me talk when he wanted to find out something, you know. But I learned a lot, we were together sometimes three, four nights a week, for weeks and weeks.

Harry would call these meetings, the two of us, I never really knew why, I look back and think that there was some aspect of keeping me in reign in those meetings, but I really couldn't say for sure. But sometimes I'd wonder what the hell I was doing there listening to this, but I liked Harry Van Arsdale, so I really didn't mind because I thought much like he did.

And Harry would come to the meetings [of the Unity Committee] usually two from each union, so that would mean, what, twenty or twenty-five people sometimes more sometimes less. But Harry would be in the middle of it, and he was a real pro about dealing with labor leaders and so forth, and often times he would put out the fire. The fire being [breaking ranks and going] back to work, or fighting within the group.

He'd put it out by his common sense approach about sticking together and so forth, and he was very, very helpful to me. Maybe the pressmen were thinking he wasn't very helpful because they wanted to go back, or the drivers, but Harry played that role of unity, most of all unity. And of course he had contacts with Wagner, and Wagner was an important force being the Mayor, and he had contacts with Kheel. Kheel being a most experienced mediator, found himself involved in this.

[Harry] said to me once, he said, "Well, you know you're going to be heavily criticized when this strike comes about, and the press is going to rip you apart, and they're going to slander you or liable you or whatever; they're going to really do a number on you." And I said, "Well, Harry, they're not going to do that to me if they're not printing." He laughed at that, because the magazines were still going to be published, and there'd be an emergency paper that would do a number on us. But the [New York] Times didn't do anything to us, or the [Daily] News, because they weren't printing.

Harry [also] predicted that I would be criticized by the President of the United States. He said, "And what are you going to say when the President criticizes you and blames you for the strike?" And I thought for a moment, and I gave him a formulation, which was kind of a wise-guy one, and he said, "No, that's no good," he said you should say this: "You should say, 'The President is misinformed.'" And I filed that away.

Sure enough, Kennedy attacked me and my union, and blamed us for the strike. Or he said that it began to look as though the purpose of the Typographical Union and its leader was "to bring the publishers of the Queen City to their knees." So the reporters came to me and said "What do you say to this?" I said, "The President is misinformed." And people said to me afterwards, "How did you ever think of that? Such a cool answer, you know? You didn't fight with the President, you said he was misinformed."

Of course, the answer was I had been coached by Harry to that and he was absolutely right. But it appears that President Kennedy was coached by "Puck" [John Hay] Whitney of the [New York] Herald-Tribune, because I learned afterwards that Whitney had a meeting with Kennedy somewhere in Florida, I think, about a week before his attack, so I'm sure that Whitney told Kennedy his opinion of my union and its leader.

We also didn't believe that the Mayor would allow the police to be used by the publishers to break us. Everybody felt that Wagner was pro-labor. He and Van Arsdale worked very closely. Van Arsdale had been able to get recognition for public employees and we felt more secure with Wagner.

The unions in New York City, in the five boroughs, by [19]61, had demonstrated that they had a lot of power in the primaries.

In fact, when Wagner got in trouble with the Democrats at one point, Van Arsdale supplied the number of people in the primary to guarantee that he got on the ballot. The same thing was done for Lindsay, when Lindsay ran as a Democrat when the Republicans dumped him. Van Arsdale was able to supply the primary participants to guarantee his being a candidate. Wagner had some other difficulties similar to that and Van Arsdale was able to give him what he needed. So Van Arsdale, politically, was an insurance policy for Mayors.

Ted Kheel became involved in the negotiations as a mediator, brought in probably by Wagner. He went for a settlement. He was not pro-labor, nor pro-management. His role—he made it very plain—was to get a settlement. And if you didn't correctly analyze the settlement, and you bought the settlement, and it wasn't a good deal for you, well then you were stuck with it. You the publisher or you the union president, because if he could sell it to you, he would sell it to you, because he was for a settlement. And even if there were some other way to do it better, he wasn't going to tell you that. He said now how about this, and if you agreed, then that was agreed to. . . . He was always pro-settlement which is what his role was and should have been.[8]

Kheel put Wagner's proposal before the union negotiators, and Van Arsdale brought his weight to bear. As Kheel put it, "Harry stayed with the local union all night until five o'clock in the morning and convinced them to accept the mayor's recommendation. And a vote was taken to settle the strike. But it was the confidence they had in Harry that he had created by sitting with them [that got them to agree]."[9]

Powers discussed Kheel and Van Arsdale further and provided additional insights into Van Arsdale's character and method of operation.

Harry Van Arsdale and Ted Kheel were about as different as two people could be. Harry was single-minded and Ted was all around the place.... Ted Kheel always got a kick out of Harry Van Arsdale. He used to tell me what Harry said and laugh about it, because he considered him to be a character, which he was [but] sound and very effective.

Harry had no fear. None that I could see, he had absolutely no fear of anybody. He said what he thought and was very direct. He'd be at a meeting and somebody would get out of hand and yell, or criticize him, and he'd say, "I don't think that's very fair, what that member said. How many people here agree with that member? Will you raise your hands if you agree with that member?" And of course nobody raised their hand, and Harry would go on from there. He wouldn't argue with the guy, he'd just say, "Say it that way."

And I used to watch him operate at the Central Labor Council and other meetings. I went to some of his meetings that he'd had with his own members and delegates and some contract negotiations. He had some very, very good techniques of dealing with situations. He'd have a meeting, and I remember one meeting he had where the delegates were rambunctious and asking a lot of questions and how about this and why not that and so forth. Harry took their questions one by one and didn't answer them. He'd say, [loud and nasally] "Now this delegate has asked me this," and he'd write it down. And he'd get ten or fifteen, until they'd start repeating themselves and then he'd say "I have that question." And after he had all those questions and replied to none, he'd come back with an answer which was: "Now this question was given to us." And he'd reform the question. Now he's stating the question the way he wants it stated. And then he'd give his answer. And he went down the ten, and it'd be all over. Well I learned from it, I do that myself. I've been doing that for years.

Another thing that was characteristic of Harry was how he tried to control how long you spoke. He'd say, "I want you to speak at this meeting." And I would agree and then as I'm going to the podium he'd say, "Two minutes," you know. And then when I'd get to about a minute and a half, he would say "You're almost through, almost through."

He orchestrated everything, you know; he just controlled the whole goddamn show. Didn't let anything to chance. He controlled when you were on, and when you came off. If he had to use a hook, he would have done that too. But, you know, you could hear it in the audience, "All right now, all right." That was time to go.

Harry was a throw-back. He reminded me of my grandparents' generation. He really was my father's generation. He wasn't like his contemporaries. He had his own style and was very different from anybody around him. And he didn't apologize for it. This was the way he was. He was so single minded in anything he did.

Ted Kheel told me a story about him, that Ted was a mediator in a negotiation with the Taxi industry and Van Arsdale was representing the Taxi workers. Harry wouldn't tell the employers what it was that would settle it. He hadn't told anybody. He knows what would settle it but he hasn't told Kheel, and he hasn't told the employers and the employers are there to get it settled. They know that it's not going to be something they can't pay, but they don't know what it is and they're waiting for it to break. And finally after days of this stand-off and everybody's waiting for Harry to really announce what it's going to be, Harry says to somebody, a spokesmen for the Taxi owners, he says, "Ah, Jones, come over here Jones, Jones, come over here." So, Jones comes running over, I think this is it, you know, we're going to get the announcement, we're going to get the word, what it's going to be, and Harry's got the paper spread out and he's looking at the comics, and its Maggie and Jiggs. And he says to Jones, "Look at what Maggie's doing to Jiggs!"

That was the "big breakthrough," and [it was] nothing, they had to go back to their corner of the room and wait until Harry would give them the word. And that's the way he was. Harry thought ahead; he was a planner. It was obvious that he knew where he was going at all times, and knew what he would do under any circumstance.

He told me something one time about planning to overcome difficulties within the union. He said that when he was young in the Electrical Workers Union, there was a lot of chaos and infighting and violence at the union meetings that he was conducting—with fist-fights and throwing of chairs and all kinds of ruckus. And he realized that couldn't continue and he had to find some way to overcome that. And the way that he did, he told me, was that he got the opposition people one by one into a group and then got the defenders to get with the movers and shakers, he'd call them, the activists, the ones who had influence, ones who had respect, who stood above the ordinary rank and file, and he spent time with them. [Therefore], he would assemble the movers and shakers of both factions, and say: "Look, to them, look, this is a problem that the union has. I think that this is a solution, but I may not be right, you tell me if you think I'm wrong, so I can correct my course of action. Tell me what you think, give me your ideas" and get their input, and then change whatever he had to change, as little as possible I'm sure knowing Harry, but he did give them input.

And he'd get a consensus, and by so doing, he would really cut that automatic opposition. And they would become supporters of a program that they had helped to formulate. And that's another thing that I learned from Harry. I did the same thing. . . . I call it a meeting of movers and shakers. I'm careful to always invite the opposition. They don't always come, but they're always invited. And then we discuss a problem, just the way he described it to me, and it works. But he was doing that years ago. That technique of his is not manipulative; actually it works. And my experience is that you always get input that you didn't expect to get and you avert problems that you didn't realize would be problems by having this discourse on a given problem.[10]

Following the strike, Van Arsdale warned there could be another stoppage when contracts expired in two years "if the attitudes of both sides in the newspaper dispute do not change drastically." Speaking on the radio program, "Let's Find Out," Van Arsdale said he hoped that "after tempers cool and there's time to look back at this sad experience" the opposing sides would fashion an "industry-governmental" structure to deal with differences. It can reasonably be assumed here that he meant a structure akin to the JIB, which had been so successful in the electrical industry. Van Arsdale suggested that it might be useful to create a national study of the newspaper industry in light of other recent newspaper strikes such as those in Milwaukee, Minneapolis, and Cleveland. The fears of automation, he continued, would not be corrected "until management and the unions make a genuine effort to try to find the solutions to each other's problems and face up to the necessary adjustments that go with finding long range solutions." Van Arsdale also praised the efforts of Mayor Wagner to end the strike. "I think he did a tremendous job and in a situation so complicated," he said. "With all the years of my experience, I've never been involved in a situation that had so many, many ramifications and difficulties as this particular dispute."[11]

The peace-keeping organization envisioned by Van Arsdale for the newspaper industry, however, never came to be. The competition between the publishers and within the unions proved an insurmountable obstacle. Of the latter, Powers said: "We decided we ought to get closer in [to stop] the publishers from singling out one from the herd, you know? So we said, 'We better get a—let's get a constitution.' It was after the [19]80 settlement. We got together—the Drivers, the Pressmen, the Typos and the Guild, the Stereos and the Electricians, the Machinists and the Photoengravers. The first subject for discussion was, 'What shall we call ourselves? What shall our name be?' Never got past that. So I guess we came to the conclusion, if we couldn't agree on a name, we couldn't agree on much else."[12]

Later in 1963, Van Arsdale's talent for fence mending was shown in his welcoming Attorney General Robert Kennedy to speak at the CLC's third annual Civil Rights Conference. Van Arsdale and Kennedy greeted each other like old friends with absolutely no hint of acknowledgment of the reputed FBI investigation of Van Arsdale. Van Arsdale would later endorse Robert Kennedy for the U.S. Senate in New York.

The city's teachers also occupied him again as contract talks between the UFT and the city's Board of Education stalled and a strike was threatened for the start of the school year (September 9). Van Arsdale and Kheel were again "in the thick of it" trying to achieve a fair settlement. Van Arsdale arranged for a closed meeting with Mayor Wagner, UFT President Charles Cogen, and officials of civil service unions at the mayor's residence at Gracie Mansion.

Van Arsdale and David Dubinsky were asked by Board President Charles Silver to use their personal influence to try to avert a strike. However, Van Arsdale later warned that a sympathy strike of city employees was possible. "Other civil service groups feel that if the teachers or any other group is victimized by this law [Condon-Wadlin Act] that their turn will soon come." He further cautioned that the CLC was not given to "idle threats." The strike was averted at the last minute. The Condon-Wadlin Act barred a strike by public employees.

Recognition of Van Arsdale's concern for African Americans and other minorities came at the end of 1963 when the Urban League presented him with its "Equal Opportunity Award." In presenting the award, A. Philip Randolph, the president of the Brotherhood of Sleeping Car Porters, said: "Harry richly deserves this honor because of his fine imagination, courage, vision and integrity. I am honored to present this award to you because, as the head of Local 3 you are the first to provide a large number of apprenticeships for Negro youths. Second, because you had the vision and understood the significance of the march of science, technology and automation and what it would mean to workers, you started the campaign for the reduction of the work-day and obtained the 25-hour week. Third, because you have resourcefulness and inexhaustible energy."

Further recognition of Van Arsdale's work in promulgating civil rights came when he was named by President Lyndon Johnson to serve on the National Citizens Committee for Community Relations established to ensure compliance with the 1964 Civil Rights Act.

Van Arsdale began 1964 doing one of the things he did best: attempting to settle a labor dispute. This one involved the Transport Workers Union and its colorful president, Michael Quill. Van Arsdale had been appointed by Mayor Wagner to a Transit Labor Board. He and other mediators spent hours with Quill to convince him to accept the bottom-line proposal of the Transit Authority as the clock proceeded toward a strike deadline. (Van Arsdale used the same approach months before in getting Bert Powers to agree to Mayor Wagner's proposal to settle the newspaper strike.) Quill gave in after Van Arsdale convinced him to drop a demand dear to the heart of Van Arsdale— a shorter workweek. Quill, taking a leaf from Van Arsdale's book, had long said a four-day, thirty-two hour week at full five-day rates was the bedrock of his list of demands. However, Van Arsdale, ever the pragmatist, got Quill to understand that the goal was unattainable. The Transit Authority did not have the money to pay for that and other wage increases. Quill gave in. The strike was averted. The problems, however, would occur two years later.

But if labor had lost a battle for the shorter workweek, the war went on. Van Arsdale threw the CLC fully behind efforts not only for a shorter workweek, but also for a higher minimum wage, and the elimination of poverty. Again, Van Arsdale was attempting to create enlightened entrepreneurs, such as those he had fashioned in the electrical industry, and to have them share more of their gains with their workers. His role would be to broker that agreement.

Van Arsdale prevailed on Mayor Wagner to declare a war on poverty by the city, a reflection of President Johnson's war on poverty. City Council President Paul Screvane was named to head the campaign, and Van Arsdale became a member of the Mayor's Council against Poverty. Screvane told Local 3 members at their regular meeting on February 3, 1964, that "if I had to single out the most important problem confronting us today, not only in our city, but in our state and nation, I would single out the existence of poverty."

Van Arsdale shortly afterward led a delegation of labor leaders to Gracie Mansion to confer with Wagner on the urgent need for a rise in the minimum wage. This was "preaching to the choir" because Wagner was actively supporting this. He signed a law mandating a $1.50 per hour minimum wage for city employees.

Van Arsdale traveled around the United States to spread his gospel. For instance, he spoke before the Industrial Relations Research Association of Wayne State University's Institute of Labor and Industrial Relations in March 1964. He argued that more people working, even at fewer hours, would pump more money into the economy by creating additional consumers with money to spend. He criticized the immorality of employers with "the mentality to hire a human at a wage that he can't sustain his family." One of the major problems, he continued, is that "nobody cares . . . enough" about others, especially those on the economic bottom.[13]

As mentioned previously, Van Arsdale had an abiding interest in aiding the disabled. Bayberry Land was an example of this and so was the CLC's Rehabilitation Liaison Project. It was the first of its kind ever initiated by a city labor council and served to coordinate the rehabilitation and reemployment of disabled workers. Van Arsdale was later to become a champion of Dr. Henry Viscardi, Jr., and his Human Resources Center in Albertson, New York. Viscardi overcame his own severe disabilities to open an industrial facility that provided jobs to other handicapped persons and showed that they were able to work effectively. To aid Viscardi's organization, Van Arsdale established a program whereby all Local 3 officers and representatives and JIB staff who had been members of Local 3 contributed $10 weekly into a payroll fund, administered by the Joint Industry Board. The interest from the funds went to Viscardi's rehabilitation center. This fund continues today.

Van Arsdale would soon lead the CLC into the toughest and most turbulent organizing campaign they would ever undertake: organizing those whom many thought were unorganizable—taxi drivers.

12

Van Arsdale at the Wheel

The struggle to organize New York City taxi drivers was a history of defeats. The first taxi fleet was born in 1907 and eight years later the Chauffeurs Division of the International Brotherhood of Teamsters attempted to organize it, but they were defeated by the fleet owners. The United Auto Workers tried again in 1937 and they failed as well. Michael Quill of the Transport Workers Union took a turn and he gained union recognition in several garages before he, too, was defeated by the fleet owners' roughshod tactics. "Drivers were intimidated not to pay their dues, shop stewards were brutalized by fleet-hired thugs and many were forced to sign petitions denouncing the union if they wished to take out a cab," wrote Charles Vidich in his book, *The New York Cab Driver and His Fare*.[1]

In 1949, John L. Lewis of the United Mine Workers took a turn. He tried to muscle the fleet owners into submission by organizing a strike on April 1, but also to no avail, partly because independent drivers continued to work during the stoppage. Moreover, drivers who had supported Lewis were blackballed, and this made others wary of attempting to unionize.

Dave Beck and the Teamsters Union tried in the late 1950s and failed. Local 102 of the Auto Workers Union was next in 1951, but "they were strictly a racket-ridden union, run to extort monies from the drivers and the management," Vidich wrote.[2]

The past defeats were added onto the mountain of difficulties facing any prospective organizer. Part of the difficulty was the nature of the taxi industry itself. The drivers were individualistic and competitive. Their pay was mostly dependent on how much time and effort they wished to devote to the job, but to approach anything near to a living wage meant a sixty- to seventy-hour week. The competition also made them vulnerable to being manipulated by the taxi fleet owners. The fleets themselves were diverse, centered in individual garages, and this made organizing difficult as well. There were also a great many temporary or part-time drivers and this pool kept changing. Edward Rogoff, in his thesis, "History of the New York Taxicab Industry," wrote "Many who work permanently find it difficult to do so for an extended period of time because of the frequent long hours, constant tension of driving, being treated like a 'servant' by passengers and the danger associated with crime." Unions were put "in the constant position of having to organize and recruit new drivers who often care little about job security, pension benefits or health plans."[3]

Theodore Kheel also said that "it was difficult to organize the drivers because (1) almost half of the taxis in the industry were driven by driver-owners, (2) strong anti-union employers who opposed elections adamantly and also had considerable influence in the city, and (3) it was difficult to reach drivers since they had no central location."[4]

But the full-time drivers felt the need for a taxi union. Needing a decent basic wage scale and benefits, they formed a group called the Taxi Driver Alliance (TDA) and sought a labor leader who could best help their cause. On June 29, 1964, they met with Harry Van Arsdale Jr., and he suggested that they gather 10,000 signatures on a petition to show they had a real base of support within the estimated 22,000 drivers.

The TDA responded by supplying 13,000 signatures. Van Arsdale was mindful of the failures of those before him in attempting to organize this very independent and volatile group of workers, but they had indicated their need and desire and that was enough. Van Arsdale was deeply moved by the plight of the drivers. They were, he felt, badly exploited. The drivers felt that Van Arsdale spoke their language and was not only with them but one of them. He also had influential ties. Former city Labor Commissioner James McFadden said, "His strength is his perseverance. Once he has made up his mind on something he will go after it. Very few people, if any, could talk him out of any of these things."[5]

Van Arsdale established the Taxi Drivers Organizing Committee on September 4, 1964. Jack Townsend, president of the Bartenders Union was named as committee chairman. Chris Plunkett, Van Arsdale's feisty assistant at Local 3, was designated as director, and six other members of Local 3 filled out the Committee. Local 3, moreover, would give inestimable help to the committee by providing the usual shock troops to aid in organizing. Van Arsdale told the Local 3 members: "You are not doing it for me. You're doing it for the workers. You are trying to help them get a better life for their families."[6]

The help given by his Local 3 "legionnaires" was in addition to bringing the full strength of the CLC behind the organizing attempt. Thus, the drivers had financial support, office space, legal staff, and the benefit of experienced, dedicated organizers. No union dues would be assessed against the drivers until the Organizing Committee achieved representation.

Peter Brennan, then president of the Building and Construction Trades Council of Greater New York, described how Van Arsdale went about setting the stage for organization.

> And of course, again, like with the teachers, Harry said, well, let's meet with some of the people who want a union. Let's meet with them. Let's let them tell us why they think they need a union and why they should be part of the AF of L/CIO. And he brought the people in. Harry brought some leaders in, they sat down with some of us . . . okay we know you people know about cabbies that have got things going on the side and making a buck, but that's only a few. There are thousands of taxi drivers [who are] not going home with a decent living and they're putting in twelve hours a day, fourteen hours a day, under rough conditions and trying to support families and educate themselves. So their story, when you listened to it, was no different than the other worker. Regardless of what he or she was working at, it was the same struggle. Look, we want to go home with a decent wage; we want to give our children food on the table, we want to pay the rent; we want to give them an opportunity for an education, have clothes on their back—it was the same story. Everybody was playing it, maybe in a different background, but it was the same thing.
>
> [But] they're so loosely knitted, you had all these different garages all over the city. You had a lot of cab drivers very loyal to the owners of the cabs and you had to break them down. You had to also examine [motives for wanting a union, that is] whether [some] people were looking to raise hell or perhaps were fired for good reason by the owners and this was their way of getting even. Were they sincere and serious about union or were they just doing it to try to give a hard time to the owners of the cabs that they worked for?
>
> So all this had to be sorted out. And Harry appointed a committee to do that. Now one of the unions that really gave its time and effort and money was his own union. Harry's own union took the lead. He and his union members went out and worked hard on the picket lines. I myself went on picket lines with Harry as we did for the teachers and the hospital workers. We did that with the cab drivers. And Harry was able then to show the Central Trades that the majority of the cab drivers were serious. They wanted to belong to a union, would pay their dues and would be a part of the labor movement.

It was a struggle. It was a tough struggle. Because the employers, most of them, fought back very hard. They used all kinds of gimmicks, including muscle. Bringing in goons to try to discourage the cab drivers from joining the union. There were a lot of scuffles on picket lines, involving the police and so forth. But Harry stayed with it. He had a number of the union leaders with him and of course his own union being out front.[7]

Van Arsdale enlisted the support of Mayor Wagner in the drive to organize the drivers, a move calculated to bolster the spirits of the drivers and show that they had the sympathy of powerful politicians. Wagner told 260 driver representatives on September 14 that "the greatest thing that working people can do is to join a fine and good union to see that they get a break." He also told the representatives that he meant to ensure that a proposed increase in the taxi fare be of benefit to the drivers and "not enhance the coffers of the taxi owners."[8]

By September 30, 18,287 signatures had been secured on membership enrollment cards and petitions, and Van Arsdale told a cheering audience of drivers at a mass meeting at Manhattan Center: "I hope that there are enough modern-thinking fleet owners whose wise judgement will make it possible for you to achieve your goal without resorting to a strike. We are serving notice that the taxi drivers in New York City are closing ranks and will not any longer be subjected to harassment or intimidation by fleet owners."[9]

But the fleet owners were a tough bunch, used to the rough-and-tumble world of making a living on the streets of New York. They fought back hard. First, despite the petition drive, they used the proposed fare increase as an argument against unionization, saying that the increased revenue would add, *ipso facto*, to the driver's wages inasmuch as they were entitled, by previous practice, to 44 percent of the fare. Thus, if the fare hike was approved by city agencies there would be no need for a union.

Van Arsdale charged the fleet owners with blacklisting and harassing drivers who were pro-union. He called on Mayor Wagner to investigate. The fleet owners retreated. The fare increase was voted and the owners promised to give more to the drivers. Van Arsdale pursued other inequities, such as "shape-ups," in which men would gather in a group to be selected individually for work. The method was open to corruption and bribery of the dispatchers who made the selections. Van Arsdale forced a crackdown on the practices by the Police Department's Hack Bureau.

Van Arsdale continued to marshal his forces for the fight. At a rousing meeting of drivers February 10, 1965, he told them of the CLC's full support and said: "I tell you that since we have come to help you build a decent union, I have seen men grow 10 feet tall." Their fight was not only one against injustice, but "it is also a fight to insure that men and women can enjoy a better way of life." He spoke of the plight of garage workers—mechanics, washers, greasers—who were not receiving the protection of the federal wage and hour law.

"We compiled cases and protested to the Wage and Hour Division," he continued. "We were shocked to learn that in 1961 the nation's fleet owners had sufficient influence to have the inside workers exempt from Wage and Hour Law provisions. The issue is being investigated and we have discussed it with Senators Robert Kennedy and Jacob K. Javits because we think there was a miscarriage of justice in granting that exemption."[10]

The following day, Van Arsdale told Local 3 members at their regular general meeting "we are going to organize every garage 100 percent. . . . We don't like strikes. We don't like the hardships which come with strikes, but the taxi drivers are ready and impatient and if there is a strike of taxi drivers in this city, it must be a successful strike and must have the support of every trade unionist. . . . We must demonstrate to the taxi drivers' employers that we are not going to tolerate any continuation of injustice."[11]

As the organizing campaign gathered momentum, the organizing committee decided that a show of strength was needed and the threats of work stoppages became more insistent. A troubled Mayor Wagner met with committee representatives at Gracie Mansion on March 6 in an effort to stave off the threatened walkout, but Van Arsdale could offer no guarantee.

In the midst of the organizing drive, Van Arsdale and Morris Iushewitz went to Selma, Alabama, at the invitation of Dr. Martin Luther King, Jr., to lend support to a drive to enable African Americans to register and vote. But he also spoke to the embattled drivers in New York by a special telephone hook-up to a special meeting on March 14. He compared the tactics of those in the South who opposed granting civil rights to African Americans to the situation in New York.

"This hypocrisy is very similar to the hypocrisy of the Metropolitan Taxicab Board of Trade which would like the public to think that they are standing by democratic procedures in wanting the taxi drivers to have an NRLB election in which they would attempt to split the taxicab drivers' vote between two unions and lessen their chances for any union. . . . All I can say to one and all is to close ranks and keep things rolling and we'll be back after we meet with Reverend Martin Luther King; that is, we hope we'll be back. Morris and I wish you well."[12]

The prestige of Van Arsdale and the CLC was at stake even as it was during the hospital workers strike. The walkout began March 23 and 8,000 Local 3 members helped man the picket lines at ninety garages. They had voted to spend a "holiday" on the picket lines and would make up the time lost the following Saturday, working at regular rates.

To show the all-out nature of the drive and the importance with which it was viewed by all of organized labor, Van Arsdale got George Meany to send a telegram to the strikers, and it was read at a March 24 rally. Meany wrote, "Please assure the New York taxicab drivers that the organizing campaign has the unqualified support of the American Federation of Labor and the Congress of Industrial Organizations. It is high time that these workers who are so important to the life of our city, are paid the kind of wages, hours, [and achieve the] working conditions that their services deserve."

An estimated 9,000 taxi industry workers attended the rally at Madison Square Garden. Van Arsdale, ever mindful of the effect of labor actions on the public, counseled an end to the strike, saying in part: "If that power of organization that you have could be directed only against the fleet owners, I might go along with you, but that power also affects the public and a lot of people who have no way of getting around." The workers then voted to end the walkout eighteen hours after it had begun.[13]

The taxi workers appeared to have won a victory when a three-man panel, chaired by Theodore Kheel, recommended that a citywide secret ballot election be held to determine representation. Only those who worked three or more days a week could vote. The owners rejected the recommendations, however, and insisted on garage balloting with part-timers voting.

This brought new conflicts, and six wildcat strikes occurred before May 7. Mayor Wagner ordered that a nonbinding election be held by the city Labor Department with only workers who put in three or more days a week on the job allowed to vote, thus excluding moonlighters who would have little to lose. The NLRB supervised the balloting. The owners opposed the move, but the election was held, with 12,326 workers voting out of an estimated 16,000 who were eligible. But because of the fleet owners' request for an injunction, the ballots were uncounted until a federal judge could rule on the application to bar the vote. The Taxi Drivers Organizing Committee reacted by authorizing a strike either citywide or against individual fleet owners. Angry drivers began selective walkouts. More fuel was added to the fire when the NLRB dismissed charges brought by the committee against thirty-six fleet owners and their bargaining agent, the Metropolitan Board of Trade, for refusing to bargain. Van Arsdale told Mayor Wagner that the situation "has reached its most critical stage because the employers haven't shown any inclination to recognize the fact that the men want a union." Thus, on June 28, drivers went on strike against the owners of 7,000 cabs in every borough except Staten Island. On the same date, the NLRB ordered that union representation elections be held in thirty-eight garages, turning down the committee's request for citywide elections. The NLRB also allowed drivers who worked only two days a week to vote. Opposing the committee on the ballot was Teamsters Local 826. Violence mounted with 132 incidents in the first four days of the strike. The Teamsters charged that Van Arsdale was "trying to bring the industry to its knees." Van Arsdale countered by saying that sympathy strikes were also possible.

Michael Mann, AFL-CIO regional director, had this comment on the turbulence of the period and also offered an insightful anecdote on how Van Arsdale operated.

> During the course of the struggle to organize the cabs which took several years, we had several strikes. And talking about the guts of this man Van Arsdale, I remember in particular one strike situation we had [involving] the Classic Cab Company which is up in the Bronx somewhere. And we were in the middle of a very, very vicious strike.
>
> We couldn't agree with the employers on a contract. This was pretty much in the early days of the drive and we decided there's only one way in which we could handle this and we called a strike, a citywide strike. We closed down the City. And it lasted for several days until we got word that the Classic Cab was going to open up its doors and roll the cabs as an incentive to the other employers of the Taxi Association that they also could break the strike in that way.
>
> So what we did was we mobilized our people—we had about . . . around a hundred and fifty, two hundred taxi drivers in front of the Classic garage on the day that we heard that they were going to roll the cabs or try to roll the cabs during the period of the strike.
>
> Well, I remember there was a great big wagon load there with the tactical police, not the regular cops, but with the cops that they use for real strong arm stuff. They were all packed in a great big blue van and they were parked just outside of the doors of the garage.
>
> And then in addition to that, the precinct had about fifty or seventy-five uniformed cops and God knows how many plainclothesmen they had. We had about two hundred fifty or two hundred people there in front of the garage. And as the doors were opened to let a new cab go in there to get gas and be ready to roll, we could see more cops inside.
>
> In any event, the situation got to be pretty bad. And this is where I saw what Van Arsdale meant when he used to be working very closely with big business organizations [or] so-called civic organizations. . . . And I often wondered why he gave so much time in being at their meetings and addressing their meetings, and he was always very, very nice in terms of, "Look, you do what's fair to us and we'll do what's fair to you" that kind of stuff. And I wondered why he wasted his time in meeting with these big men of the city on the opposite side of the labor movement. I found out at the taxi drivers' Classic situation why.

The cops were giving us a real bad time even before the doors opened up to roll out the cabs. And there was a little mom and pop candy store on the corner and then Van suddenly said to me, he says, "Mike, come on! Let's go!" and Van had a habit of running. He never walked. He kept running in a sort of an ungainly fashion. And he got in [the store]. There was a little telephone booth in there. And there was a man on the telephone. And Van very politely asked the man if he would leave, that he had an urgent call.

And this guy, whoever he was, a very nice man, he hung up. And Van got in there and he says, "Mike, listen" and he called City Hall. And he asked for the Mayor. At that time that was Bob Wagner. And the people who answered the phone at City Hall said that the Mayor was not in. He was sick at Gracie Mansion. Van had his little notebook and he got the number right away and called Gracie Mansion. And somebody answered the phone and they say, "the Mayor is ill and he can't be reached." So Van said, "It's important." And the guy says to him, whoever it was, he says, "No, the Mayor can't talk to you." Van says, "Well, you go in and tell the Mayor that Harry Van Arsdale is calling." And sure enough, the Mayor got on the telephone [from his] bed, and he and Van had a discussion. Now, Van told him he didn't want to bother him, but there was going to be an ugly situation here at Classic. The cops were more than rough. And he recognized they were entitled to protect property, life, limb and all that, but at the rate they're going all hell would break loose and he wanted the Mayor to know that the Union—the Central Trades Council and the Taxicab Drivers Union would not be responsible for whatever took place. So the Mayor evidently told Van, "Get the captain in charge of that to calm down and talk to me." And Van asked me to run back to the line. I got ahold [sic] of the captain, brought him down. The captain talked to the Mayor. Rather, the Mayor talked to the captain. The captain went back and inside of a minute the doors rolled up and nearly all the police who were in there came out. The big truck with the tactical police moved on. A few more police remained, and that was the end of that. The cabs never rolled. And that was when I realized why Van had given so much time to the City organizations even though they weren't actually a part of the labor movement.[14]

Representatives of the fleet owners and the committee were subsequently called to City Hall for talks on July 3. Van Arsdale said he would "be glad to do anything I can do to settle the strike." As a result of the meeting, Vincent Impellitteri was named to be a taxi industry "Czar" to hear and settle grievances until representation elections covering about half of the garages could be held on July 21. Van Arsdale felt the move "could end the strike [and was] a genuine effort to find a solution." The strike ended on July 4—its seventh day.

The committee won in the great majority of the garages. "The sweeping victory by the taxicab drivers should make clear for all time that these men are going to build a successful union and the maneuvers that have been used by the employers have not worked and will not work," said Van Arsdale. "These taxicab drivers are the best trade union men I've seen in a long time. It will be a great union and a tribute to the community. We hope the employers have learned to enter into general collective bargaining with us."[15]

But the battle was far from over. The fleet owners stalled on holding elections in the remaining garages. They also challenged the results of the July 21 voting. Van Arsdale collected 15,000 signatures on a new petition, which was sent to President Johnson asking him to order the NLRB to settle the matter. When the NLRB continued to delay, the committee threatened another strike. This threat got the NLRB to move and the Committee was confirmed as the bargaining agent in a majority of the garages. The owners still stalled. The issue had now dragged into a new year and there was a new mayor at the helm: Republican John Lindsay. Van Arsdale felt he had no recourse but to threaten another strike against the fleet garages unless a contract was achieved by May 15, 1966. "Our men do not want a strike," he said. "It would be an unfortunate thing. . . . But we have been 21 months forming this union and we can't go further than May 15 to get a contract."

Nevertheless, 2,000 drivers walked out of thirteen garages on May 11 over the key issue of a higher share of fares. Mayor Lindsay began marathon talks at City Hall between both sides. On the sixth day, after a twenty-two hour bargaining session, the strike ended. Van Arsdale and Lindsay jointly announced the settlement: Mayor Lindsay would decide on the wage increase in binding arbitration. He issued his decision on May 28, 1966, and the drivers achieved most of their demands. That July, the drivers union was chartered by the AFL-CIO as Local 3036, New York City Taxi Drivers Union, representing 28,000 drivers and other workers in eighty-two garages.

In a message to all Local members, Van Arsdale compared the union success to a newborn baby that would require care and nourishment in order to grow. "The future advancement of workers depends on intelligent thought and intelligent action," he said. "There are no shortcuts. Building an effective union is a difficult job that needs the active help of every individual member. Eternal vigilance is the price of good trade unionism."[16]

Van Arsdale directly took on the task of nurturing the infant he had brought into the world. He was named interim president of the Local on June 29, 1966, and then officially its president, taking no salary, the following November.

He was now the leader of two union locals: Local 3 and Local 3036, with a combined membership of about 65,000, and president of the Central Labor Council, which represented more than 1 million city workers. He was without a doubt, as if any had existed before, "Mister Labor" in New York City, the man to see about labor matters.

But the crown of the taxi union was not one he had sought. It was thrust upon him:

> Harry was the President of that union, while he was President of the Central Trades, in order to get the thing sorted out properly. Harry agreed, not that he wanted it—he wasn't looking for that job, that wasn't his reason for organizing them. They asked him to take the leadership, the AFL/CIO wanted him to take it, because they had to have somebody who was an experienced man in the labor movement and could help them to get together, and he did that. And once they elected officers and worked with Harry, he'd seen that they had the ability. He suggested . . . to them that they go ahead and elect their own officers and run their own affair.[17]

But before Van Arsdale was to turn over the reins of office to others, he led the taxi drivers through other tumultuous negotiations while building them into a strong and progressive union. He led the drivers out on a fifteen-day strike that began December 4, 1970, on issues that included wage increases, better pensions, vacations, holidays, and sick benefits. After the strike was settled, the situation remained contentious due to Mayor Lindsay's proposition for a taxi commission to regulate the industry and the drivers. Van Arsdale opposed the plan because he feared it would put gypsy cabs on a par with medallion taxis. The commission proposal was "garbage," he said. He criticized Mayor Lindsay's support of the commission as a "charade to legalize gypsy cabs and to penalize owner-drivers."[18]

The commission, however, was created. The drivers again struck—for one day—in 1974, and negotiations were again marked by acrimony and divisiveness. Irving Stern, director of the United Food and Commercial Workers International Union, described the situation:

> The taxi drivers were indeed an unruly lot and, as one might observe, unappreciative of the effort to bring the benefits of collective bargaining to their industry. Many of them were transients, and unappreciative, and lacked the understanding of the work and effort that went into their organization.
>
> Some later turned against Harry, and even though he was an unpaid president of the Taxi Workers Organizing Committee, they expected that he would deliver at first blush a contract comparable to the benefits of perhaps the electrical workers that had had 75 years of organization. After all, hadn't they not been gracious enough to sign a card and weren't they entitled for their signature to the benefits of 75 or 100 years of organization?

I was constantly amazed that despite Harry's tough-minded attitudes, he really believed that taxi drivers would make good trade unionists and never anticipated that they would turn against him and others in the union. Despite everything that this union had done for them in terms of benefits, and coverage and improvements in conditions.

I think it has something to do with sitting 8 to 10 hours a day on a hard seat and navigating New York traffic, [which] makes you surly, belligerent and difficult, and Harry was the victim since seemingly the employer was now under control and who else was there to blame for the hard life they were compelled to live. . . .

Harry never regretted for one moment and even though, in my judgment, knowing what he put into it, knowing the nights and days and effort and vigor and determination and the heartache he suffered in this campaign to organize these people he never once complained in all the years and in all the hours I was with him about their attitude particularly prior to the period when he resigned as acting president of the taxi driver's union.

Harry never complained about the taxi drivers. He always thought it was some personal shortcoming that caused it. I don't think he really meant it—just that he had a need never to criticize workers. They were after all rank and file workers and you had to accept them as they are and he wouldn't condemn them—at least some of those who were outrageous in their behavior—for their attitudes. In every sense of the word he was a man, a mensch is really the word and he only relished the joys of the organizing and never the sorrows or the pain of some of the bad times flowing from that organization.[19]

It was reported at the time that Van Arsdale intended to resign from his post as president of the Local, but that did not happen until March 21, 1977. By then he had succeeded in giving the taxi drivers an organization that shared many of the same types of benefits he had achieved for workers in the electrical industry.

In his remarks to the executive board, he urged that Local 3036 Vice President Benjamin Goldberg replace him as president. Goldberg did. (Goldberg was later to say that "If Harry tells me to jump out of a window, I jump first and then I ask why did he tell me to do it?")[20] Van Arsdale also spoke of the achievements made by the local leadership including the establishment of a pension fund in their first contract, which he said no other union that he was aware of had ever accomplished, a scholarship fund, and death benefits. And, he added, this was from employers not known for their generosity.

So sometimes you wonder if whether the effort you make is worthwhile. Somebody in your family may ask why do you give so much time to that union and accuse you of neglecting your family because of it. But even if nobody else knows it, you can be proud you played a part in bringing the union into existence. . . . I'm very proud of having been associated with you men and having the responsibility and taking on the responsibilities and taking on the abuse that went with it [and] working for most of the time for less than if you had put in that many hours in your cab, and that is going on today. And the fact that you have done it, well—I am always proud to be associated with people like that. And I don't just say that to blow smoke or just on this occasion or in this room. . . . And if my advice means anything, I say "close ranks behind your union" . . . and when you run across a fella that says "What am I going to get out of it? Why should I be interested in it? Why should I go to a meeting? Why should I help strengthen the union?" Just let that fella know there wouldn't be a union if it hadn't been for people like yourselves or others . . . who made a contribution. . . . When I was young, one thing I heard over and over again was "Keep the union strong. Keep the union strong."

Van Arsdale also expounded on the idea that a union is not measured in wage increases or monetary considerations alone, but also in brotherhood: "I think that the brotherhood, the friendship, the fraternalism, the assistance that you have extended to so many hundreds, so many thousands of the members has a value that you can't add up," he said. "And what you have done in your own way to be helpful to your brother and sister members and that should not be overlooked in any analysis or discussion of the work you are involved in." He also urged the executive board members to seek out other workers who need help in organizing and give them what they now enjoyed in their own local contracts.

Van Arsdale apologized for not being able to spend more time on local affairs in the past year, but explained he had been busy trying to help deal with the city's fiscal crisis. He also pointed out that he had worked without salary as their president and had been reimbursed only occasionally for expenses.

He had high praise for the taxi drivers in the city whom he said had made a great contribution to it and pointed out that they were engaged in the second largest means of transportation in the city. "They perform a public service," he said. "They are out in the cold, [they are out] in the warm weather and in what everybody agrees is the worst traffic in the nation and possibly anywhere else in the world." He said the taxi driver often has to work long hours to make ends meet and must endure danger and the abuse of riders.

The taxi driver should be appreciated. He doesn't get any percentage of the credit he is entitled to. And I'm saying this very seriously based on my association with you men and things I knew about taxi drivers before I met you because I grew up in a neighborhood where working people drove cabs and I knew something of the problems they had. . . . I have been paying my dues and I will continue to pay my dues. And I will be honored to be a member. And in some time in the future I hope to have more time to spend with you because being associated with you has been one of the most interesting experiences I have had in all the years I have been in the American labor movement.

Van Arsdale left the podium to thunderous applause, causing him to admonish the local leaders that "if you keep that up, you will wake the neighbors."[21]

As a sign of gratitude, Van Arsdale was declared president emeritus of the Local and a $5,000 scholarship was established in his name to be awarded to the son or daughter of a member of Local 3036.

The taxi wars of 1965–66 had given Van Arsdale his first experience with John Lindsay. Lindsay had always enjoyed CLC support while he was a congressman because of his pro-labor stance even though the Council endorsed (albeit barely) Abraham Beame in the race for mayor. Van Arsdale publicly took a positive view of Lindsay, saying "He has youth, vigor and vision." However, he would never enjoy the same kind of relationship with Lindsay that he had with Wagner and Rockefeller. Theodore Kheel stated that "Lindsay was not an easy man to get along with; he was rather pompous and stiff. Harry didn't get along with Lindsay and that was Lindsay's loss."[22] Armand D'Angelo was more blunt. The relationship between Lindsay and Van Arsdale, he said, was "very cold. Distant and cold. And if Harry could avoid him. He'd avoid him."[23]

One labor leader who did take an active and extremely vocal dislike of Lindsay was Michael J. Quill, the peppery leader of the Transport Workers Union (TWU), with 35,000 subway and bus members, who called the Yale-educated mayor "a pipsqueak." Quill led the TWU into a crushing thirteen-day work stoppage that began on New Year's Day 1966. Van Arsdale once more had a strong hand in the settlement and in helping the TWU achieve its goals.

The TWU had informed the city's Metropolitan Transit Authority (MTA) of its contract demands in July 1965, but negotiations had dragged on, with the MTA showing few signs of compromise. The key issue was a wage increase that the union felt was especially necessary because of the inflation caused by the burgeoning Vietnam conflict.

Following his election in November 1965, Lindsay showed no willingness to participate in the MTA talks, and the MTA, under little pressure, made no offers. Lindsay, in fact, showed his indifference to the talks by vacationing in Puerto Rico even under increasingly loud threats of a strike by the TWU.

On the strike's first day, Lindsay prompted the MTA to seek an injunction, which elicited a war cry from Quill: "If they think they can put us in jail and break the strike, they're wrong. The strike will go on."[24] The injunction was granted and Quill, with a dangerously ailing heart, was ordered jailed. He told reporters on the fourth day of the strike: "The judge can drop dead in his black robes. I don't care if I rot in jail. I will not call off the strike."[25] Van Arsdale and the Council voiced total support of the TWU. Van Arsdale also led taxi drivers onto a TWU picket line.

On January 6, Lindsay said Van Arsdale would strive to have negotiations resumed. Van Arsdale also lobbied intensively to have Quill and other TWU leaders released from jail. Quill was in custody, but also hospitalized because of his heart ailment. Theodore Kheel told of a secret meeting with Quill that took place beside his hospital bed. Quill, unable to talk, raised four fingers before Kheel and Deputy Mayor Robert Price. This represented the dollar-an-hour amount by which the strike could be settled.

After the strike ended, Quill declared that Van Arsdale had been a key figure in helping to resolve the dispute along with mediators Kheel, Nathan Feinsinger, and Sylvester Garrett. Van Arsdale helped to secure Quill's victory. Kheel told of a behind-the-scenes maneuver by Van Arsdale that cemented the raises given to the TWU and spiked the possibility of another devastating strike.

Quill died shortly after the end of the strike and was succeeded by Matthew Guinan. "And at that point, a taxpayer had commenced an action against the [Metropolitan] Transit Authority claiming that the wage increase was illegal under the Condon-Wadlin law because the employees, having engaged in a strike, were not entitled to a wage increase," Kheel said. The presiding judge called the mayor and informed him that the law would have to prevail and Lindsay replied that he, therefore, had no choice but to invalidate the settlement. "When Guinan got this news, he was in a state of panic," Kheel said. "The strike had been very unpopular and if the settlement was set aside what does Matty Guinan do? Have his men go out on strike again or accept the decision and [in effect] get no increase. "Matty Guinan went to Van Arsdale in a state of panic. 'I don't know what to do.'"

Van Arsdale then did what he often did in such cases, which is what he also did during the taxi dispute: he called on his friends in high places. In the transit situation, it was Nelson Rockefeller.

"Harry Van Arsdale called Nelson Rockefeller on his private number in Albany and got him on the phone and explained the dilemma Matthew Guinan was facing, and Rockefeller [then] introduced legislation that amended the Condon-Wadlin law as it applied to the Transit Workers only—retroactively—so there was no violation. It was unheard of. And that saved the day and

Harry Van Arsdale did it. I don't know what would have happened if he had not done that."[26]

After the strike, both Lindsay and Rockefeller created committees to study legislation to replace the Condon-Wadlin Act. Van Arsdale and other state and city labor officials vehemently opposed the action. "Let's stop thinking that by passing bills and passing laws and enforcing them, that we're going to change everything," Van Arsdale said. "The Condon-Wadlin Law indicates it could not be done. So, I think it would be another mistake to pass more laws. I think that organized labor will oppose any such action by legislators."[27]

Van Arsdale also issued a statement at another time apparently in view of the contemplated legislative action. The undated statement read:

> A city is made up of people—some are union members, some are not. *All* of them, regardless of union affiliation have suffered greatly as a result of the impasse in bargaining in the recent transit situation. *All* of them, re-gardless of union affiliation are determined that it must not happen again and yet we know that unless there is a substantial accommodation of view and positions and unless new agreed-upon procedures are developed, it *could* happen again [emphases in original].
>
> Speaking for the Central Labor Trade and Union Council, I want to assure the people of this city that the Council is determined to assist all men of good will in a search for ways to avoid in the future the hardships suffered by all in the first 12 days of 1966. If we do not exert ourselves to the utmost to advance that objective we do not deserve to be in the union movement.
>
> Fortunately, acting wisely in advance of the present situation, ex-Mayor Wagner, last Fall established a committee to review all of the problems of bargaining between the City and representatives of City Employees. Mayor Lindsay on taking office warmly endorsed and continued this committee. . . . The important feature of this committee is that it is tripartite. In addition to important city officials and distinguished public members, it includes, as full partners in its deliberations, the leaders of the principal organization representing city employees.
>
> The committee is embarked on its work. First priority consideration on its agenda is being given to the possibility of working out agreed-upon procedures for dealing with the difficult problem of deadlocks in city bar-gaining.
>
> The Council wishes it to be known that this committee has its unstint[ing] support. This committee, in my judgement, offers the greatest promise of finding ways to avoid the unfortunate experiences of the past. The com-mittee should be given a full and fair opportunity to develop its ideas and to seek to reach agreement around the table. Precipitating moves by other

well-meaning groups may satisfy a compulsion to act rapidly in the wake of the transit strike, but without labor participation such action might not achieve the desired goals. Without the good-faith partnership, assistance and responsible commitment of the New York City labor movement, who can feel confident that any new procedures or gimmicks will work?

This is a time to cooperate and exercise restraints in the interest of making this a better place in which all of the people can work and live. Nobody has a monopoly on this project, We must all form a partnership to strive for the good of our city and the welfare of all its people.[28]

Van Arsdale also moved to strengthen ties with Mayor Lindsay as part of his constant strategy to win the friendship and cooperation of officials in a position to help or hurt the working man. "Lindsay is much bigger in the city and nationally as a result of his performance in this thing," he said. Did Lindsay gain a pro-labor image? Van Arsdale was asked. "He's got a pro-people image," Van Arsdale said. "I think everybody feels he made a great effort."[29]

It was typical of Van Arsdale to try to put the best face on everything. He was a bridge builder, not a bridge burner. And part of his image was of a man busily racing around the city trying to build those bridges between labor and management or to repair them. Moreover, in a city the size of New York, many bridges would need attention simultaneously so that Van Arsdale had to attend to several at one time. He was undoubtedly the busiest labor fireman of any city labor leader.

One conflagration was a strike by welfare workers. It preceded the transit strike, and was to have an even more profound effect on public employee labor relations in the state.

As a member of a fact-finding committee, Van Arsdale helped to try to work out a formula to settle the strike by the Social Service Employees Union and Local 371 of the American Federation of State, County, and Municipal Employees. The strike began on January 3, 1965, and lasted through the month. The fact-finders reached a "basic agreement" that called for the city to submit all issues in the strike to "advisory" arbitration. The sticking point was the state's Condon-Wadlin Act, which barred a strike by public employees on pain of automatic dismissal. However, after a hearing, the employee could be reinstated, but would be docked two days pay for each day on strike, among other penalties. The fact-finders could see no way around it, but the unions wanted amnesty. When they believed they could not achieve that, they rejected the fact-finding panel's recommendations.

Van Arsdale and the CLC, however, continued to work. Van Arsdale and David Dubinsky met with AFL-CIO president George Meany in New York to try to help mediate the dispute, which was intensified by the arrest of sixteen strike leaders for ignoring an injunction to halt the walkout.

Mayor Wagner responded to the entreaties of the labor leaders by empaneling a citizens' task force to reopen direct negotiations. The panel's recommendations called for economic issues to be considered by a fact-finding unit; the city and the unions to join in legal action to free the jailed strike leaders; the union to obtain a stay of the Condon-Wadlin provisions against the strikers; a court test of the constitutionality of Condon-Wadlin provisions on pay docking with the outcome binding on all parties; and no retaliation against those who struck nor against those who crossed the picket lines. The city and the unions accepted the recommendations and on the twenty-eighth day the strike ended. The machinery was also set in motion to repeal the Condon-Wadlin Act. However, it would be two years before the state legislature would enact a substitute bill: the Taylor Law.

Although Van Arsdale and other labor leaders had lobbied against penalizing a striking union, the Taylor Law mandated a $10,000 fine against a union for every day it was on strike and loss of dues check-off privileges for eighteen months. Each striker could also face penalties ranging from a reprimand to dismissal. Through Van Arsdale's efforts, the Council softened the provisions of the measure, which had put a strain on his friendship with Governor Rockefeller—as had the governor's veto of a $1.50 per hour minimum wage bill.

Van Arsdale and the CLC had lobbied to prevent Rockefeller from vetoing the bill, which the governor said would drive industry from the state. It was one of the few times that Rockefeller would not take Van Arsdale's counsel. Van Arsdale said he was "shocked" by the veto, which he said had "dealt a devastating blow" to the aspirations of low wage earners. A campaign was begun to induce the state legislature to overturn the veto.

A New York Times editorial had praised the governor's action. In a letter to the Times, Van Arsdale countered that low-income families might be forced to accept welfare payments in order to make ends meet: "As trade-unionists we abhor the idea of workers in a democratic society forced to live on municipal charity, which is what relief is, because however hard they work, their reward is insufficient for decent human existence." He said the labor movement could not wait for the federal government to get around to raising the minimum wage, but would attempt to achieve it through collective bargaining, which might lead to strikes or other "needless difficulties." "We cannot and will not wait. The labor movement of this state, during the days of Al Smith, Senator Robert Wagner, Franklin D. Roosevelt and Herbert H. Lehman helped to pioneer great social experiments. We intend to revive the traditions of that era."[30]

Through the efforts of Van Arsdale and other trade unionists, a labor-backed compromise bill was passed by the legislature, signed by Governor

Rockefeller in mid-1966, and went into effect on January 1, 1967. It gave New York State the highest minimum wage standard of any state in the nation.

Another victory for Van Arsdale and Local 3 was the passage of the electrical industry's self-insured Workmen's Compensation Bill on March 29, 1966. Local 3's legislative committee had waged an intensive campaign for the bill. It provided for increased Workmen's Compensation Benefits for Local 3 members employed by electrical contractors. The new benefits were far above the previous $60 maximum. Members of Local 3 could enjoy generous benefits without having the employers pay exorbitant premiums.

Van Arsdale continued to strengthen his ties with Lindsay. The mayor conferred with him on the appointment of a city hall labor liaison aide in March 1966, with Van Arsdale commenting that such an appointment "might help to develop greater understanding between the administration" and labor in the city.[31] Lindsay later appointed Van Arsdale as one of the labor members of the Public Development Corporation, which was established to stimulate industrial growth in the city. Van Arsdale and the CLC also proposed a plan to improve community relations in the city following the rejection of the Police Department's Civilian Review Board by the voters.

Van Arsdale, Local 3, and the CLC had also campaigned hard for the passage of a state Medicare bill, and Governor Rockefeller signed the bill in a ceremony at the JIB auditorium in Queens with Van Arsdale and other Local 3 and CLC leaders, as well as Local 3 members, looking on. Rockefeller said it was an "honor and a privilege" to sign the legislation in the presence of hundreds of members of Local 3 because "Harry and this union" had fought hard for its passage.

But shortly after that, personal tragedy struck Van Arsdale. On May 26, 1966, his wife Molly died at home of a sudden heart attack.

She had been his childhood sweetheart, and she had kept their family together when he was away. Molly cared for his parents as they became elderly and ill. Her loss affected him deeply, causing him to reflect on his own advancing age. He had greatly broadened his responsibilities with the presidencies of the Central Labor Council and Taxi Local 3036. He was also becoming more and more involved with the public employee unions and this meant greater involvement with the elected officials who dealt directly with those unions. Moreover, he came to see himself as a spokesman for all the city's unions, and champion of all causes that affected working men and women. He wanted to achieve for all unions the higher standards that he had secured for Local 3, but the battlefield was now bigger and the union leadership more diverse and independent. The latter included the officials of public employee unions, like Victor Gotbaum of District Council 37, Jerry Wurf of the American Federation of State, County, and Municipal Employees, and Albert Shanker of the United Federation of Teachers. Although they had the highest regard for Van Arsdale, they also were uneasy about his close relationship with Governor Rockefeller. The governor, they feared, may have been using Van Arsdale more than Van Arsdale was using the governor. Some observers felt that Rockefeller was polishing his liberal Republican image by taking labor's part when it suited him and cementing the support of the state AFL-CIO and the CLC by endorsing capital improvements that provided jobs for the building trades.[32] But they failed to give Van Arsdale enough credit for his pragmatism. Van Arsdale sought to have a united trade union movement that he could use as leverage for gains with the powers-that-be who controlled the fate of workers. He was unaffected by flattery from on high. He accepted myriad committee appointments, on federal as well as state and local levels. Those appointments gave him the opportunity to meet and influence power brokers, and to further educational and social causes he believed in.

But something had to give in his schedule as his civic responsibilities grew. His work with Local 3 was behind him. The structure he had built was strong and needed only maintenance and nurturing in order to remain healthy and grow. With that in mind, he began preparations to turn the reins of the Local over to his son, Thomas, so that he could deal with burgeoning labor, social, and fiscal problems in the city.

13

A Wider Garden to Tend

"Harry was like George Meany, the president of the AFL-CIO, in that he was the man that unions appealed and applied to when there was trouble in the House of Labor; Harry played a parallel role in New York City," said Donald Menagh, Sr., who, as attorney for the Central Labor Council, worked closely with Van Arsdale for many years.[1]

On August 12, 1968, the way was made even clearer for Van Arsdale to play this role because that was the date he stepped down as business manager of Local 3. His son Thomas replaced him on a vote of the Local 3 executive board immediately after Harry announced his resignation. Thomas had graduated from the electrical engineering curriculum at Rensselaer Polytechnic Institute and joined Local 3 upon discharge from the World War II navy. He was well prepared for this position. Harry remained an officer by filling the position of financial secretary, replacing Albert Mackie who had retired.

Elected to Local 3's executive board in 1953, Thomas was appointed an assistant business manager in June 1965 after a long and distinguished union record of service in a series of responsible, prestigious posts. His father told the local staff, "we worked as a team throughout our long association and I am confident that this same teamwork will prevail during your relationship with your new business manager, Thomas Van Arsdale, who has the experience, training and dedication to do his job as Business Manager for the good of the members of Local 3."[2]

Harry Van Arsdale then turned to aid unions in the public sector. James McFadden, former assistant labor commissioner under Mayor Wagner, said: "When Wagner got elected in 1953, one of the first things he pledged was a Little Wagner Act, recognizing the public employee unions. . . . Van Arsdale is a trade unionist and believed in the fact that there should be government employee unions. So Harry Van Arsdale can certainly take credit for the support he gave to the idea [of the Little Wagner Act]. . . . And it was constant support. . . . The real growth in the labor movement in the last ten or fifteen years has been in the government sector and certainly it got its start with Van Arsdale."[3]

Theodore Kheel also observed:

The public sector unions became more important in labor/management relations. The private sector unions weakened in this last ten or fifteen years [of Van Arsdale's tenure]. The public sector union leaders became interested in recognition: Victor Gotbaum, Al Shanker, Johnny DeLury, the firemen and so forth. They had common interests and they began to look to each other rather than to the Central Labor Council. Harry was very anxious to be of service to them and he called upon me to be of assistance. But they weren't particularly interested in assistance. They weren't interested in giving credit to anybody. They wanted to handle it themselves and you couldn't fault them and the result was the Municipal Labor Coalition. . . . What does the Central Labor Council do? The unions are all autonomous. The Central Labor Council is a service organization. It is to the unions of New York City what the AFL-CIO is to the International Unions. Looking at it another way, it is what the NAM [National Association of Manufacturers] or the Chamber of Commerce is to business.

It's a service organization. It does not represent the workers. It doesn't bargain for them. Now, I think the absolutely splendid example of what Harry did is that he set out to be of service to the member unions. In that respect it was tremendously important for him to have access to political leaders. See? All of the unions, but most particularly the public sector unions, have dealings with government, whether it's on legislation restricting their rights or guaranteeing their rights, or collateral matters having to do with whatever. All of them have lobbyists in Albany and they're very much involved in political affairs, but they are also dealing with their employers. In the private sector they deal with politicians because of what politicians can do to their employers so there is a difference. Now, Harry's usefulness to the members depended on his access to political leaders.

The man he had the best access with that was absolutely a work of art on both sides, was Nelson Rockefeller. When Harry met Rockefeller, who was a genius in his own way, he said, "Harry, here is my private number. If you've got any problem, call me on this number. You get me directly."[4]

And that is what Van Arsdale did in the transit strike in 1966 and on other occasions.

"Mr. Van Arsdale moves endlessly around the city, using telephones to offer advice to unions, politicians and businessmen and trying to ease troubled situations, hopefully to labor's advantage," wrote reporter Peter Millones in the *New York Times*.[5]

To businessmen sometimes that advice could be aimed at nothing more than getting them to understand the personality and problems of the working man and woman and to empathize with their needs. Brian McLaughlin speaks of this and also of Van Arsdale's asceticism and self-denial in putting the needs of others before his own.

> Harry felt that many difficult negotitations and even strikes could be re- solved more easily if some of the influential business leaders knew the labor leaders on a first name basis, and what they were involved in, and what made them tick. He also felt that some of the important things that challenged our City could be worked on more successfully if business and labor tackled them together. [At the same time, Van Arsdale didn't care about acquiring wealth and the trappings of power.] Take his own dress, his home, it was below modest. I mean, a little black and white TV and very, very old, plain furniture. He was a man of most modest means. Wealth and power meant nothing to him. . . . Harry could have been a wealthy man if he wanted to abuse his power but he never did.[6]

How Van Arsdale used his networking with big businessmen to explain the world of the worker is illustrated by an anecdote that Van Arsdale related to the executive board of Taxi Local 3036 when he announced his retirement as its president in 1977 and while he was deeply involved in trying to help pull the city out of its fiscal crisis.

> I serve on some of these committees to try to save the city and they are taking up a great deal more of my time. You get with some of these impor- tant people and occasionally one of them will say "I had one of your taxi drivers today and I want to tell you he was about the most impossible person I ever met." And these guys would tell you a story and I don't know if they thought I would be ashamed because I was the president of the taxi driver union or what. But when they get finished I say, "It doesn't happen every day, but only occasionally, right?"
>
> I say to them, "Do you use many cabs?" "Oh, yes," they say, "I use four or five taxis a day." And now there is a group there hearing this sad story and I say "Four or five cabs a day at five days would be about 400 to 500 cabs a month [for all within the group] if [they were] in the city 20 days. Is this the only driver who acts the way you say he acted?" And they say, "Yes." And I say, "Why don't you talk about the other 499?" Invariably, they will look at you and it's proof that cab drivers don't get the credit they deserve.

But there is a good chance that those who heard this story would bear it in mind in considering matters concerning the drivers from that point on. And this would be but one of the ways in which Van Arsdale proved his value to the labor movement. And, as others have said so often, he would never assume credit for what he did, but would assign it to others.

Lindsay was initially puzzled by Van Arsdale whom he believed to be a "power broker." Van Arsdale told former Mayor Wagner how he clarified Lindsay's thinking in that regard.

> Shortly after Lindsay took office. He sent deputy mayor Robert Price to see Harry and in the name of the mayor, he told him—and this is what Harry told me: "You know those jobs that Wagner gave you? We're now willing to give them to you." And Harry said, "What jobs?" And Price said, "Oh, the jobs he gave you." And Harry said, "Name one." And that was true. Harry never asked for any patronage. And you know, that was his answer to them. And they were rather stunned. The power broker never asked for anything, except what he thought was good for the working people of this town.[7]

Van Arsdale had a hand in helping to settle every major, as well as quite a few minor, labor disputes in the city—many of them involving public employee unions—during the administrations of Mayors Lindsay, Beame, and Koch. There was not, in fact, any labor event during his watch of which he was not aware. But he was, moreover, destined to play a crucial part in the shoring up of city finances when the city faced bankruptcy in the 1970s. It can be argued that if it were not for his efforts as a cohesive force, rounding up disparate elements and keeping them in check, the crisis would have been deeper and lasted longer than it did.

Prominent among these elements were the public employee unions. Van Arsdale had already brought the power and prestige of the Central Labor Council to bear in several major disputes involving employees working for public- or government-regulated entities, for example, the hospital workers, teachers, social workers, and transit workers, and he was about to do so again in Mayor Lindsay's labor-beleaguered administration.

Shortly after the Taylor Law went into effect in January 1967, city welfare workers struck again on pay issues. The walkout lasted three days before the workers agreed to return to their jobs and await the results of fact-finders.

As part of his consistent philosophy of attempting to avoid painful strikes if at all possible, Van Arsdale helped establish (and became a co-chairman) of a fifty-member Labor-Management Council in the city on November 14, 1967. Van Arsdale declared that the Council would champion better understanding between labor and management and work to resolve differences. "Strikes and the threat of strikes have not contributed to industry coming to or staying in New York City," he said.

Governor Rockefeller, who attended an organizational luncheon along with other dignitaries, including Mayor Lindsay, declared that the council "was in the tradition of enlightenment that made this city great."

The Council had been the brainchild of Van Arsdale and Ralph Gross, president of the Commerce and Industry Association of New York. They had reportedly discussed the idea at length in June 1967 when they attended a conference in Rome, New York sponsored by the American Foundation on Automation and Employment headed by Theodore Kheel.

The Council's goals were: "To improve the city's labor image through programs for better labor-management understanding in major industries in the city; to cooperate in programs to expand existing industry and to attract new industry and new jobs into the city; to work together in identifying and eliminating the obstacles, government and otherwise, to the city's economic growth; to assist in realistic workable programs for finding jobs and to educate and train people to fill these jobs; to help provide the necessary leadership and support to make the city a better place in which to work and live."

Other labor leaders who were on the executive committee of the Council included: Peter Brennan, president of the New York Building and Construction Council; Matthew Guinan, president of the Transport Workers Union; Arthur Harckham, president of the Building Service Employees Union; Michael Sampson, business manager of Local 1–2 of the Utility Workers Union, and Louis Stulberg, president of the International Ladies Garment Workers Union.[8]

The philosophy of the group would cause banker David Rockefeller, the governor's brother, to say in later years that "Van Arsdale believed in the free-enterprise system. He recognized that employees and members of the work force depend on profitable business if they were going to be well off themselves so he never begrudged the profitability of business as long as the labor force was treated well."[9] David Rockefeller and Van Arsdale were to work together on similar groups and formed a close professional relationship. For example, through the Working Group they pushed for a $5 billion investment in business and industry in the city and they also were aggressive advocates of the proposed Westway project to replace the West Side Highway, which had crumbled. They pushed for an "economic regeneration" program for the city that rankled the sensibilities of some progressives and environmentalists. Van Arsdale, however, advocated the program that would result in more jobs. The plan called for, among other things, tax cuts, an end to rent control, and a reduction in air pollution standards. "Our ancestors would be somewhat amazed to say the least at the prospect of a lifelong labor leader and a lifelong capitalist joining together in common cause at a union headquarters," said David Rockefeller, speaking at a news conference held at the CLC offices. Their differences had been put aside in the face of the need to produce new jobs in the city, Rockefeller said. And Van Arsdale declared that "labor as much as business has a stake in the future of New York and maybe even more because companies can leave but the workers are left behind to stay here."[10]

Van Arsdale had moved into the upper realms of civic endeavors bringing the voice, image, and influence of labor and the working class to the boardrooms and executive chambers and other courts of economic power. He became the voice of conscience that the lords of business, industry, and government listened to because of the legions behind him. He was among those, as a member of the New York Full Employment Action Council, who pressured President Jimmy Carter to keep his promise to put the jobless to work. He lectured the Carter administration on the inequity of taking more money from the city than it returned. As a burgher of the city, Van Arsdale addressed all problems that affected its citizens, including crime. He became part of a committee of the City Bar Association to aid in efforts to reduce crime and make the criminal justice system more efficient and fair.

In 1967, Van Arsdale was appointed vice chairman of a citizen's group to persuade voters to approve a $2.5 billion bond issue for transportation. He also was appointed to serve on the City Board of Collective Bargaining, which dealt with procedures for city employee unions to be certified as bargaining agents and to provide guidelines for negotiations, grievances, mediation, fact-finding, and arbitration.

He was soon to become active in his new position. The Uniformed Sanitationmen's Association (USA), which represented the city's refuse collectors, moved to set up its first strike fund in its fifty-year history. Their action, in April 1967, took place in the shadow of the Taylor Law, which was to take effect that September. The law would permit the city or state to fine striking unions $10,000 a day and eliminate dues check-off procedures for eighteen months.

They were just one of many public worker unions that meant to test the new law. Police and firemen's unions were increasingly restive during the period. The Transport Workers Union, Local 2 of the United Federation of Teachers, and District Council 37 of the American Federation of State, County, and Municipal Employees, planned to raise more than $1 million to pay the Taylor Law penalties and fund campaigns to unseat the legislators who had voted for it.

First up at bat against the beleaguered Mayor Lindsay, who was getting a hard lesson in labor relations, were sanitationmen (the USA), led by John DeLury. It was to strike for nine days, choking the city in its own garbage amid a barrage of ultimatums from Mayor Lindsay, threats to bring in the National Guard, appeals to Governor Rockefeller, and active attempts by Van Arsdale and other labor personages to bring a just settlement.

The city and the 10,000-member union had been attempting to negotiate a new contract without success. In a summary of actions: The contract expired on June 30, 1967, and on January 29, 1968, the union rejected mediator proposals. Lindsay, who again had adopted a "hands-off" policy until the last moment, now stepped in, but it was "too little, too late." Both sides were still far apart on wage and pension issues.

On February 2, the strike began and the union ignored court orders to return to work. On February 6, as mediators continued work in negotiations, DeLury was sentenced to fifteen days in jail for contempt of court and fined $250. He entered jail the next day.

On February 8, a union contingent met with Lindsay at Gracie Mansion, the mayoral home. The contingent included a score of sanitationmen, consultant Jack Bigel, union attorney Paul O'Dwyer, Van Arsdale, Joseph Trerotola, vice president of the International Brotherhood of Teamsters (IBT), and president of Teamster Council 16, and Paul Hall, president of the International Seafarer's Union.

But Lindsay would not meet with the representatives from the sanitationmen. He met with Van Arsdale, Trerotola, and Hall; the mayor, however, held fast and the talks were broken off at 6 A.M. He then issued a call for the National Guard to be activated to collect the garbage.

The *New York Times* lauded the mayor's stance and said his call for the National Guard "was precisely the kind of action required to save the city from disaster." The governor, a *Times* editorial continued

> . . . will have no choice except to call out the National Guard to clear the streets of strike-accumulated filth, snow, and any other encumbrance. This strike is far more than a labor dispute. It is an effort to coerce the community in flagrant disregard of state law, of court order and of machinery that the city has established jointly with organized labor, for the fair and peaceful settlement of all civil service labor disputes. . . . The mayor has shown both courage and leadership in asserting the primacy of the public interest over any reckless abuse of union power. He has recognized that municipal bankruptcy would be the end result if negotiations, held under the club of civic enslavement, upset the wage pattern established for policemen, firemen and workers in other essential city services.[11]

The USA suspected that Lindsay was influenced by the *New York Times,* and, in particular, by editorial writer and former labor reporter Abraham H. Raskin, just as he had supposedly followed their lead in the Transit Strike.

But Van Arsdale warned that a general strike by all the unions of the Central Labor Council would occur if the National Guard was called. "We will not tolerate the use of militia against any workers," Van Arsdale said.[12] Rockefeller refused to call up the guard. Then, at the urging of Van Arsdale and other labor leaders, Rockefeller set up a unit of himself, the union, and mediators, but Lindsay rejected the plan they offered. Rockefeller, again following the appeals of Van Arsdale and other union leaders, offered to have the state take over the city Sanitation Department temporarily and then did so with the blessing of Van Arsdale and other union leaders.

Union members also agreed to Rockefeller's request to return to work on February 10, and the strike ended. Van Arsdale praised Rockefeller for "having the guts a public official should have."[13] However, Lindsay denounced the governor for "capitulation" to the "extortion" of the union.

The USA was fined $80,000 and its dues check-off rights were suspended for eighteen months. On February 17, the city and the USA agreed to binding arbitration. Later, DeLury said he had been opposed to binding arbitration because it represented "a breakdown in collective bargaining . . . but it was either that or blood in the streets."[14]

On February 29, Vincent McDonnell, chairman of the state's Mediation Board granted the union the wage raise it had sought. Jack Bigel praised Van Arsdale's aid to the USA. In an interview, he spoke of the value of Van Arsdale's influence with Rockefeller and other aspects of Van Arsdale's participation included repeated visits to picket lines. Van Arsdale, Bigel told the interviewer, was "a titan."[15]

Peter Millones, a labor reporter at the *New York Times*, also had praise for Van Arsdale's negotiating abilities while at the same time comparing them to the mistakes he believed were committed by DeLury.[16] He pointed to Van Arsdale's tactics during a contract dispute with the Taxi Drivers Union in 1967 in which his hotheaded members wanted to strike. Van Arsdale felt that a strike would have damaged their cause and was against it. Millones noted that Van Arsdale early on invited McDonnell into the talks. He also downplayed strike declarations in order to try to cool the situation, Millones continued. But most dramatically, Van Arsdale took a bold action during a meeting of the drivers at Sunnyside Gardens in Queens in 1968 in which they were to vote on whether or not to continue negotiations or to go out on strike. A negative vote would have meant a strike. As Theodore Kheel tells it: "When it was put to a vote, there were just a few ayes and a lot of loud shouted nays. Harry said, 'The ayes have it.'"[17]

The sanitationmen's strike led to a reexamination of the Taylor Law. Rockefeller wanted to strengthen it. Van Arsdale argued against this in a meeting in 1969 and predicted that additional penalties "would not deter strikes." One mitigating amendment, attributed to Van Arsdale's advice, called for an extension of the functions of the Public Employment Relations Board to include the "adjudication of 'improper practice' charges which can be brought by either negotiating party."[18]

But Lindsay's education at the hands of labor continued. In 1968 he was a different mayor than he had been in 1966 when he chided Mike Quill and other TWU members to soften their contract demands because "we've got to remember there's a war on in Vietnam." Quill responded by describing Lindsay with a pair of Yiddish obscenities. But in 1968, when another strike loomed, Lindsay's tactics had changed and Matthew Guinan, Quill's successor, announced "This agreement would not have been possible except for your intervention in this dispute." An intervention that was counseled by Van Arsdale.

Van Arsdale's help was available in the other labor disputes that plagued Lindsay. Parcel deliverymen walked out. Lifeguards refused to swim. Hospital workers struck. And there were slowdowns by firemen and policemen with strikes threatened. Van Arsdale worked behind the scenes in each situation. The United Firemen's Association (later to be renamed United Firefighters Association) was a member of the CLC, but the Patrolmen's Benevolent Association was not. Van Arsdale pledged the full support of the CLC to the firemen and policemen and met with Lindsay several times regarding their contracts. Lindsay's continuing labor problems led him to form the city's new Office of Collective Bargaining (OCB) with the aid of a municipal labor committee. Van Arsdale and Paul Hall were named as labor members of the seven-man board of the OCB. Van Arsdale's influence with the Lindsay administration was shown when he complained to the city's Welfare Department about a dispute between the Association for Homemakers Service and its homemaker employees. The association bitterly opposed a drive by the low-paid home aides to unionize. Van Arsdale sent a telegram to Welfare Commissioner Mitchell Ginsberg, whose department paid some 45 percent of the bills for the association, protesting that "we consider it untenable that public funds are used for organizations that are anti-union." Ginsberg responded by mediating the dispute between the Association and Local 1701, Community and Social Agency Employees Union.

Van Arsdale also had a critical role to play in the explosive situation involving the UFT, which, in the 1967 and 1968 school years, was involved in a series of strikes, highlighted by a particularly acrimonious dispute on the issue of decentralization of school administration.

The first of these strikes, starting on September 11, 1967, the beginning of the school year, lasted fourteen days, and, more than salary increases and increased benefits, centered on the issue of quality of education. The UFT wanted an expansion of the More Effective Schools (MES) program, which included smaller class sizes and the inauguration of more stringent means to handle disruptive children. In the end, the UFT was forced to scuttle most of its demands for MES.

In 1968 there were three strikes swirling around the fiery issue of decentralization. The move toward decentralization had actually begun in 1966 and had gained the support of some educational and vociferous public circles, especially black militants. To answer these demands, the city Board of Education established three experimental districts in poverty stricken areas, IS 201 in Harlem, Two Bridges on Manhattan's Lower East Side, and Ocean Hill-Brownsville in Brooklyn. The latter district spawned the strikes. The transfer of twenty teachers from the district caused initial strife. The UFT said the transfers were illegal, but the local board said they were routine. It wanted the teachers out of the district because it claimed that they were attempting to sabotage the decentralization experiment. The issue became a larger one over the right of a local board to hire and fire teachers and the specter of union negotiations with a separate board over contractual obligations. The UFT struck in the final weeks of the 1967–68 school year. Over the summer, the local board retaliated by hiring young nonunion teachers with the result that when the schools reopened in the fall, the union teachers found they were essentially locked out. The UFT began a series of negotiations to try to settle the issue, but the school board under the leadership of superintendent Rhody McCoy was adamant. Anti-Semitism was injected into the dispute, making it more explosive. Mayor Lindsay straddled a political fence attempting—unsuccessfully—to avoid brickbats from either side.

The dispute polarized the city. There were heated demonstrations by parents in front of schools in the Ocean Hill-Brownsville district. The media were in their usual feeding frenzy. Van Arsdale called for "absolute and complete support for the United Federation of Teachers."[19]

Van Arsdale saw the conflict as a case of union-busting and a threat to other unions in the city. But some Council members were publicly opposed to the strike along racial lines. A group of union leaders, with a growing African-American membership, appealed to Van Arsdale to use his influence to have the Council withdraw its support of the UFT and end the teachers' strike. Van Arsdale stood firmly behind Shanker and union principles and defended Shanker and the UFT against charges of racism.

Van Arsdale became the man in the middle between the UFT and the union dissidents, led by Victor Gotbaum of District Council 37. On January 14, 1968, Van Arsdale met with approximately fifty irate African-American and Puerto Rican union leaders who warned him that they would lead a racial revolt in the council unless they received prior notice of any strikes affecting their communities. "If we have to split the labor movement and go our own way, we will," said Lester Roberts, general organizer for District 65 of the Retail, Wholesale, and Department Store Union, who acted as spokesman for the group.

Thomas Mitchell, a vice president of Local 1199, Drug and Hospital Employees Union, added: "Those of us who are black and Puerto Rican and Hispanic will set up our own labor movement." Van Arsdale also met later with Leon Davis, 1199 president; David Livingston of District 65, and Gotbaum, in an effort to cool the heat of the moment.[20]

The dispute escalated, and the courts, the state legislature, and state mediation chief Vincent McDonnell became involved. The state ordered the suspension of the school board and the use of UFT teachers in classrooms. Shanker supported the state formula for settlement despite strong internal UFT opposition. The formula was accepted. Shanker was later ordered jailed for fifteen days for his part in the strike on charges of contempt of court.

There had been a lot of pressure on Shanker from many sides to settle the dispute, including from Van Arsdale, who enjoyed Shanker's special confidence and esteem because of the help Van Arsdale had always given the UFT. Van Arsdale had worked hard in his usual way behind the scenes, attempting to quiet the situation and achieve a settlement. The *New York Times* reported that Van Arsdale reportedly made a number of suggestions to Lindsay that would be acceptable to both the African-American community leaders and the UFT.[21] The need for a settlement was especially urgent, Van Arsdale felt, because the situation was having an adverse effect on public perception of all unions. Because of this, "Van Arsdale took Shanker behind the woodshed and read him the riot act," said Jack Schierenbeck, a reporter for the *New York Teacher* newspaper and a UFT historian.[22] In the end, the experimental school districts were erased and the teachers' position was upheld: school districts do not have the right to change established practices and contracts.

In a weekend conference at Arden House, in Harriman, New York, on January 6–7, 1968, Shanker voiced his appreciation for the help Van Arsdale had given in the recent crisis. His efforts and presence were extremely instrumental in helping teachers reach their objectives.[23]

While Van Arsdale nurtured the UFT during this period, as always, he was kept busy with other parts of the labor garden that he tended: for example, farm workers. All workers, not only those within the boundaries of New York City, were within his sphere. He supported efforts to make employers of migrant farm workers subject to minimum wage laws. "It's time for action," he said.[24] Van Arsdale's interest in the plight of the downtrodden migrant workers encompassed the campaign of the United Farm Workers. Irving Stern, director of the United Food and Commercial Workers International Regional Office, told of that interest and of how Harry's actions helped further the UFW's grape boycott in the city and their organizational efforts in California.

> One year, I was attending a meeting of the state AFL and, like many others, stayed through all the sessions. Toward the conclusion of the session, a resolution on the grape boycott was coming up before the convention. And Harry Van Arsdale approached me, since I was from a food union, and asked me if I would speak on the resolution. Since it was Harry, and Harry asking me, there was no question of what I was going to do. It was of course in the affirmative. Naturally I had heard a great deal about the effort to organize the farm workers, about [Cesar] Chavez, and Harry's invitation, and the indication that the Central Labor Council was supporting this campaign was a heartening thing. And I was very happy to say yes to Harry.
>
> Harry's support for the farm workers was consistent with his attitude. The underdog had to be supported, had to be organized, and he naturally gravitated toward that kind of support. . . . I made a speech before the AFL/CIO convention in support of the resolution, and felt very good that I had been involved by Harry in that campaign. We later discussed what my union could do in that connection. Since I was one of the leaders of the food workers in New York, I headed a food labor council, composed of all the food unions in the city of New York, I brought that campaign into this food council, and went to the industry to discuss that campaign.
>
> Simultaneously, the farm workers conducted picket lines in front of many of the grocery store chains. These picket lines were of great concern to some of these supermarket operators—some of whom were very decent people. And while their attitude was determined by the impact on their business, they nonetheless—they also [were] people with some degree of feeling and concern, and the "grapes of wrath" syndrome had not yet run its course, and they were still remembering that period. I met with many of them on an individual basis to discuss the whole question of the boycott, what was happening to their business as a result of the picket lines, and convinced some of the more decent supermarket operators that they had to take some actions to change the situation in California.

I kept Harry posted on all of these developments, since it flowed origi-nally from his interest and concern in support of the Farm Workers. He had sent some organizers out to California to support their organizing efforts and subsequently their strike efforts, and some of them were badly injured in some of their labor struggles. [Stern related how he and other city labor leaders went to California for a firsthand look at conditions and were hor-rified at what they saw.] At any rate, when we came back I reported to Harry . . . [and then] . . . I brought together some of the supermarket people, and we instituted a non-buying policy and at least 95 percent of the grapes were cut off in New York. We instituted a thorough, thorough boycott. And the grape growers capitulated soon after. And that was their first major victory, of course, the Farm Workers union has been ever grateful to Harry.

As a matter of fact when I went out later they wanted me to negotiate their first contract with the growers, which I refused to do because I thought that would be a diversion and a new factor in what was already a bad situa-tion. At any rate, the farm workers victory was in large part the result of Harry's interest, support, and mobilization of the unions in New York, in terms of the resources, in terms of the boycott that he had me bring about, because of my support of the Council, and of course the Farm Workers.[25]

On another front, Van Arsdale had also encouraged the assignment of Jose Lopez, who helped to found the Santiago Iglesias Educational Society of Local 3 and who was its second president, to aid in the organizing of the incipient Farm Workers Union (FWU). Lopez had become a Field Representative of Region No. 7, AFL-CIO, and had been appointed to the AFL-CIO's national field staff by George Meany on Van Arsdale's recommendation. He was then assigned to work with Cesar Chavez and his organizing committee. He worked with Chavez from 1967 to 1973 to help establish the FWU and effect their first contract. During a strike action, Lopez had been severely beaten by police and had to be hospitalized with back injuries, which plagued him for the rest of his life, said his son, Edwin, a Local 3 business representative, who also served as president of the Santiago Iglesias Educational Society from 1986 to 1992.

"Local 3 and Harry were very proud to have made that contribution of talent to the AFL-CIO and to the farm workers," said Edwin Lopez.[26] He went on to point out that Van Arsdale always sought to "empower workers at the lower end of the totem pole to fight their own battles." For instance, he encouraged the formation of committees of Local members from within the Society to bring the weight of the organization against landlords who dis-criminated against Latinos, Lopez recalled.

Van Arsdale's broad interests and responsibilities came to include the finances of the International Brotherhood of Electrical Workers (IBEW) when he was named international treasurer in 1968, which gave him more national exposure. As treasurer he was to stress the importance of affiliation with state and city labor bodies and the importance of financial and personal participation in political activities. He particularly urged the other IBEW unions to adopt benefit structures similar to those in Local 3, especially the Annuity Plan.

He also threw the full weight of Local 3 and the CLC into the support of the embattled copper workers who were engaged in a long-fought strike nationally. Among the strikers were 1,000 Local 3 wire and cable workers employed in the Habirshaw Division of the Phelps Dodge Corporation in Yonkers. The plant was effectively shut down except for the shipment of reels of copper wire needed by the military in Vietnam.

The Local, by the way, sent $10 checks monthly to each member serving in the armed forces in Vietnam. Appreciative letters from servicemen were printed in each issue of the *Electrical Union World*. In another Vietnam-related activity, Van Arsdale was also named as a labor chairman by the AFL-CIO in the 1968 U.S. Savings Bond campaign.

Van Arsdale joined the fray for public unions again in a mass protest demonstration on December 20, 1969, for Mrs. Lillian Roberts, director of organization for the American Federation of State, County, and Municipal Employees Union (AFSCME), in front of a city jail in New York. She had been imprisoned for leading a strike to organize state hospital workers.

Van Arsdale's relationship with Mayor Lindsay soured completely when he refused to endorse him in the 1969 mayoralty race. At first, Van Arsdale had thrown the endorsement of the Central Labor Council to Robert Wagner in the Democratic Party primary—the first time in 100 years the CLC had made a primary endorsement. "Most people think that I don't like Lindsay, but of all the mayors, no one has been kinder to me," Van Arsdale said. Then why was he supporting Wagner? "Because he can and will do more for the working man," Van Arsdale replied.[27]

But Wagner lost in the primary to Mario Procaccino who then became Van Arsdale's choice. The mayoralty race that year also split the ranks of labor. Victor Gotbaum of District Council 37 endorsed Lindsay and was critical of Van Arsdale for what he called Van Arsdale's "heavy-handedness" in throwing Council support to the Democratics. Van Arsdale and Gotbaum also crossed horns in a racial arena. Gotbaum, whose union was largely composed of African Americans and other minorities, had said that the labor movement is no longer respected by African Americans, a not-so-veiled attack on Van Arsdale and the CLC, which he considered to be conservative and old-line. Gotbaum's remarks had been inspired by a dispute between African Americans and whites in the Pittsburgh construction trades unions and markets. Van Arsdale, speaking on a television news program, countered that he did not believe New York City would have such antagonisms because of the CLC's continued efforts to bring more African Americans and Latinos into the construction trades. Certainly, Van Arsdale's record in Local 3 supported that. Gotbaum's attacks were "reckless," Van Arsdale continued. "I think Victor Gotbaum thought he would get his name in the paper and get some wide publicity by making a statement of that kind."[28]

Gotbaum was to get his name in the papers quite a bit between 1974 and 1975, during the heat of the city's budget crisis. Van Arsdale's name was hardly mentioned in comparison. But that was the way both men wanted it. Van Arsdale's modus operandi was to get as much accomplished without fanfare and personal aggrandizement. Gotbaum also sought to accomplish much, but not in the same manner as Van Arsdale. As a result, the media, and even to some extent some scholars, slight Van Arsdale's role in pulling the city out of its financial mess, but it would be ludicrous to think that a man who had been so integral a part of the city's economic and labor picture for decades would not have been involved completely in helping to save the city and its people and workers, which he loved. The fact is, because of his contacts and ability to persuade, Van Arsdale was a key player, albeit a largely unsung one, in reaching the final solution whereby union pension funds bailed the city out. And it must be remembered that it was not Van Arsdale's habit to take credit for his achievements. He always allowed others to do that, preferring to remain behind the scenes as labor's gray eminence.

In 1974, the city faced default. Thousands of public employees faced the prospect of losing their jobs. The entire city economy would have been damaged and would have resulted in the loss of countless other jobs. Van Arsdale worked tirelessly with other labor and business leaders in the crusade to save the city, and, in the final analysis, was the midwife of the deal that accomplished it.

The eroding foundation of the fiscal downfall of the 1970s was laid in the 1960s when the economy of the nation began to go sour and federal aid to cities was cut. There were also higher costs in New York City because of increased welfare and contractual labor obligations. However, revenues were dropping in the city because of a flow of business and the white middle class to the suburbs. Bond debt was high because of fiscal practices by Mayor Lindsay and Governor Rockefeller, and, in the early to mid-1970s, the bubble burst. By early 1975, New York City's deficit had reached $3 billion, outstanding notes were $12.3 billion, and $7 billion would be needed to keep the city afloat in meeting operating expenses. Bankers, however, were becoming more loathe to lend the city money because of its higher risk position. Overseas opportunities had become better banking investments.

All of this landed in the lap of Mayor Abraham Beame, the former city comptroller, as he faced his first year in office in 1974. That fall, he announced that he would have to lay off city workers to trim the city payroll. The municipal labor unions, led by Victor Gotbaum as head of the Municipal Labor Committee, vehemently protested. Fingers were being pointed at both the bankers and the unions as the prime scapegoats.

In the first half of 1975, verbal brickbats flew amid threats of city bankruptcy, default on loans, dismissals of city workers, the specter of wage freezes, and strikes by city workers. By May 1975, more than 13,000 city workers had been laid off. Labor began to make a number of belt-tightening actions as tourniquets to stem the bloodletting, but it continued nevertheless.

Forces outside the city tried to come to its aid. The state floated Municipal Assistance Corporation (MAC) Bonds. The city's real estate industry induced changes in the city charter allowing for a prepayment of real estate taxes in return for long-term fiscal considerations.

Unfortunately for the UFT, its contract expired in September 1975. The city dug in its heels and the UFT was forced to strike. Negotiations continued and UFT demands were reduced in the face of the fiscal dilemma, and the strike ended in October after five days. However, the pact was voided and tossed out by the state fiscal watchdog, the Emergency Financial Control Board (EFCB). After a year of further talks, the UFT contract was revised to the liking of the EFCB.

With Governor Hugh Carey in the statehouse in Albany, the EFCB turned its eye toward other municipal unions. In May 1976, it issued guidelines that barred wage increases and mandated that other increases had to meet acceptable criteria. The unions reluctantly went along and in that way helped to deal with the crisis. But an even more meaningful way of helping came in a bailout by the unions in the sale of city and MAC bonds and it is here that Van Arsdale played a powerful—even critical—behind the scenes and largely unheralded role. Gotbaum, in fact, stated he did not want the help of Van Arsdale and the "private" unions of the CLC.

> We had unanimous agreement in the public sector unions that we would keep the private sector out. We didn't want them. We just did not want them really. Were they bad or were they negative? No, but we really didn't know what Harry Van Arsdale could possibly contribute. The other aspect that worried me, I want to be honest about this since this is supposed to be historical, is I wanted to make sure Teddy Kheel was out of it. Was Teddy a bad guy? No, but once Teddy gets in there, Teddy takes over and we weren't about to allow that to happen.

The truth is that it wasn't even an issue, we never thought of inviting them in. We knew if we had a militant action [which we didn't want] they'd be supportive. I think they really would have been supportive, but in terms of the negotiation, in terms of what we were going through, in terms of . . . maybe it was an error of omission. But they never came to Washington with us. They never really came to Albany.

We carried it. If we needed them, fine. We didn't need them. By the way, there's an aspect here that I think is totally important. Jack [Bigel] used to say . . . [that] those who make history are unaware. A tremendous change took place in the labor movement. Here it's now taking place much later in the national movement. You went from a construction leadership to a public sector leadership. We suddenly became the leaders. Matthew Guinan, Victor Gotbaum, Al Shanker, Barry Feinstein, were the growth unions and so this change took place. We didn't need them [the private sector unions] and I would be less than honest if I said that we wanted them. We really did not want them.[29]

But Van Arsdale did go to Washington. He did go to Albany. Gotbaum's self-serving comments were an illustration of his ambition to become head one day of the Central Labor Council and a leader, in fact as well as fancy, of all the unions in the city.

The municipal unions, with Gotbaum, Feinstein, and Bigel taking the much publicized helm, bought $2.5 billion worth of bonds using pension funds. The cherry on the cake was a last-minute, crowning investment by Shanker and the UFT, which added $150 million to the $138 million it had already submitted to the cause.

But it has to be remembered that Van Arsdale was not only the president of the CLC, but also a confidante of the brothers Rockefeller, Nelson and David, and a board member, or formerly active member, of a number of other civic and economic institutions, including the Mayor's Council of Economic and Business Advisors, the Temporary Commission on City Finances, the Mayor's Management Advisory Board, the Institute of Collective Bargaining and the American Arbitration Association, Lincoln Center, the Mayor's Task Force on Youth and Work, the New York City Urban Coalition, the National Citizens Committee for Community Relations, the Bicentennial Committee Advisory Council, the Carnegie Hall Corporation, the New York City Public Development Corporation, the United Fund of Greater New York, the AFL-CIO Mortgage Investment-Trust, the New York State School of Industrial and Labor Relations, the Labor College Advisory Board, the AFL-CIO Labor Studies Center, the Workman's Compensation Advisory Board, the State Savings Bond Committee, the Advisory Committee of State and Local Central Bodies AFL-CIO, the temporary Commission on

Powers of Local Government, Coalition Jobs, the New York Labor-Management Council of Health and Welfare Plans, the National Advisory Council on Economic Opportunity, the Governor's Committee on Scholastic Achievement, the Labor Advisory Committee of the Office of Economic Opportunity, the Mayor's Task Force on Youth and Work, the Advisory Committee on State Construction Programs, the Board of Education Selection Board, the Mayor's Council Against Poverty, the Labor-Management Council of New York City, the New York World's Fair Corporation, the Manpower Utilization Council, and the Regional Plan Association—among others.

With such a list of associations—not complete—and the contacts they represented, it is clear that Van Arsdale had the power to shake the money tree. "Van Arsdale played a constant major role in the fiscal crisis," said Ted Kheel.[30] It was Van Arsdale, for instance, who arranged a meeting with Municipal Assistance Corporation Chairman Felix Rohatyn and Victor Gotbaum at the Unity House Resort in Pennsylvania. At the meeting, Van Arsdale strove to persuade Gotbaum to help guarantee city bonds with the use of union pension funds.[31]

Van Arsdale frequently attended UFT meetings during the crisis to make the case for investment of UFT pension funds in city bonds. Jack Bigel tells of a meeting arranged by Governor Carey in order to try to get UFT President Shanker to agree to invest UFT pension funds in city bonds. The meeting was to be between Shanker and Richard Ravitch, head of the New York State Urban Development Corporation, but Shanker insisted that Van Arsdale also attend.[32]

Mayor Robert Wagner accompanied Van Arsdale to a meeting at Gracie Mansion. Subsequently, they all went to Ravitch's apartment where Shanker agreed to ask the UFT Board to approve an additional $150 million investment of pension funds into city bonds.

The UFT was given continuous support by Van Arsdale during the fiscal crisis. Shanker thanked Van Arsdale in a letter dated February 11, 1977, for "intervening with the Governor and the State Controller and urging approval of the UFT contract before the Emergency Financial Control Board. . . . I sincerely appreciate your immediate and unqualified support and the actions you took. It was part of an essential educational process for non-elected state officials who are trying to build political careers by stomping on labor contracts and union leaders. . . . Many thanks for jumping in at a crucial moment."[33] Shanker said that Van Arsdale played a "mid-wife role" by persuading Shanker and the UFT that helping the city would be in the best interest of the union.[34] "Al Shanker was a key vote and Harry Van Arsdale was a key player in helping to bring about the decision to invest. . . . I think the union leadership came to the conclusion that this was the best thing to do for the city and the best thing for the unions," said Theodore Kheel.[35]

Central Labor Council records show that Van Arsdale made constant appeals and arguments for unions to join in the bailout of the city. Van Arsdale also traveled to Washington to present the case for more federal aid for the city. Bernard Rosenberg, a Van Arsdale aide, said:

> During the fiscal crisis, I attended a joint House-Senate fiscal meeting in Washington, D.C. I went with Mayor Beame, Harry Van Arsdale Jr. and Frank Vivert, who was a business representative with Local Union 3. The purpose of the meeting was to have the Mayor request Congress to guarantee the City's bonds. To this day, I can recall almost every word that was said. The Mayor asked Congress to guarantee the City bonds. The unanimous responses from our distinguished and honorable representatives in Congress to Mayor Beame sounded to me as if I was in a foreign, enemy country. The Senators and Congressmen told the Mayor that he was fiscally irresponsible; go sell the Brooklyn Bridge and all of the other assets that the city had. They said they would not help the Mayor and would allow the city to go broke.
>
> I am paraphrasing what the Mayor said. It went something like this: "After World War Two many cities in the South, many from your own states, sent their Blacks north. They gave them one way bus tickets and took them to the buses. The reason for this was that the South was no longer a primary agrarian economy. During the war, they became industrialized, but there were not enough jobs for your citizens of your respective states. We must remember that this [forced migration] took place before the Civil-Rights Act of 1964. Not many whites would choose to work with a black worker alongside of him or her. . . . The Southern States did not have welfare and social benefits to support and assist in the unemployed black population. There were only two major cities in this country that could provide for those impoverished people at that time. One was New York City and the other city was Detroit. . . . Many of the people who are receiving welfare and social services in New York City have come from your own states. You deported your own citizens to New York City. Now you do not want to guarantee the bonds, so that the City can continue providing services for your former citizens. All of you are denying them the right to have food, clothing and shelter for themselves. . . ."

The Mayor's plea to save New York City went unheeded. I can still see the headlines in the *New York Daily News* [October 30, 1975]: FORD TO CITY: DROP DEAD.

Harry Van Arsdale Jr. wanted to make a statement before the committee. During the lunch period, he told me to ask the committee's secretary for him to be able to speak when the session would commence after lunch. I told the secretary Van Arsdale had to speak at that time. He had a meeting in Queens with the Electchester Housing Committee at 4 P.M. and he had to catch the 3 P.M. shuttle back to New York. The secretary told me that he would be the first person on the agenda after the break. Van Arsdale left the room and came back as soon as the session was about to start. As the Senators and Congressman sat down in their respective chairs, Van Arsdale gave each one of them a copy of his remarks that he thought he was about to make.

The secretary next passed out the agenda for the afternoon. Van Arsdale's name was last on the list. He was scheduled to speak at 4:30 P.M. As soon as Van Arsdale read the agenda, and saw that his name was last on the list of speakers, he dashed up to where the Congressmen and Senators were sitting. He pulled the sheets of papers out of their hands.

He told them that he was told that he would be the first person to speak after lunch and his name appeared last on the afternoon agenda. He said that he was leaving and as he turned to leave, he shouted to the seated Congressmen and Senators: "Your minds are made up . . . if you ever invite me to come back and if I have nothing else to do, I would consider it."

The congressman and senators said in chorus: "Mr. Van Arsdale, please stay! Please stay! You can speak right now. . . ." But Van Arsdale did not change his mind. We caught the next plane back to New York City. I do not believe many people would have the nerve and courage to do that. I never forgot that scene.

At Van Arsdale's urging, AFL-CIO President George Meany issued a strong statement on behalf of the organization, criticizing President Ford's snub of the city and exercise of a double standard that permitted federal bailouts of corporations and unfriendly nations, but not of cities under Democratic party rule. Speaking at a dinner in New York, Meany expressed "a fervent hope that Congress will have the guts to defy the President of the United States and give to the city of New York . . . the federal backing for its bonds that it must have."[36] Van Arsdale continued his lobbying for aid for the city with the succeeding Democratic President Jimmy Carter and his role in achieving this aid was substantiated in a warm letter of praise and thanks that he received from Carter. The president wrote on October 13, 1978:

As New York City moves toward completion of its financing package, I want to express my personal appreciation for the substantial contribution you made to the enactment of the New York City Loan Guarantee Act of 1978. This legislation represents a historic point in New York's path to economic recovery and financing independence. It provides the necessary long-term commitment which will permit a rational resolution of the city's financing and fiscal problems. Less than a year ago, many people believed that the guarantee legislation proposed by the Administration could not be enacted. Our subsequent success reflected the efforts of many groups and individuals, and your help was instrumental in achieving this critical legislation. I am grateful for your assistance, and I look forward to continuing to work with you on other important issues before the Congress.

Lewis Rudin, a realtor and builder, worked with Van Arsdale on the fiscal crisis.

I was privileged to work with Harry who was a great man and a great New Yorker. It was the problems of the late '60s and early '70s which put us together. I got to respect Harry Van Arsdale on the basis of trying to solve the fiscal crisis of the city of New York. Some of us saw it coming and we formed a civic association with business and real estate people and we felt there was no way we could turn this town around without a real alliance of business, labor and government. And we were very lucky that it was Harry Van Arsdale, who understood what we were talking about, who joined us and became a partner with us in what was one of the major resurrections of a major city in the history of the world.[37]

Further evidence of the extent to which Van Arsdale was involved in the negotiations to shore up the city's finances is also shown in Van Arsdale's own words to the executive board of the taxi union he founded on March 21, 1977. At the same time, he also asked for their secrecy, showing no desire to take personal credit for what he had done—a continued sign of his method of working effectively and quietly away from the spotlight. His statement was made actually as a form of apology for not being able to spend more time with the taxi union because of his active role during the fiscal crisis.

I serve on some of these committees to try to save the city and they are taking up a great deal more of my time. In the past year, I have been in the position of spending very little time [with you]. . . . But the city is faced with such problems. . . . I was in a conference with the governor of this state and the head of the Teachers' Union sometime back. This is not generally known and I would just as soon it not be spoken about outside the room. But the teachers were not being treated fairly and I was the only one with Governor Carey and President Shanker, and this city would have been faced with bankruptcy if as a result of those discussions the teachers did not make available the amount of money the city needed.

And I learned later that while we were in the meeting discussing the problem, there were people outside calling up anybody and everybody they could call who they thought had enough money to make up what the teachers might not have, which was a substantial number of millions of dollars.

And I always remember it was close to 3 o'clock and the discussions had not concluded—the bank decided to stay open until four. At four o'clock, there was still no conclusion and the bank agreed to stay open until five o'clock. At a quarter to five, the president of the teachers' union contacted his trustees. Just as many of you are trustees on your funds, they needed the vote of some of those teacher trustees under the law to be able to make their pension funds available.

And I don't think it serves any purpose to have these things talked about publicly and on TV and headlines but I was very happy that the city [would] not face bankruptcy. I am only mentioning it so you will have an understanding of how you are affected. You make your living in this city. The unions I represent—their members make their living in this city. This city is in desperate circumstances.

And [the city] is not going to come out of it right away. That's how close they were [to bankruptcy]. It is hard to visualize . . . hard to believe that anything like that could happen. But that is how close [it came to bankruptcy].[38]

14

The Kid Goes Down Fighting

In 1978, Van Arsdale was 73 years old, a time of life when many men happily spend retirement years in easy harmony. Their only hats might be those of golfers, gardeners, or fishermen. But Van Arsdale continued to own a swirling console of hats, one of which was that of IBEW treasurer. It was largely an honorary post requiring that Van Arsdale deliver a financial report, prepared by IBEW auditors, at each convention. Although it was not planned that way, a tradition was being established to fill the post with Local 3 officers. Prior to Harry Van Arsdale Jr., it had been held by Local 3 officers William A. Hogan and Jeremiah P. Sullivan. As an International officer, Van Arsdale attended regional progress meetings where he spoke about the benefit of annuity plans and other educational benefits. One of the major accomplishments of IBEW President Charles Pillard and Secretary Ralph Leigon, while Van Arsdale was treasurer, was the establishment of reciprocity procedures. Resulting from a diligent coordination effort among locals by Wesley Taylor, IBEW members who worked in various jurisdictions could have pension contributions sent back to accrue, and to earn pension credits in their home Local. Prior to that, pension benefits accrued only in individual jurisdictions and were lost if that string were broken.

Van Arsdale remained a power within the IBEW and within the AFL-CIO, first, because of his accomplishments as head of Local 3, IBEW, and then as IBEW treasurer and head of the New York City Central Labor Council. As stated earlier, he eschewed a higher post in the IBEW and in the AFL-CIO because he felt his energies could be better used helping people directly. In other words, Van Arsdale liked to run his own show, dealing with those willing to work toward a common objective, without the strain of having to deal with adversaries seeking to supplant him within his own organization or following private, self-serving agendas that hampered achievement of a worth-while goal. Van Arsdale also knew the field very well and was a master at reaching out to, motivating, and influencing others. His son Thomas said:

> He would go to dinners and meetings and meet people. And he was always interested in discussing one thing or another. He took great satisfaction in trying to coach other leaders. . . . One technique he used at conventions was to position himself in the lobby of a hotel late when people were coming back from their functions and he would greet them.
>
> I remember being with him at a convention out of town . . . he would walk down the street with the leader of the plumbers or steamfitters and if say the business manager of one was not getting along with his president, he would talk to one about the good qualities of the other. Or he might be encouraging them to have an annuity plan or a vacation plan or an education program or give scholarships. . . .
>
> His foremost objective was to further the well-being of the organization and the trade union movement. He probably had a lot of associations he did not favor, but he would set his personal thinking aside and worked with that person as long as that would be in the best interest of achieving the objective. When the objective was achieved, he would move on. It wasn't so much that he was abandoning that relationship except that he was moving on to other relationships. Over the years, he was always fair and wanted to be fair to people and give them what they were entitled to, but if they showed signs of not being willing to go along, there would be a cooling and a disassociation.[1]

Van Arsdale's position and work within the IBEW and the esteem in which he was held was also described by IBEW President J.J. Barry in a 1987 interview. "As time moved on he became recognized far and wide as an elder statesman and very highly regarded, and his company was sought by everyone across the country and Canada," Barry said. "He made so many contacts that it was unbelievable. Always people looking to get information or to find out how he accomplished certain things and to see if he could help them set up a certain program."[2]

Barry said that other IBEW locals, but not all, followed the pattern established by Van Arsdale with the JIB. The reason not all did was because: "They didn't have a Harry Van Arsdale to pursue it," but he did name a few that more or less copied the model set by Van Arsdale. "They're patterned maybe not exactly like the Joint Board, but they've come close to it. Chicago, Local #134 is an example of one. The larger locals that have a little more, shall we say control of the area, insofar as the work that's developing. I use Chicago as an illustration. I'm thinking maybe of Pittsburgh, I'm thinking of Atlanta, #613. Harry spent time down there trying to explain to them how to set up these various operations."

Barry went on to say that at the IBEW conventions Van Arsdale "was very popular and when he spoke, as I said, everyone listened, because he always had a message that was timely."

> Instead of from the podium he would get clusters around him after the convention had adjourned. And he would conduct a little seminar of questions and answer and try to be helpful. I know this one convention, I think it was Atlantic City, after the convention was over. . . . During the convention you get daily proceedings. He was around collecting them, I mean by the armload, and he had some of his guys with him, and I was curious as to what he was going to do with them. I said "Harry, what are you going to do with all those?"
>
> "Well," he said, "these people apparently don't want them. I'm going to bring them back to the apprentice class so they can see firsthand what transpires at a convention." So I thought that here's a man [who] at that time was well into his 70s and he was concerned at that point about someone getting firsthand information about a convention proceeding. It was a mark of a man, follow me, that really and truly loved the brotherhood. He loved the trade union movement and he loved the people he represented. . . . I just can't find adequate words to express my admiration for the man.

Barry recalls that Van Arsdale also always kept focused on the job at hand and was not much for "small talk."

> He always talked about something relating to our common endeavor. I can remember he asked me to go to England with the study group to meet with the electrical workers of the world. And the chairman of the program was an English trade unionist, and said that he was outlining the projected schedule and said "That will take us up until Wednesday and then maybe the people will want to do some sightseeing." Harry vetoed that. He said: "We came here to work. We'll work until Friday." And we worked every day, and we discussed all the various aspects of collective bargaining around the world and the various things that we could do to help each other across international boundaries to develop the best thing for the people we represented.

Barry also spoke of Harry's humanity and willingness to share his time with him when he was a junior officer in the IBEW.

> I can remember when I became international vice president of the 3rd District [and] we call a progress meeting. All the delegates from the various

local unions convene in the city that we select. And he called me after the meeting. It was a Sunday morning and people were ready to leave to go home because the meeting is Friday and Saturday. And he said "I would like to speak with you for a few minutes." Now here's a man of world renown coming to meet a neophyte. And he said: "If there's anything that I can ever do for you in your position all you've got to do is call me. And if you don't call me I'll be very upset." Those were his words, and I never forgot.[3]

But Van Arsdale's position in the IBEW became more of a strain as his work in New York as head of the Central Labor Council began to demand more and more of his time and energy. And time was catching up with him. At the age of 73 he was beyond the normal retirement age for IBEW officers. The time had come to shed one of his hats—that of international treasurer. He was allowed to stay on in the post past the retirement ceiling in order to qualify for an IBEW officer's pension, which, according to his son Thomas, was secondary to Van Arsdale. Primary was that he enjoyed the job. Thomas said that this touched on one of the prominent—and to others most astounding though laudatory characteristics of his father—his indifference to personal income.[4] So, in 1978, after serving ten years in the post, he passed on the baton of international treasurer to Thomas. The younger Van Arsdale was named treasurer by International President Charles Pillard and then ratified by the IBEW's Executive Council prior to a formal election in October 1978.

The importance Van Arsdale placed on his work in New York was indicated in remarks he made at the Progress Meeting of the IBEW's Third District in Atlantic City, on June 8, 1979, in which he exhorted delegates to affiliate with regional councils as the best means of accomplishing political aims.

A harsher political climate had settled in New York in the form of Edward Irving Koch who had succeeded Abraham Beame as mayor. During his 1977 campaign, Koch had warned that cutbacks and retrenchment, following the fiscal crisis, were needed. He sharpened his knives in preparation for negotiations with city unions, and the relationships soured between him and Van Arsdale and other labor leaders. "It was a very negative relationship. Koch did not like Harry and Harry did not like him," Theodore Kheel said flatly.[5] In opposition to Koch, the CLC supported Mario Cuomo in a primary runoff election.

One of the biggest labor difficulties that occurred early in the Koch regime was an eleven-day transit strike in April 1980. Koch made political hay and mugged for the television cameras by prancing on the Brooklyn Bridge alongside commuters walking to work. "Never give in to intimidation," he shouted. "Never give in to political or physical threats."[6]

After the TWU won a 9 percent increase in their contract with the Metropolitan Transit Authority, Koch cried that it was "too much" and proclaimed that "the city had won the battle in the streets, the Metropolitan Transit Authority lost it at the bargaining table."

His words angered Van Arsdale and other CLC members. "Harry was anxious as president of the Central Labor Council in order to be helpful to other labor unions to have access to the mayor and the governor and other people in political office. Harry saw his job as helping the affiliated members. He was constantly rebuffed by Koch. . . . Koch came to the very cynical conclusion that there was no benefit to him in mediation. If a strike resulted in a price increase, people would blame him . . . so he stood on the sidelines and denounced the unions for striking. He had no interest in settling although Harry would seek his assistance in settling," said Kheel.[7]

In 1981, Van Arsdale and the CLC again tried to use the voting booth lever as a way to pry loose uncooperative politicians. "Harry feels very strongly that the labor movement has become fat and lazy and too inclined to take the easy course," said Kheel who was instrumental in getting Van Arsdale to oppose Koch politically.[8] So, the CLC endorsed State Assemblyman Frank Barbaro in the Democratic primary. Although Van Arsdale knew that Barbaro would not win, he decided to make his stand on principle, but not all labor leaders stood with him. Barbaro said:

> Victor Gotbaum and Al Shanker were vehemently opposed to our campaign. They were afraid of Koch. They said, "You can't win. We don't want him to be angry at us. He would retaliate against us." And Al Shanker, in particular, said, "I don't want you to run and if you do and there is a rank and file committee organized in the teachers' [union] I would stop it. Victor Gotbaum also wanted in no way for DC 37 to support me. In fact there was a meeting of delegates and somebody made a motion to endorse my candidacy and it passed. And the leadership said it was a violation of the rules and therefore it was null and void. Gotbaum and Shanker actively undermined my campaign.
>
> And to the credit, the courage and the vision of Van Arsdale, he was able to get the CLC to endorse [me] in the primary. . . .
>
> They were so narrow in their thinking. Here Ed Koch had consciously tried to break the Transit workers strike by standing on the Brooklyn Bridge and urging people to walk to work. This was right on the heels of what many of the labor people were saying: we cannot allow an anti-labor mayor to be re-elected.
>
> Harry Van Arsdale had healthy working class instincts and knew that this could not go unpunished, just like when he supported the hospital workers and Leon Davis. He was an incredible guy. . . .

I go in to meet with him and we talked about nothing for an hour and at the end he looked at me and he said, "You don't want to change our government, do you?" And I said, "No, I just want government to be sensitive to the needs of working people." Then Harry handed me an apple and said, "Lad, you just go do what you gotta do." And from behind the scenes he began his engineering to get the Central Labor Council to endorse me.

Now, I still didn't know the kind of a guy he was and I would go around speaking: We have a great coalition. We have a labor leader on the left— Leon Davis. And we have a great labor leader on the right—Harry Van Arsdale and the two of them do not even talk to each other while they are in the same room and here they're both supporting me until one of the progressive labor leaders took me aside and said, "Do you understand that Harry and Leon are very good friends and that Harry helped Leon?"

And then I got a new perspective of Van Arsdale. Van Arsdale was very critical of phonies and if he believed that you were dedicated and truly in favor of helping working people, he was with you. There were many times when he and I were eating and then I would drive him back and walk with him and he would say to me, "You know, Frank, half of these labor leaders if they called their workers to go out, the workers would not follow them." He was very critical of . . . weak labor leaders. . . . He never mentioned any by name. . . .

He was very interesting. He had invited myself and my wife to Bayberry. Now almost nobody gets invited to Bayberry. When you get invited to Bayberry by Harry—that meant that he cared for you. We were walking one day and he said, "How's it goin'?" And I said "I have problems. . . . Mario Cuomo is giving me a hard time. . . . I think it was on workman's compensation." And he said, "Oh." And not another word. So I thought, he blew me off. And then the following Monday or Tuesday, I get a phone call, and it's Harry and he said, "Frank, you have a tuxedo?" And that night or the next night he called and he said you are coming to the construction industry dinner which nobody—no politician was ever invited to—so I said okay and I [went]. Now, the seating arrangement had me on the dais directly behind him and who was the speaker, but Cuomo and then Van Arsdale is introducing people on the dais and he said, "Our friend, Frank Barbaro who is always fighting for the working people." And then came Cuomo, so the message was very clear to Cuomo. Frank Barbaro is a good friend of mine.[9]

Harry was always there. When there were rallies he would take me there and he would say, "Alright, Frank, rouse them up. You are the only one who is not afraid to speak out." I respected him like a father. I knew . . . I could tell he really cared about working people. He used to have a little card. It said: "Be kind. Everybody you meet is putting up a hard fight." And he would give these cards out to people. He had a deep love for working people and was dedicated to making life better for them.[10]

But a bigger adversary to labor than Koch had sprouted nationally: Ronald Reagan, whose beliefs were the antithesis of Van Arsdale's beliefs about helping the working man and woman. Reagan was inaugurated on January 20, 1981, and immediately showed that his allegiances lay with those at the upper end of the economic spectrum by calling for massive tax cuts over a three-year period while at the same time strongly increasing defense spending. Social programs were to be severely cut to account for the fiscal shortfall.

Reagan's labor philosophy was akin to the robber barons of the nineteenth-century United States or the burghers and lords of Victorian England, even though at one time he had been the president of the Screen Actors Guild. He showed his true stripes after almost 13,000 air traffic controllers went on strike on August 3, 1981, following the failure of months of negotiations. While their union, the Professional Air Traffic Controllers Association (PATCO), sought a pay raise, a cut in the workweek, and better benefits, they also wanted recognition of the pressures they faced on their job, and that was as primary a concern as were the economic issues if not more so.

Reagan responded by threatening to fire all controllers who did not return to their jobs within forty-eight hours. A relative handful did and the rest—11,350—were fired. Their critical work, on which the lives of passengers and crews depended, was filled by supervisors and new hires. Organized labor quickly rushed to PATCO's defense.

In a news conference called to announce aid to PATCO in the New York area, Van Arsdale compared Reagan to Hitler.

> This is a sad period that the nation is going through now. From my viewpoint as a long time representative of working men and women it appears that the United States government is involved in an effort to destroy professional workers unions. It brings to my mind that fellow in Germany who crushed the whole labor movement in that country which had been one of the strongest in the world. His first name was Adolph and he did not make much of a great contribution to the people of this world. He caused a lot of people to be killed or maimed. Our country took the right stand at that time and our country is taking the wrong stand now. It is difficult for me to believe that the intention of our government is to destroy these professional workers' efforts to have their grievances heard.[11]

Regional AFL-CIO Director Michael Mann said Reagan's action posed "the greatest threat to organized labor in the history of the American Labor movement."[12]

Some members of the press were openly hostile to Van Arsdale, Mann, and the other labor representatives present. Their questions became contentious and scoffing and no doubt augmented Van Arsdale's already deep belief that most of the press served as mouthpieces for the moneyed establishment.

Van Arsdale wholeheartedly supported the cause of the traffic controllers. He attended a number of their meetings and walked with them on picket lines. He vehemently opposed the argument of some that the air traffic controllers were elitists who did not want to fit themselves into the working class mold. To Van Arsdale it was enough that they were men and women with families who were suffering because of unjust treatment. He pointed out the tragedies within PATCO families because of the economic stress, citing a case of a wife who allegedly "laid out all of the bills that were long overdue on the kitchen table. She then committed suicide, leaving behind her [now] motherless children and unemployed widower husband."[13]

In subsequent days, Van Arsdale sought to rally the flagging forces of labor by organizing a mammoth Labor Day Parade, to mark the 100th anniversary of the American Labor Movement, as a show of strength. But Koch sought to belittle labor and Van Arsdale. Permits from the Police Department to march down Fifth Avenue came only after several months of repeated requests, a far different situation than it had been when friendlier heads and hands were in City Hall. "Success has had an adverse effect in many ways on the labor movement," said Van Arsdale in commenting on the many powerful enemies of labor that sought to beat down its reared head.[14]

Defiantly, more than 200,000 marched in the parade on September 7, 1981, and, among the largest contingents, were members of the striking PATCO, led by their president Robert Poli. AFL-CIO President Lane Kirkland was grand marshal.

On September 19 in Washington, DC, more than 400,000 union members demonstrated in "Solidarity Day" to answer Reagan's charge that "labor leaders don't really speak for their membership." AFL-CIO President Kirkland countered by telling the huge assembly of unionists: "Look around you. You are not alone. Behold the numbers as far as the eye can see."[15] There were also 2,000 Local 3 members present.

Reagan was further lambasted at the AFL-CIO convention held in New York City later that year. Van Arsdale used the occasion to attack Reagan again for his actions against PATCO. "If your children make any mistakes, you want to correct them," he said. "You might want to punish them. But no president should destroy 12,000 men and women and their families and I hope he gets the message."[16]

But Reagan did not get the message, which illustrates how much more difficult it was for organized labor and Van Arsdale to be heard in those colder times. A headline in the *New York Times* of September 4, 1981, declared: "For Van Arsdale, Glory Days as Labor's Political Broker Are Now in the Past." The article, by Michael Oreskes, said that Van Arsdale had lost influence in City Hall and that his effect on the statehouse in Albany was greatly less than it had been when Nelson Rockefeller was in Albany.

"The old blue collar work force that he came from is nearly gone," Oreskes wrote. "The old Democratic coalitions have collapsed. Public employees and other service workers now make up more than half the city's union membership—which overall is declining—and politicians from the White House to City Hall are finding that they can get along quite well without people like Mr. Van Arsdale," Oreskes wrote.

He followed this with quotes from Robert Wagner, Jr. and Albert Shanker.

"His access to City Hall and his importance from City Hall's perspective is less than it has been in past administrations," Wagner, then deputy mayor and son of Van Arsdale's old friend and ally, was quoted as saying.

"It mirrors what has happened nationally," Albert Shanker told Oreskes. "George Meany and the other labor leaders of that era were more comfortable with the old-fashioned political bosses who made a deal and shook hands and kept it. Harry had a relationship like that with Mayor Wagner and later with Beame and with Nelson Rockefeller. Obviously, the relationship with Koch is pretty hostile."

Van Arsdale's political clout was also reportedly hemorrhaging because of his support of labor-friendly candidates who had lost at the polls, including Beame in his reelection drive, Cuomo in his runoff against Koch, and then Barbaro. "The Labor Council has picked too many losers" said "a political operative for a major city union," according to the Oreskes.

But it would always be a mistake to count out Harry Van Arsdale. He backed a winner in Mario Cuomo, who, as lieutenant governor, ran in a Democratic primary against Koch for governor in 1982. Afterward, Van Arsdale became a strong campaigner for Cuomo in his successful gubernatorial race. Cuomo remembers Van Arsdale's contributions with warmth and gratitude.

> In 1982 the labor movement in the country was debilitated, to put it mildly. Reagan was in the ascendance still. He was popular in 1980 and was even more popular in 1982 and the Republicans were strong and virulently anti-labor as we all know. The labor movement was not itself strong.
>
> I was an extremely improbable candidate again Ed Koch, most people thought, because he had not only the power of the mayoralty, he had Rupert Murdoch. He had the entire state committee virtually at least. He had the regular Democratic party. He had even some segments of Republicans for him and he was 38 points ahead in the polls when we started the campaign.
>
> I had only one thing: that was Harry Van Arsdale and "Chick" [Sol C.]

Chaikin of the ILGWU [International Ladies Garment Workers Union]. Labor was the only real strength that I had and labor is the reason I won the primary. They turned out the bodies; they turned out the emotional charge we needed. We had a cause. The other guys did not. And I ran as an unabashed, proud labor candidate. I remember the Labor Day parade that year was a sensation and got a lot of ink. Harry, of course, was the giant in the labor movement and just his name meant a lot, but his name and Local 3 which has always been one of the most intelligent and most active unions were very, very substantial parts of my campaign. I remember it well and I am grateful still.[17]

Specifically, Cuomo said the labor chiefs provided "people who manned phones for us, distributed literature. . . . It was one of the last old fashioned campaigns. I had no money for television. And it was not like today . . . five people in a little room and 100 millionaires. . . . We did it in the streets. We did not have television. We had to do it with placards . . . mano a mano . . . by handing out bills, by contacting people, by driving them to the polls. . . . We outmanned them and out-womaned them."

Prominent in the ranks were members of Local 3 who were always his biggest supporters, he added. "They were always the point of the spear."[18]

Koch, known for holding a grudge, never forgave Van Arsdale. In 1984, still rankling from his defeat in the primary, he refused to march in the Labor Day Parade with Governor Cuomo, Democratic presidential candidate Walter Mondale, and vice presidential candidate Geraldine Ferraro. Van Arsdale commented on the absence. "We've got lots of good company today," he said. "Why should we need him?"[19]

That Van Arsdale did not have a rapport with Koch put him on a par with every other labor leader in the city. The Reagan White House was hostile to all labor, not just Van Arsdale. But Van Arsdale still represented all of labor in the city, even though half might be in the municipal or service unions. And Van Arsdale's contacts, friendships, and rapport with leaders in industry, business, and banking made him a great deal more influential than the leaders of any public union. Van Arsdale's power had shifted to another plane. And while it may have been lessened by the loss of associations with Mayor Wagner and Governor Rockefeller, it was not lowered by much. In short, Van Arsdale still bore the mantle as "Mister Labor" in New York, the most powerful and influential city in the nation other than Washington, DC. And though advanced in age, he was no shrinking flower, and continued to make his voice heard in labor circles, large and small.

Van Arsdale marked the 100th anniversary year of the birth of Franklin Delano Roosevelt with a wide-ranging, prescient, and thoughtful speech to a seminar at Bayberry on July 7, 1982. The speech was remarkable in providing an overview of how Van Arsdale viewed the status of labor at that time and events leading to his conclusions. It also revealed the depth of his convictions about the need for social justice and fair and decent economic balance in the United States.

Early in his remarks, he spoke of the growing problem of unemployment and the competition for minimum-wage jobs even among college graduates. "Now just try to visualize a man or a woman, graduated from college, how long they must be out of work to be willing to take this job that pays so little that they possibly couldn't meet expenses? And if you would visualize that [then] it would give you an idea of what a long period of unemployment does to people and to their families."

He pointed to the inability or the indifference of many in the privileged class to empathize with the plight of the unemployed because they had never experienced such hardships. He pointed to the Supreme Court justices who opposed most of Franklin Roosevelt's attempts to help the downtrodden and then made a comparison with then President Ronald Reagan.

> We have a repeat . . . a similar situation [today], not quite as bad, but it could be, and there is very little, if anything, being done about it. And we have a President who, most of his life, was an actor and then he was the Governor of California and if we try to familiarize ourselves with him we come to the conclusion that there were a group of very important, influential, wealthy men and corporations that made him the Governor of California. And I believe on two occasions a group similar to this raised millions of dollars to try to get for him the Republican nomination [for President].

He spoke of the need for unions to rectify such evils as child labor.

> [The need to organize by workers] was a fight for justice and it took a lot of guts in those days [to organize. The value of education as a way to improve the quality of life was early recognized by both the wealthy and the poor alike]. One of the first efforts [of] . . . organized workers in this city and country was to get a free education for workers' children. And the people in control . . . their representatives testified in the legislature that if you want to spend money on education, spend it on manager's children because they are going to grow up to be managers. Don't waste it on the workers' children because they're just going to grow up to be workers. . . . The union just doesn't exist to get more money for each individual; the labor movement was formed for a better life for workers, a better life for people.

Van Arsdale also took aim again at one of his favorite and most deserving targets: the press, which harps on isolated instances of union corruption while neglecting the good that unions have done, with the result that an entirely false picture of organized labor is given.

"Why would the news media just give wide publicity to these kinds of things?" he asked. "And there is a reason. Ask yourself if a newspaper could exist without advertising. Could a radio station exist without advertising? Could a TV corporation function without advertising?"

The answer, of course, is no, and that included public broadcasting, Van Arsdale said, in that public broadcasting depends greatly on corporate grants. The regular credits announced on air are a form of commercial, he noted. "If that's not advertising, you tell me what is advertising because it plants the seed in our brain that this is or was an interesting program and [you should be] thankful to the big corporation for making it possible. . . . There's no union that I know of that has enough money to be able to pay for those kinds of broadcasts and then have it said that this program [for instance] was made possible by the Brotherhood of Painters and Decorators. They just don't have the money for those matters."

Van Arsdale also criticized the stance of the Reagan administration and Congress toward public welfare, unemployment, and unions. President Reagan was set on crushing unions, he said, and referred once more to the blackballing of the air traffic controllers as an example of Reagan's strategy.

He also spoke strongly against the ever increasing cost of running for office. "If that continues, we're going to lose the services of good, decent, honorable men and women . . . and the people who have a lot of money aren't going to support people that are going to help the vast number of citizens; they're going to help people that are going to help them and that creates a serious problem for [all of us.]"

Van Arsdale predicted that the labor movement would grow stronger in the next 100 years "because it's sound, it's basic, it's fundamental," but he also warned of the growing use of labor consultants by corporations who wished to break a strike or keep their workers from organizing. "They're going to create situations where the people are going to have to go through terrific hardship and sacrifice to maintain something that they ought to have without extra effort," he said.

Moreover, he warned against the strong campaign for right-to-work laws in many areas and used a local situation, a bitter strike by lay teachers at Christ the King High School in Queens as an example of that philosophy. Opposition to the beleaguered unionized teachers was led by a board of trustees headed by a strong advocate of right-to-work laws, he said.[20] Van Arsdale had firsthand knowledge of that situation because he, other members of the

CLC, and his stalwarts from Local 3—his "minute men"—could often be found on the picket lines of the teachers who were members of Local 1261, American Federation of Teachers.

Van Arsdale also was a strong voice in a national and international protest against the repression of independent unions by the Polish government. Van Arsdale mounted a flatbed truck outside the offices of the CLC on January 30, 1982, to condemn the action and support the Solidarity Union Activists led by Lech Walesa. Van Arsdale became a continued vociferous opponent of the Polish action.

Van Arsdale continued to answer every call for help by labor organizations in the city or in the nation in alliance with city locals or national unions. He threw the full force of the Central Labor Council behind a nationwide boycott of Greyhound Bus Lines called by the AFL-CIO.

He was also a strong supporter of trade union women. The New York Central Labor Council underwrote and endorsed the founding of the First Trade Union Women's Conference, held on January 19, 1974, in Manhattan. He also spoke at the conference in support of the strikers, most of them Chicano women, at the Texas and New Mexico clothing plants of the Farah Manufacturing Company, which had sought to bar organizational attempts by the Amalgamated Clothing Workers union. He had been asked to speak because of his involvement and CLC support in battling the company since the strike had begun nineteen months before. Following the conference, he joined in a protest march to a downtown Manhattan department store that carried Farah pants.

Van Arsdale also gave his weight and the bulk of the CLC and its member unions to a 1977 national boycott of goods made by the J.P. Stevens Company, which engaged in union-busting and paid substandard wages to its workers, most of them women, in their plants—plagued by substandard, hazardous working conditions—in the South.

"We asked for help often and the answer was always 'yes,'" said Clara Wright of the Storeworkers Union and treasurer of the Coalition of Labor Union Women (CLUW). Van Arsdale was honored for his help at an International Women's Day celebration held by the CLUW on March 1, 1981.

"He always encouraged the idea of bringing more women into the labor movement, but not just to bring them in for the sake of being women," said Paul Sanchez, of the regional AFL-CIO. "You know, bring them in because we know that they can make a contribution to the cause of the workers. In the Central Labor Council, for example, he was the first president appointing women to key positions in the labor movement."[21]

Van Arsdale's backstage strategies in helping to bring about a settlement in the J.P. Stevens strike involved Richard Shinn, chairman of the Metropolitan Life Insurance Company. It was also further evidence of the powerful role Van Arsdale played in labor circles—a role that rippled not only in the city but nationwide. Met Life was a major creditor of J.P. Stevens. Shinn and the Met were unhappy at being picketed by the Amalgamated, which also reportedly threatened to run two dissidents in an election to the Met Life's Board of Directors.[22] To head off the election, Shinn asked Van Arsdale to intercede with the Amalgamated and a meeting was arranged between Shinn and Murray Finley, Amalgamated's president.[23] Shinn subsequently met with James Finley, chairman of the board of J.P. Stevens, and the tide turned toward settlement. A.H. Raskin, writing as associate director of the National News Council, observed, in an op-ed piece in the New York Times:

> Perhaps the most ironic footnote to the strange upshot of the Stevens campaign as a victory for union money power is the extent to which relationships forged in New York City's fiscal crisis proved influential in opening the gateway to a labor advance that may profoundly affect the industrial future of the Sun Belt—the promised land for corporate refugees from union heartlands in the Northeast and Midwest.
>
> Richard Shinn, chairman of Metropolitan Life; E. Virgil Conway, chairman of the Seamen's Bank for Savings and Harry Van Arsdale, president of the Central Trades and Labor Council here, all deeply involved in the intricate negotiations that helped rescue this city from bankruptcy, found themselves thrust in key roles as intermediaries in the talks that brought Stevens and the Amalgamated to their current state of armed truce, if not of enduring peace. That may be the happiest augury for the emergence of a new spirit in an industry as troubled as this in this city.[24]

Van Arsdale also showed that he was a strong proponent of helping women achieve prominence in the labor movement by placing Sandra Feldman, executive director of the United Federation of Teachers, at the head of that year's Labor Day Parade on September 5, 1983, as its grand marshal. She became the first woman ever so honored. "It's certainly an historic and overdue moment for the Labor Day Parade to have its first woman Grand Marshal," Van Arsdale said. "We were looking for a dynamic, militant, respected New York trade union leader. Sandy has all the right qualifications."[25]

Another vivid exhibit of the Van Arsdale style occurred two weeks after the parade on Saturday, September 17, at Bayberry. It was a balmy day. Twenty-six members of Local 3 who had attended week-long classes in "Critical Thinking" at Bayberry were winding up their studies, thirty retirees and their wives were enjoying the weather, and 400 members and their families were preparing for a picnic at the Solidarity Family Center when a helicopter landed on the Great Lawn.

Out stepped Van Arsdale's friend, David Rockefeller. After breakfast, Rockefeller addressed the class on critical thinking. The students questioned him closely about the effect on the American economy and labor of imports from low-income nations. He then toured the camp and was impressed by the yeoman work done by Local 3 volunteers who had cleared more than a mile of thick brush to build an access road to the picnic grounds and also erected a deck and stairway to the beach.

One of those who had worked on clearing that stretch was Brian McLaughlin, a close aide of Van Arsdale (and, as previously mentioned, a future state assemblyman and president of the Central Labor Council). David Rockefeller's visit to Bayberry and what McLaughlin had to say about the work he and other volunteers had done illustrates the methods used by Van Arsdale to build his edifice. It also tells a lot about the reasons for the esprit de corps of Local 3 members and other trade unionists inspired by Van Arsdale. McLaughlin said:

> Harry had a way of communicating, aside from his leadership qualities, and promoting anything that he felt was of tremendous value to him or to the organization. For instance, when we went out to Bayberry Land to build the Solidarity Family Center, we had to get fifteen volunteers [each from various divisions and clubs] including myself and Lou Stein from Manufacturing and Jose Lopez from the Santiago Iglesias Educational Society. So we had forty-five men out there. And we started with some machetes and some chain saws, sawing down trees and making a roadway a mile from where we were. Nobody even knew where we were going to wind up. We left on a Saturday. We decided we'd come back the next Saturday. Then we started to work Saturday and Sunday. Now, after the third or fourth day, we started losing some people. You know? We went from forty-five down to thirty-eight, thirty-six and we said: "Mr. Van Arsdale, might we—you know—reach out to get a few more people here?" He said, "No." He said, "We got a committee of fifteen men from each of you, and it's important that each of these fifteen men, when we're done, would be part of this from beginning to end so that they can tell the other members what was involved here and how important this opportunity is to the Union."[26]

It was one of Van Arsdale's ways of building up the self-esteem of his membership. He also encouraged them by asking them to do nothing he would not do. McLaughlin continued:

> After we were about six weeks into the project, Harry was working out there with everybody. He'd come in with his legs bleeding at the end of the

day from the thorn bushes that were out there and he'd have the little snipper. Till seven o'clock at night he was still snipping away, you know, at these vines. But he broke us up and he had one crew start working from the other end and we were going this way and now you'd hear the chain saws [from the other crew] and you thought that you were near completion, but you still were four weeks away from getting to where you were going to get. But it had a tremendous value to all the workers because they said: "Oh, you know, we're going to do it. You know? We're going to make it." The point is that here's forty people. Almost everybody knew what we were doing out there, though, because the fellows would come back and tell all their co-workers. Harry would talk at meetings about how the Committee was doing. It became widely known in our industry.

Thus, the men were able to feel pride in their work and bask in the esteem of others because Van Arsdale made sure they would get the credit, McLaughlin explained. "He was inspirational. He was a motivator with unparalleled skill."[27]

The injection of David Rockefeller into a lazy afternoon at Bayberry was an example of how Van Arsdale differed from other labor leaders in that he expected his members to view broader horizons and make them proud to be part of a bigger canvas. McLaughlin again:

Our members were unusually exposed to a far bigger picture than members in another Union. Bert Powers or anybody else would come to a meeting and they'd talk about what? Printing. Or they would talk about collective bargaining. They would talk about a problem in the *Daily News* or the *New York Times*. But when you came to a Local 3 meeting you're likely to have the Governor there or the Mayor or a Committee on building Electchester or a Committee on forming a Labor college or organizing the taxi drivers . . . or some African prime minister.

Gradually people began to set higher goals for themselves. They were exposed to something that was much broader than would have ordinarily been intended for them as electricians or as workers in a factory and many responded to it. They became more interested, more diversified.

Harry was able to organizationally structure committees and through a system that started with the stewards talking to their people, the foremen talking to their workers, fraternal clubs talking to their members, bringing in all segments of the industry where when someone volunteered their time to go somewhere, it wasn't like, "Hey, I'm going to get stuck doing all the work." Everybody had a role to play. It wasn't like it was just the same five people all the time and I think that was one of the secrets to his success.

Our members, over a period of time, began to take pride in the fact that there were changes in the life of our City or the lives of other workers.

Harry didn't take the credit for doing it then. Harry was an unusual leader that gave the credit back to them and when others came to Local 3 meetings, they gave the credit to the members. They would say, "We know. Harry has told us what you have done." You know? It wasn't: "Harry had told us what he had done. Harry told us what you have done to make this housing possible or to make this Taxi Drivers Union possible or to make the Hospital Workers Union possible or to stop our Union from losing its membership."[28]

And that too accounted (headlines in the *New York Times* notwithstanding) for Van Arsdale's never-ending power: his ability to motivate and lead coupled with his astonishing record of accomplishments in labor, education, and plain morality. Enter now the Moral Rearmament Movement.

"Just like anything else, Harry never did anything half-way," said Hy Greenblatt, who would serve as president of the Harry Van Arsdale Jr. Memorial Association. "Whenever he got interested in something, he jumped in with both feet."[29]

Van Arsdale got interested in Moral Rearmament. "It was right up his alley. He was always trying to do good for people and that is just what the Moral Rearmament Movement was all about," Greenblatt continued. As a result of his interest, Van Arsdale posed this question to many: "When are people going to join the human race?"

The Moral Rearmament program had its beginnings within the Oxford Group, which sought to deepen the spiritual life of its adherents. It was particularly popular with students and faculty of Oxford University in England. The founder of the nondenominational group was actually an American churchman, Frank Buchman, who, when Europe was teetering on the cliff of war, expanded its basis and pleaded for a worldwide "moral and spiritual rearmament" to attack the causes of conflict and seek a "hate-free, fear-free, greed-free world."

His campaign was dubbed Moral Rearmament (MRA) and it sprouted actively after World War II. An international center for reconciliation was opened in the Swiss village of Caux in 1946. It has been the site of conferences of world leaders twice a year ever since. The aim of MRA is to change the course of history by changing human character for the better and causing people to help each other.

Van Arsdale and then Joint Industry Board Chairman Joseph D'Angelo attended the 1982 conference and a photo shows him seated at a table conferring with Francis Blanchard, chairman of the International Labor Organization, Archie Mackenzie, a former British Representative to the United Nations, and Fritz Philips, former chairman of Philips of Holland, among others.

Van Arsdale encouraged other JIB and Local 3 officials to go, and the following year Greenblatt and William Fiedler, Local 3 recording secretary made the trip. Dr. Harry Kelber added:

> When he got interested in something, he got everyone to do it. They all had to go. And some of them were not particularly keen on the thing. But he got obsessed with it. He went around asking the same thing "When are people going to join the human race?" That's what he asked. Well you could say in one way it's a ridiculous question because people are in the human race, but he didn't mean it that way, he meant when are we going to become human, moral? When are we going to start treating each other decently? And he picked up some data about the number of wars over past years. And he kept repeating it and saying, "Why are we this way?" And that bothered him. And it bothered him that he was making no progress on that.[30]

But another problem was soon to face Van Arsdale and though he fought against it, it would overcome him: prostate cancer.

It is difficult to say when the cancer first began to affect Van Arsdale because he was not the kind of man who would complain publicly of ills and he would strive to ignore ailments.

"He would never complain to me about anything," his second wife Madeline said. "He would keep things to himself."[31]

And Hy Greenblatt recalls, "He never took care of himself. He would always be more interested in taking care of other people, not himself. I remember when he would go to a dentist and have a tooth pulled. He had to have it pulled because he neglected it too long. And then he'd leave the dentist with some cotton wadding in his mouth and go right to a meeting. He would never baby himself. But he was very concerned when I had a heart bypass and went back to work. He said, 'What are you doing at work? You should be home.'"[32]

Van Arsdale apparently knew that something was wrong with him long before he did anything about it. Prostate problems are painful and debilitating. His grandson, Christopher Erikson, recalls speeches his grandfather gave when he was in obvious pain. As difficulties mounted, he took a leave of absence from his job as president of the Central Labor Council. Van Arsdale began to take long stays at Bayberry, conducting business from his spartan room there because, as Madeline pointed out, "Wherever there was a telephone, Harry would [carry out] his business."[33]

In that final period, his attention turned more and more to Local 3, which was his home.

"[D'Angelo] and I met with him at Bayberry several times," Greenblatt said. "He was working the same as he always did, worrying about the members of Local 3."[34]

And D'Angelo said, "He was thinking about what he could do because time was getting short—he knew that [even] if we didn't—and there was so much to do. So, he stayed there and had people come to him to save him all that time. He was concerned about where people were going to live. He was concerned about how Bayberry would continue on once he wasn't around. He was concerned about the very high costs of hospitalization and illnesses, particularly sudden family illnesses."[35]

When the pain became too great, Van Arsdale visited the JIB medical unit. The unit chief, Dr. Alex Maurillo, was away at a convention and Van Arsdale was seen by another physician who immediately ordered that a catheter be inserted. Van Arsdale gave a speech that same evening at a function. When Maurillo returned in a few days, Maurillo examined him and sent him immediately to New York Hospital in Manhattan, which had one of the city's best urology departments. Business agent and good friend, Bernard Rosenberg, tells of the day he took Van Arsdale to the hospital.

> He was very ill. He concealed it from everybody. He never told anybody he was ill. He would always say, "There is so much to do and there is so little time to do it." That is what he always used to say. In his last days, he would call me up and I would take him to the hospital, New York Hospital.
>
> New York Hospital has a parking lot in front of the main entrance to the hospital and there is a horseshoe driveway which allows you to park right in front of the door. So, I drove up there and he could hardly walk. So I got him out of the automobile, locked it up in front of the door, walked inside with him and there is a marble bench there and I left him there and walked in to register and the people there said, "Mister Van Arsdale has to come in and sign the papers." And I said, "Give me the paper and I will bring it out to him, he's sitting out there." And then they said, "Well, you're going to have to have him come in to take an X-ray." And I said, "If you want an X-Ray, after you put him in a bed, then you take a portable X-Ray and take an X-Ray." And then they said, "He needs a wheelchair to go up." And I said, "No, he refuses to have a wheel chair. He's going to walk up." And this is all against hospital rules and procedures. But he was a very, very proud man. He didn't want a wheelchair. So they agreed. And they escorted him up to his room.[36]

He was examined there by Dr. E. Darracott Vaughn, Jr., a surgeon, and later chairman of the Department of Urology. Surgery of the prostate was ordered, but during this ordeal Van Arsdale always kept up his spirits. "On his way to the operating room, he tried to organize some of the hospital workers," Maurillo said. "He was one tough guy, I'll tell you."[37] The surgery revealed prostate cancer so widespread that an operation would be useless. Van Arsdale stayed for a short time at the hospital, and working in his hospital room, continuing the habits of a lifetime. Among the well-wishers was David Rockefeller, who sent a dozen roses to the room, according to Maurillo.

Rosenberg was one of the regular visitors to Van Arsdale's hospital room/office.

"I would visit him days later and he asked me to massage his feet. 'Massage my feet,' he said, 'They're cold and feel numb.' And I was speaking to the doctor. Harry was in a lot of pain. You could see it on his face. And I said to the doctor, 'Why don't you give him some pain medication?' And the doctor said, 'Mister Van Arsdale told me that his body is poisoned, but he doesn't want his mind poisoned.' So, until he passed away, as far as I know, he never took any pain medication. He wanted a clear mind."[38]

The story tells volumes about Van Arsdale. He worked through the pain. He could have had an ambulance take him from home, but he eschewed that because of the expense, just as he rode subways or walked to save fare money, just as he spent next to nothing on clothing or on anything but basic foods, just as he constantly sought ways to economize in spending any union money on himself, just as he refused to take any money for any post except for his salary as business manager and later financial secretary of Local 3, just as his wife Madeline had to pressure him to buy a second suit to supplement his one and only basic blue.

"He did not care for material things, not for a car or money or luxuries," she said. "The man just had two suits and I had to argue with him to do that. I said, 'Harry, a man has to have at least two suits so you'll have one if you send the other one to the cleaners.' He just didn't have time to get a second suit. He never had time for anything for himself."[39]

And he didn't need a wheelchair to get to his hospital room. He was a fighter who wanted to remain on his feet, rather than use a crutch or a chair when he could still stand up.

And his hospital room became his office, his bed of pain, his desk.

"I had two phones put into his room," D'Angelo said. "One he used to make outside calls and the other he used to receive calls."[40]

Greenblatt recalls that he prepared some complex reports for Van Arsdale "and I prepared the information for him and I sent it up [to his room] with [his daughter] Kathryn and then a day or so later after he had a chance to look it over, he called me. We talked about it. He asked questions about the figures and I had them in front of me and we resolved it as we had always done—usually this was about Sunday night at 11 o'clock and I said to him

'Harry, is there anything else you want?' And he says, 'I'd like you to do me a favor and I'd like you to think of anything you can to help our members, any kind of program.' I said, 'Harry, I'll be very happy to do so.' We said goodbye and that was the last time I spoke to him."[41]

D'Angelo added his recollection of a final meeting. "He had something he wanted to go over with me. . . . He could hardly talk, but he had some kind of a report that he wanted me to review for him and I went over it, but I knew he was bad. So, I said to the doctor before I left there—'You know, what is he going to go through now? Is he going to be in pain or. . . . And the doctor said, 'Yes, he'll have some pain, but we'll be able to take care of that. But there is not much more we can do now.'"[42]

Van Arsdale wanted to return to his home in Electchester for his final days and the hospital allowed him to do so with round-the-clock nursing care. And that is where he was to die. "Before he passed away, I visited him and he was in bed and he could hardly talk," Rosenberg said. "He motioned me to come over to him and I pressed my ear against his mouth and he said, 'Tell me the truth. How many students do we have at the labor college?' He knew he was dying and he wanted to know how many students there were at the college."[43]

He died peacefully at the age of 80 on Sunday morning, February 16, 1986, in his bed in his Electchester apartment with his wife Madeline and his two daughters at his side. The date was also that of the birthday of his son, Thomas.

His estate was modest, a reflection of the way he lived. Thomas explained that his father had refused to take a salary from the Central Labor Council because he was on salary at Local 3 and there were periods during which he even stopped accepting that.

> He didn't believe in people being paid big salaries or holding down several jobs and adding-up the big salaries in the trade union movement. He knew that the success of the trade union movement depends on having membership. And if you raise the dues to a certain point, you risk the loss of membership and the membership was more important than the money. And if you increased the cost of the union beyond a certain point, you jeopardized the whole situation.
>
> Of course, there were examples of people who were leaders of very large unions [who] got big salaries and, of course, he just didn't think it was good. But he followed his principles that he lived by and when he became the treasurer of the IBEW there was a small salary which I think he took. But when he reached the age of 72 [and] being on social security, he periodically said, "I don't want to accept my salary from Local 3, like, for

whatever period it was." [Because of social security income] and then I guess the bills would catch up with him and then he'd say, "Oh, I'd better go back on the salary." And so it was amazing. Of course, the tax people, when they would come in and say "This man is working without a salary, there must be some gimmick here, some angle. What . . . what is it?"[44]

But there was no gimmick, it was just Van Arsdale's way of doing things. But that way of doing things posed problems for William Blain, who had been recording secretary of Local 3 up until the time of Van Arsdale's death and who also succeeded him as financial secretary. He said:

Well one of the things that Harry did that probably gave me the biggest headaches and the biggest problems in the course of working as his unofficial assistant in the financial secretary's office, Harry would from time to time present himself before the executive board and at his request ask that he be taken off the payroll, and the board would act on his request favorably, and Harry would be stricken from the payroll of Local #3, and he might leave himself off the payroll for six to eight month stretches at a time, and then when he felt the need he would come before the board and ask that he would be put back. In effect, what he was doing was he would go on salary for a short period of time until he accumulated a few hundred dollars or whatever he thought he needed to live on for the next few months, and then at that point he would remove himself from the payroll.

And then when he exhausted those funds he would go back on. Well, it wasn't a bookkeeping problem so much as it gave me a lot of headaches with the Internal Revenue Service, because Harry would file his income tax return. . . . Now picture, if you will, a man who's the financial secretary of the largest local of the International Brotherhood of Electrical Workers, also the President of the New York City Central Labor Council numbering over 1,000,000 members, and his income for the year was 0. Now if you were an IRS investigator would you buy that?

So periodically I would have these official inquiries into Harry's finances, and of course at that point it was my responsibility to have Harry fill out whatever forms they had deposited with me, and then it became my duty to try to convince those people and those agencies that what Harry said was the truth.

And of course it was simple to do because we would have the documentation, the executive board minutes, the actions, the dates, etc. to backup our claim. . . . He was not receiving a salary from the Central Labor Council, never did to the best of my knowledge, and then periodically would remove himself. . . . He did remove himself on at least three or four occasions that I could think of during my tenure as the office manager.

But his wants were simple. In his later years, he did not own a car. He had a driver's license but he hadn't driven in years. He traveled everywhere by public transportation—subway and bus. He didn't smoke, he didn't drink. He did not have any vices that I'm aware of. His biggest vice was his untiring efforts on behalf of his lifelong work.

As for his wife Madeline, she had a pension of her own, so I can only assume that she and he lived on those limited funds. And, as I said, he would take a salary when the need presented itself. And as soon as he was solvent and would be for a month or two he'd remove himself. He always felt that money should be . . . that the monies of the organization should be put to the best use, and that best use being to serve the membership and not to enhance the individual official or officer of the union.[45]

Van Arsdale's wake was held in the Martin Gleason Funeral Home in Flushing, close to his home and to Local 3. It lasted three days and throngs of mourners from all stations in life spilled into the street. Burial was at St. John's Cemetery in Queens.

A funeral service was held at St. Patrick's Cathedral in Manhattan. More than 3,000 people attended. Throngs of union members, many wearing buttons or woven insignia to show their affiliations, had gathered at the cathedral under a dark, morning sky more than two hours before the service. Dignitaries and labor leaders from the city, state, and nation attended. And those unable to attend, including foreign luminaries, sent condolences.[46]

Scores of mourners unable to get seats in the cavernous cathedral lined the walls inside and listened reverently or joined in the singing of the opening hymn, "Oh, God of Loveliness."

The eulogy was read by John Cardinal O'Connor. He said in part:

> Governor Cuomo very fittingly spoke of Harry as a giant of the labor movement. One could hardly use a better term. Lane Kirkland seconded that by saying that he was so very, very important not merely in the labor movement in New York, but throughout the entire country, and one could say, throughout the world. Last, night at the wake out in Queens, as I was arriving, Mayor Wagner was leaving. I said, you've lost a good friend. He said, I've lost a great friend. I noted Mayor Beame's tribute. I've read things by labor leaders. . . . And it is from these and from intensive reading that I believe that I have been able to come, I think, to recognize an extraordinary individual before God and before man . . . not too many have contributed so much as Harry Van Arsdale trying to advance the dignity of a union person, the working person. This Mass means so much to me because I know what this man did for this town. I was deeply gratified when assigned here to know that I was coming to a union town. I was deeply grati-

fied to [encounter] in my own Archdiocese of New York, a Teachers' Association, a Hospital Workers, Health Care Workers' Union, a Cemetery Workers' Union, and so on. And these came into being because of the efforts of a Harry Van Arsdale. Had they not come into being, they would have had to be created. I was deeply gratified simply to encourage them and do my best to support them. I was very much touched by his concern for education. One hears the word empowerment today. So many of us talk about . . . quite appropriately, about homelessness, about poverty, about hunger. And the word empowerment appears [often]. Empowerment of the poor. This was a man who recognized that the poor's cause can best be empowered by education. That would help factualize the potential of Almighty God appearing in every one of us. God knows where the union movement would be were it not for . . . Harry Van Arsdale—an enlightened union man. One who recognized, indeed, that there had to be true unionism. He said unions should be a brotherhood. Perhaps today we should have added sisterhood, but surely, his meaning was quite clear. He said a union of brotherhood is such [that] when you're sick your brother from the union comes to visit you, when you are in difficulty, it is your brother in the union who reaches out to you. This man really understood the meaning of the term union. What it should mean. A union in justice, a union in charity, a union in true love. . . .

We speak of the union of a family, that's the way he spoke of trade unions, of organizing associations.

As our Holy Father teaches, as the church teaches firmly, as Harry Van Arsdale understood, not only because of the labor schools that he himself established. . . . He understood as the church teaches. People must have the right to organize because everyone has a right to a just wage, that's a union wage. That's a wage that guarantees at least a degree of security. Everyone has the right to collective negotiations, collective bargaining and if these fail and all . . . [has] been exhausted, then indeed [they have] the right to strike. I was interested to read a little citation, of all places, a little newspaper, Newport News, Virginia, 1962. It was Harry Van Arsdale saying a union leader must . . . he must serve all of his people, he must worry about them, he must be available to the people, he must not remove himself from the people, he must live with the humility of these people. Now if anybody did that, he certainly did it in the manner in which he lived and died. . . .

Governor Carey told us that the name Van Arsdale was synonymous with the word integrity. He went beyond this. He said Roosevelt and Truman gave us the fair deal, Van Arsdale gave everybody a good deal. New deal, fair deal, good deal. Not for an isolated few but for everybody and the whole community has profited. So now, he has died, he will soon be buried. We will proceed with this Mass, aware of his accomplishments, aware of his imperfections, cared for by everyone of us. In one of the most beautiful and telling passages of the Gospel, we read of our Lord's gathering everyone in the final judgment. At His right hand, on His left. He says to those on His left hand, depart from me ye cursed to everlasting fire. To those on His right hand, come and be blessed in my Father, receive the kingdom prepared for you, from all eternity. And then He goes on to tell us why He says to those on His left hand, depart from me ye cursed to everlasting fire. Because He says, when I was hungry, you gave me nothing to eat; when I was thirsty, you gave me nothing to drink; you never clothed me; you never visited me in prison; you never mourned for me while sorrowing. For those on my right, when I was hungry you gave me to eat; when I was thirsty you gave me to drink; when I was naked, you clothed me; in prison you visited me; when I was sorrowing and suffering, you consoled me. And they would say, when Lord did we do this to you? And He said, I will answer, as often as you did it to the least of my brothers and sisters, you did it for me. I strongly suspect that they'll be the words that He will extend to Harry Van Arsdale. . . . I have no greater prayer for Harry Van Arsdale than that God will look at the work of his hands, his laborers hands, union hands, and say that it was good.[47]

Of his father, Thomas said: "He was an example of a man who started out as a very young labor leader . . . and along the way, while there were plenty of reasons to be discouraged and get off the track, he never did get off the track. Up to his last days, those were the things he was thinking about the trade labor movement and its importance."[48]

Fond remembrances and praise came from around the city, the nation, and the world.

"Organized labor has lost a giant," Governor Mario Cuomo said.[49]

"Harry was one of the great figures of not just the New York labor movement but the whole American labor movement," Lane Kirkland, president of the AFL-CIO, said. "He was an extraordinarily committed and dedicated man who never spared himself and didn't spare others. When I say that, I'm thinking of the 3 o'clock in the morning calls, and it wasn't because he was carousing, he was working. He will be sorely missed. I was terribly fond of him personally."[50]

John Sweeney, president of the Service Employees International Union (and destined to become president of the AFL-CIO) recalled: "When I became president of Local 32B in 1976 we had a citywide apartment strike and we were in mediation. I came home at 2 A.M. My wife told me Mr. Van Arsdale called and said to call no matter what time I came in. I told her I don't call anyone at 2 o'clock. At 6 o'clock that morning the phone rang. It was Harry asking what he could do. He was eventually part of a three-man fact-finding team appointed by the mayor, and their recommendations settled the strike."[51]

Albert Shanker, president of the American Federation of Teachers, said:

> We [the teachers union] had a strike on November 7, 1960, on the question of whether teachers had the right to collective bargaining. The next day George Meany, then president of the AFL-CIO, called Mayor [Robert] Wagner, pointing out that here was the son of the great pro-labor senator with a union-busting strike on his hands.
>
> He urged the mayor to set up a committee to study the issue. Harry Van Arsdale was appointed chairman. It was the Van Arsdale committee that brought about the first collective bargaining rights for teachers, not only for New York City, but for the whole nation.
>
> When he took over the Central Labor Council, it was dead. He organized the teachers, the taxi drivers. He was the guy who got [Governor Nelson] Rockefeller to give collective bargaining rights to the hospital workers.[52]

"A man in continuous motion" is how Thomas Donahue, then secretary-treasurer of the AFL-CIO, remembered Van Arsdale. He recalled how he used to ride around Manhattan on the back of a motor scooter driven by Arnold Beichman, who edited Local 3's newspaper in the 1960s, to save time in traffic.

> If he were on his way to an apprenticeship meeting and he met you on the street, he would sweep you up, take you along and have you make a speech to the apprentices. He organized the taxi cab drivers. He started the Brotherhood Party around 1956 in an effort to form a labor party. He was a major figure in organizing the hospital workers [Local 1199]. It wouldn't have happened without Harry. As of this past year, throughout 1984, Harry had meetings at the Central Labor Council at 5 o'clock every night with a different group of delegates to the council to ask, "What can we do for you?" He did that right up to the time he got sick.[53]

John Lawe, international president of the Transport Workers Union of America, said, "I've known him since the 1966 [city transit] strike. The mold is broken. I don't think we'll ever have another labor leader as dedicated as Harry. He never sought publicity. His work was for the membership. If it didn't serve the membership, Harry didn't think it was worthwhile."[54]

Vito Pitta, president of the Hotel-Motel Trades Council, who led a hotel workers strike in the city in 1985, said of Van Arsdale, "During the hotel strike in New York, he was out there just like a kid on the picket lines with the hotel workers. He was a model for the whole country. There isn't anyone who is going to replace him. Someone might run for his office, but they won't replace him."[55]

Norman William, general secretary of the British Trades Congress, said: "He was a good friend to many British trade unionists, especially those in the construction industry and he will be missed here."[56]

Frank Chapple, British trade union leader, said "He was known and loved by trade unionists throughout the world. He commanded respect as well as instilling inspiration."[57]

One of the deepest, most mournful and most insightful eulogies came from Local 3 in the words of its then President George Schuck who said, in part:

> Like a parent, Harry was always available when we needed him the most whether it was to seek his counsel or just to talk out our frustrations. Although we knew better, we selfishly hoped that his days would never end and that he would always be there to lend us his eternal optimism when things seemed dim or give us words of encouragement when our goals were unsure.
>
> Just as a parent nurtures and guides a growing child, so it was that Harry loved and devoted himself to the labor movement in general and the IBEW in particular. He recognized that mistrust and skepticism would divide us unless we got to know and understand each other better. Therefore, Harry always made the time to listen to what someone else had on their mind.
>
> So it was that he came to share the joys and disappointments of the thousands of union members and others whom he went out of his way to meet and talk with. Often it was from those conversations that a dream was born or a program initiated.
>
> Then with seemingly boundless energy and an indomitable optimism, Harry would personally spend long hours, both day and night, motivating his associates to work with him to find the means to bring those dreams into reality. Today, many of us enjoy the fruits of his labors. Harry's intuitive foresight manifests itself in the many beneficial programs that he initiated and fostered during his 53 years as a local union Officer and which permit our members to enjoy some measure of security and dignity in a troubled world around us.
>
> Harry had an uncanny ability to seek out and nurture the worthwhile qualities within each of us. Then by stimulating our conscience, he would channel our energies towards helping others. His greatest pleasure seemed to come from watching associates grow and develop into responsible leaders and he delighted in their personal achievements, but always at a distance so as not to detract from the individual's significance.
>
> Harry saw the trade union movement as the social and economic conscience of our nation and the *only* means by which American workers could confidently provide a better life for their families. He also understood that the key to successful labor organization was the systematic involvement of

the greatest number of its members. He regarded any member's complacency or apathy to be a personal defeat and he would go out of his way to renew their interest in the work of the union.

He knew that true understanding of a problem only comes from actively participating in the solution; and that an enlightened membership would then zealously guard their union's accomplishments because they gave a part of themselves to win them.

Harry wisely recognized that membership involvement on the myriad of committees within our union was also a means for the Officers and Business Representatives to know and understand our membership better so that we can truly represent them better. Out of these activities has grown a mutual respect for each other's integrity and developed the bonds of mutual trust that are essential for a group of individuals to function in harmony as a union.

Harry looked upon education as another important factor essential to our union's success. He was constantly urging our members to return to school for many reasons. In a high-tech industry such as ours, education is a life-long commitment just to stay abreast of the rapid technological changes that threaten to engulf us and affect the security of our future work opportunities. Harry also believed that a full understanding of our nation's history and the development of the labor movement within it was the best assurance that past mistakes would not be repeated. . . . He realized that tradesmen, with all their expertise and practical knowledge were consistently excluded from key positions in our society if they did not also possess the necessary academic credentials that would attest to their abilities. He was a firm believer that practical men developed practical, workable solutions while those skilled only in theory, only seemed capable of promoting theoretical solutions to the many serious problems threatening our society.

Finally, it irked Harry to witness the latent talents of others go undeveloped because of the individual's disinterest or reluctance to gain the formal education that was required; or because no educational facility or program was available with the flexibility necessary to accommodate the schedules of working men and women; or because of the burdensome cost of education. He constantly pressed to remove these obstacles so there would be a better future not only for a worker's children, but for the worker as well.

It delighted him to be able to tell the story of a manufacturing member's child who was doing better in school because his father had returned to the classroom to achieve a high school diploma. I can vividly recall his obvious pleasure when he would describe how father and son did their homework together each evening, each learning from the other. That was typical of the inner joy and personal satisfaction that Harry derived from his work. It also characterized Harry's view of his work as the opportunity to learn from each other.

Throughout his life, Harry shunned personal rewards or flowery accolades for his many accomplishments. In fact, he constantly gave all the credit to others for what in reality was the small part they had played in bringing forth his dreams. I believe his only desire for tribute was his fervent hope that the lessons that he had attempted to teach us had not fallen on deaf ears and that we would not neglect the spark that he had carefully kindled within each of us.

If we have truly learned the lessons that he eloquently taught by his own example, Harry Van Arsdale's influence in the world he lived in and loved so much will be eternal. May his personal integrity and total dedication to his fellow man inspire in each of us the will to carry on his work. Then and only then will Harry's ultimate dream be realized that "Someday, EVERYONE on Earth Will Rejoin the Human Race."[58]

To help fulfill that design, this book was written.

Afterword

This book leaves no doubt that the Trade Union Movement and Local 3, first and foremost, were Harry's life. The complexity of his union and all of the events and activities that had been a part of it were voluminous. Some of the important mileposts had "Harry" written all over them. There were many mergers of smaller IBEW locals into Local 3. Local 20 of the IBEW merged in 1934, having the outside jurisdiction for high voltage linemen and splicers throughout the New York metropolitan area including Westchester, Nassau, and Suffolk counties; the merger incorporated a group of highly skilled workers into Local 3. In 1946 IBEW Local 277, whose members performed marine electrical work on ships in dry-dock, merged into Local 3. IBEW Local 664 which was chartered in 1910 had the jurisdiction in the Brooklyn Navy Yard, and in 1961 it also merged becoming the JGB Division of Local 3.

There were also mergers of independent unions into Local 3; most notably was the union formally representing the members of what is now the Electric Elevator Division of Local 3, a division of over 1,800 men and women. It is important to note that many of the officers of these groups maintained their leadership positions in Local 3 as business representatives and served the members and the Local with distinction.

Organizing was the other means by which Harry grew the Local. The F, the I, J, DBM, and the Sign Divisions were some that were born out of those successful early efforts to have Local 3 represent all electrical workers in the City of New York—from the lowest paid manufacturing worker to the higher paid skilled electrician.

Harry also took an interest in helping to strengthen the IBEW and particularly Local 3's relationship with the Canadian members of the IBEW. In 1982 he hosted a week of intensive study and an exchange of ideas among International Vice President Ken Rose and twenty Canadian IBEW business managers and the officers and business representatives from Local 3. Broadening the education of his own officers through international travel was something Harry had been doing for some time. More than twenty-one senior staff members traveled extensively throughout the world during the 1950s. They attended international labor conferences and met with foreign trade unionists. Later study tours to South and Latin America were Harry's way of keeping his staff fine-tuned, to the needs of newly organized immigrant workers. Recognizing the changing face of the American workforce early on, in 1983 Harry founded the Chinese American Cultural Society within Local 3. He also shared the knowledge and experience of his organization and that of the Joint Industry Board with many visiting labor delegations from foreign countries. Harry and Local 3 were renowned worldwide.

To sum it up, if I had to say it in one word what Harry held most dear, it would be *education*. It was what Harry was most concerned with and he saw education as the means to help find solutions to the challenges that will continue to face working men and women. He saw education as the justification for higher standards and ultimately he saw education as the path to a better and more just society.

On behalf of the Harry Van Arsdale Jr. Memorial Association, it is our hope that this book will encourage additional research and that it sparks an interest to further the goal of this organization, namely, to perpetuate and foster the ideals of this great Trade Unionist. We are happy to add this fine work to the other memorials and honors that have continued to accrue to Harry Van Arsdale Jr. since his death on February 16, 1986. They include:

- The planting of 10,000 trees in Israel in his honor.

- Renaming of Empire State College's Center for Labor Studies, State University of New York, as the Harry Van Arsdale Jr. School of Labor Studies.

- Establishment of a college scholarship through the Educational and Cultural Fund of the Electrical Industry in the name of Harry Van Arsdale Jr.

- Renaming of Eli Whitney High School in Brooklyn, New York, as the Harry Van Arsdale Jr. Vocational High School.

- Naming the intersections of 161st and 162nd Streets in Electchester as Harry Van Arsdale Jr. Plaza.

- The establishment of periodic seminars by Cornell University to study labor and management relations.

- The renaming of Jewel Avenue in Flushing, New York, as Harry Van Arsdale Jr. Avenue.

- A Web site was also established: www.harryvanarsdalejr.org with links giving his biography and listing his achievements. There is also a "guest book" to allow Web site visitors to write comments. The hundreds of comments are from those who knew Van Arsdale and/or his work. His tributes continue to grow in number. The great majority are from the rank and filers, and further reveal his legacy in the minds and hearts of those whom he served so well.

- On December 5, 2001, Harry Van Arsdale Jr. was inducted into the AFL-CIO's, Labor's International Hall of Fame at the George Meany Center, Silver Spring, Maryland.

Hy Greenblatt
President
Harry Van Arsdale Jr. Memorial Association

Notes

Chapter 1. From the Revolutionary War to Hell's Kitchen

1. The major source for the history, descriptions of the day, and its main characters is a pamphlet, *Evacuation Day*, 1783, self-published by James Riker, a member of the New York Historical Society, in 1883 to mark a centennial celebration.

2. As Riker (John Van Arsdale's grandson) reported in his pamphlet, John Van Arsdale was the son of John and Deborah Van Arsdale and was born in the town of Cornwall in Orange County on January 5, 1756. He was part of the fourth generation of his family on these shores. The common ancestor of the Van Arsdales here was Simon Jansen Van Assdalen. A modification of the name was Van Osdell. Simon emigrated here from the Netherlands in 1653, soon after the arrival of the Roosevelts.

3. Riker, *Evacuation Day*, p. 18.

4. Ibid., p. 53. The Revolutionary War veteran John was honored with a prominent place in the elaborate parades and celebrations of the Evacuation Day holiday which was an annual feature of New York City life.

5. Some members of the family still live in Bullville, about 95 miles from New York City, in a house built in 1804. Harry Van Arsdale Jr. would visit there as a child with his family to enjoy peaceful days in the country. It was always a favorite spot for him. Later in life, en route to Albany to see governors or legislators, he would also stop off to pay his respects to ancestors buried in the family plot.

6. As attested in an interview with Margaret Van Arsdale Brohan, Harry Jr.'s first cousin.

7. The building might have been on West 47th Street. The name of the area known as "Hell's Kitchen" was originally Clinton. The most popular story of how the area got the name Hell's Kitchen is that it was coined when a rookie policeman watching a riot on 39th Street remarked to his partner, known as "Dutch Fred the Cop," that "This place is Hell itself." Dutch Fred supposedly replied: "Hell's a mild climate. This place is Hell's Kitchen." "The revival of the place name of Clinton for the area from West 34th Street to West 59th Street is well underway. One may at first, as I did, suspect middle class pretensions or even a lace curtain search for respectability in such a usage. Nonetheless as a name it has much more precedence in history and therefore would seem more accurate than the more colorful, but odious one. Certainly

as far back as 1918, before the parish was a half-century old, it was understood to be in the Clinton neighborhood. New York mayor and governor DeWitt Clinton, once had a mansion there" (Henry J. Browne, *One Stop above Hell's Kitchen* [South Hackensack, NJ: Custom Book, 1977]). Historian Mary Clark also notes that the name "Hell's Kitchen" was attached to a rough area of London. She goes on to say that it first appeared in print on these shores on September 22, 1881, when a *New York Times* reporter used it in a story about a multiple murder in the West 30s. He described an especially notorious tenement at 39th Street and Tenth Avenue as "Hell's Kitchen" and depicted the neighborhood as "probably the lowest and filthiest in the city." Still another version about the origin of the name has it that it referred to a German Restaurant in the area known as "Heil's Kitchen."

8. The area also produced, among others, former New York Senator Daniel Patrick Moynihan and former Secretary of Labor Peter Brennan, and movie stars Alice Faye and George Raft. Raft claimed to have used some of the gangsters he grew up with as a basis for the mobsters he played on the screen.

9. Michael Daly and John Hamill, "The Ghosts of Hell's Kitchen," *New York Magazine*, April 12, 1982.

10. Reverend Philip Carey, interviewed by Julius C.C. Edelstein (senior vice chancellor emeritus of the City University of New York), tape recording, n.d. Joint Industry Board, Flushing, New York.

11. These tenements were outlawed in 1901 under a state law that mandated more light and space for living quarters.

12. As described by Benjamin Appel in his novel, *Hell's Kitchen* (New York: Pantheon Books, 1977), pp. 7–8.

13. Browne, *One Stop Above Hell's Kitchen*, p. 9.

14. Warren Moscow, n.d. "History of Local Union 3." IBEW Local 3 archieves.

15. Maurice F. Neufeld, *Day In, Day Out with Local 3, IBEW*, New York State School of Industrial and Labor Relations, Cornell University, February 1955.

16. Harry Van Arsdale Jr., interviewed for *Apprenticeship on the Move*, sponsored by the electrical industry's Joint Industry Board (New York, 1974).

17. Family lore attested to in interviews with Harry Jr.'s first cousins Margaret Brohan and Alanson Van Arsdale, Jr.

18. Moscow, "History of Local Union 3," p. 5.

19. Leon Goodelman, "Van Arsdale Tripled Union's Size . . . Now He Faces Prison," *PM,* a 1940s article, date uncertain.

20. William McSpedon, interviewed by Edelstein, tape recording, March 27, 1987. Joint Industry Board, Flushing, New York.

21. Ibid.

22. Ibid.

23. Harry Van Arsdale Jr., interviewed for *Apprenticeship on the Move.*

24. Chris Plunkett, interviewed by Edelstein, tape recording, n.d. Joint Industry Board, Flushing, New York.

25. Browne, *One Stop Above Hell's Kitchen*, p. 48.

26. As told by Harry Van Arsdale Jr. in an address at a Local 3 Honor Roll ceremony and reported in the *Electrical Union World*, November 1, 1963, p. 11.

27. As outlined in the Announcement of Courses of Study of Townsend Harris High School.

28. Van Arsdale Jr., interviewed for *Apprenticeship on the Move.*

Chapter 2. Making His Mark: Early Struggles in Local 3

1. Warren Moscow, "History of Local Union 3," IBEW Local 3 archives, p. 6.

2. Ibid., p. 72. It is possible that Harry Jr. was helped as much as he might have been hindered by being the son of Harry Sr. in finding work. As he himself pointed out, the Van Arsdale name carried respect. As a Roman Catholic and of half-Irish descent, young Harry was also a member of the dominant membership group in the Local at that time. But being admitted to the union may have been another matter. It may have been felt that one Van Arsdale, vocal and militant against inequities in the Local, was enough.

3. Howell H. Broach, *Union Progress in New York* (published by Local 3, 1929), p. 6. This was largely a report made by Broach—then president—to an IBEW convention in Miami.

4. Joseph Jacobson, interviewed by author, December 12, 1999.

5. Moscow, "History of Local Union 3," p. 6.

6. Grace Palladino, *Dreams of Dignity, Workers of Vision: A History of the International Brotherhood of Electrical Workers* (New York: IBEW, 1991), p. 129.

7. Harold Seidman, *Labor Czars: A History of Labor Racketeering,* (New York: Liveright, 1938), p. 130.

8. As attested to by George Schuck, Sr., a former administrator of the Joint Industry Board of the Electrical Industry and a good friend of Harry Van Arsdale, in an interview for *Apprenticeship on the Move,* August 12, 1975. Schuck also said: "One of the reasons he thought so much about Bill Hogan was that his father was a close friend of Bill Hogan's. And they organized Local 3 in Bill Hogan's kitchen."

9. Harry Van Arsdale Jr., interviewed for *Apprenticeship on the Move*, September 16, 1975.

10. Identified as Allen Bedsole in Moscow, "History of Local 3," p. 13. Bedsole went on to hold many key posts in Local 3 under Van Arsdale.

11. Van Arsdale Jr., interviewed for *Apprenticeship on the Move,* June 1974.

12. This is indicative of the puffery and exaggeration evinced in this report. Official Local 3 membership rolls, based on per capita payments to the IBEW, list the Local's membership as 6,994 in 1929. This still represents, however, substantial growth from 1926 when Broach took control. The rolls then, according to per capita payments to the International, showed 4,886 members.

13. Van Arsdale Jr., interviewed for *Apprenticeship on the Move,* June 1974.

14. Moscow, "History of Local Union 3," p. 6.

15. Ibid.

16. (New York) *Daily News,* March 5, 1944. This was published one day after Buchalter was electrocuted at Sing Sing prison (in Ossining, New York) for the murder of Joseph Rosen, a candy-store clerk. He had spurned the pleas of his wife Betty to try to make a deal to save his life by telling authorities all he knew of the infamous coalition between criminals and politicians. The *News* reported that Rabbi Jacob Katz had asked then Governor Thomas E. Dewey to delay the execution by at least one day so that it would not fall on the Jewish Sabbath. The Saturday Sabbath was a busy day for him in his synagogue, Rabbi Katz explained, and if the date of Buchalter's execution was not changed, then it would be necessary for him to interrupt his duties to spend the entire day with the condemned preparing him for his departure from this world. Dewey was sympathetic to the Rabbi's plight, but he did not postpone the execution.

17. Moscow, "History of Local Union 3," p. 10.

18. Van Arsdale Jr., interviewed for *Apprenticeship on the Move*, June 1974.

19. Broach, *Union Progress in New York*, p. 18.

20. Ibid.

21. Bertram Powers, interviewed by Julius C.C. Edelstein, tape recording, February 16, 1990. Joint Industry Board, Flushing, New York.

22. Van Arsdale Jr., interviewed for *Apprenticeship on the Move*.

23. Lance Van Arsdale, interviewed by the author, July 25, 1999.

24. Joseph Cuty, interviewed by the author, September 1999.

Chapter 3. A Fight to the Top

1. Howell H. Broach, *Union Progress in New York* (published by Local 3, 1929), p. 44.

2. Based on per capita tax payments to the IBEW.

3. The troubles within Local 3 attracted the notice of some of the city's more prominent progressive intelligentsia. They signed an open letter to the members of Local 3, explaining that "All intelligent citizens have a deep interest, however, in how the trade union movement settles its problems. They know that without an effective, clean and progressive trade union movement both material and moral standards will be lowered for everybody." They went on to say that they had written to Broach asking for his answers to a host of charges (including that he had arbitrarily expelled members, revoked local charters, expelled elected leaders, suspended meetings, had opponents physically attacked, not accounted for funds, and steered work to favored contractors), but Broach essentially brushed off their concerns. The signers of the letter included Devere Allen, associate editor of the *Nation*; Roger Baldwin of the American Civil Liberties Union; Malcolm Cowley, associate editor of the *New Republic*; the writer Theodore Dreiser; A.J. Muste of the Conference for Progressive Labor Action; Rev. William B. Spofford of the Church League for Industrial Democracy; Edmund Wilson, associate editor of the *New Republic*; and Rabbi Stephen S. Wise of the Free Synagogue.

4. Grace Paladino, in her book *Dreams of Dignity, Workers of Vision* (New York: IBEW 1991), quotes Thomas Van Arsdale, business manager of Local 3, as saying that, although many thought Broach had left New York with "a suitcase full of money," he believed that this was due just to the usual barbs thrown at any leader.

5. Warren Moscow, "History of Local Union 3," p. 11.

6. By referendum votes of the national membership, the conventions in 1933, 1935, 1937, and 1939 were canceled. Funds that had been earmarked for the conventions were then transferred to the general fund. It was the only way the Brotherhood could meet its financial obligations without going into debt.

7. *Journal of Electrical Workers and Operators*, August 1933.

Chapter 4. Dealing with the New Deal

1. Warren Moscow, "History of Local Union 3."

2. Van Arsdale, interviewed for *Apprenticeship on the Move*.

3. At a membership meeting November 23, 1933.

4. According to Julius C.C. Edelstein.

5. Hearing held on November 28, 1933. Local 3 was represented by Bert Kirkman, president; William Reuter, vice president; George Whitford, recording secretary; Harry Van Arsdale, business manager; Hugh Morgan, assistant business manager; and David O'Hara, financial secretary.

6. Moscow, "History of Local Union 3," p. 18.

7. In the speech, "The Goals of Labor," given by Van Arsdale at the Cooper Union Forum, February 28, 1962.

8. Thomas Van Arsdale Jr., interviewed by Edelstein, tape recording, January 4, 1989. Joint Industry Board, Flushing, New York.

9. Peter Brennan interviewed by Edelstein, tape recording, August 20, 1986. Joint Industry Board, Flushing, New York.

10. Thomas Van Arsdale Jr., interviewed by Edelstein, tape recording, January 4, 1989.

11. Kathryn Erikson, interviewed by Edelstein, tape recording, December 22, 1986. Joint Industry Board, Flushing, New York.

12. Madeline Van Arsdale Jr., interviewed by the author, September 15, 1999.

13. Ibid.

14. From his address at Cooper Union, February 28, 1962.

Chapter 5. Growing Pains

1. Located at 205 East 67th Street.

2. At Pythian Hall, 1941 Madison Avenue.

3. Now Avenue of the Americas.

4. The firms were: Allen Bradley Company, Allis-Chalmers Mfg. Co., Clark Controller Co., Colt's Patent Fire Arms Mfg. Co., Cutler-Hammer, Inc., The Electric Controller & Mfg. Co., General Electric Co., Hardwick-Hindle, Inc., Monitor Controller Co., Palmer Electric & Mfg. Co., The Rowan Controller Co., Square D Co., Trumbull Mfg. Co., and Westinghouse Elec. & Mfg. Co. In 1938, National Electrical Manufacturers Association, Hardwicke-Hindle Company, Palmer Electrical and Manufacturing Company, and Rowan Controller Company withdrew from the case. Van Arsdale commented in Quarterly financial statement to the members of Local 3, Bulletin of August 8, 1938: "You may have noted that while certain newspapers went to great lengths to feature in a sensational manner comparatively trivial matters which reflected unfavorably towards Local No. 3, they invariably neglected to feature this important development."

5. *Business Week,* December 14, 1935, p. 23.

6. Quarterly financial statement to the members of Local 3, Bulletin of February 10, 1935.

7. Warren Moscow, "History of Local Union 3."

8. Quarterly financial statement to the members of Local 3, Bulletin of November 22, 1937.

9. *Journal of Electrical Workers and Operators,* July 1940, p. 37.

10. *New York Times,* November 21, 1938, p. 15.

11. Van Arsdale was interviewed for *Apprenticeship on the Move.*

12. Quarterly financial statement to the members of Local 3, Bulletin of March 31, 1936.

13. Quarterly financial statement to the members of Local 3, Bulletin of February 8, 1937.

14. David Kass letter to Van Arsdale in Moscow, April 16, 1937.

15. A resolution introduced by Kass at the July 10, 1941, general membership meeting, urging the American government to give all possible aid to the Soviet Union in its fight against Nazi invaders, was defeated.

16. George Schuck, Sr., interview August 12, 1975. Interviewer unknown.

17. Bernard Rosenberg, interviewed by Julius C.C. Edelstein, tape recording, June 5, 1991. Joint Industry Board, Flushing, New York.

18. Quarterly financial statement to the members of Local 3, Bulletin of March 11, 1937.

Chapter 6. Battles on Many Fronts

1. Sokolsky quoted at length from the testimony of a mercurial and eccentric former Local 3 member, Isaac Penner, who had become a contractor and then engaged his former union in a series of disputes. His charges of intimidation, extortion, and the like received a heavy play in the press. Local 3 responded in part by seeking an injunction against his lockout of Local 3 members. Penner's odious behavior was such that it caused Supreme Court Judge George L. Donnellan, who was hearing the case, to say: "I consider this man Penner a dangerous individual and some steps should be taken to stop him from making these general accusations against everybody."

2. Typography used by Van Arsdale in his letter.

3. The syndicate paid $7,500 and the Westchester group paid $15,000.

4. Austin Perlow, *What Have You Done for Me Lately* (New York: Benjamin, 1979), p. 124.

5. Harry Van Arsdale Jr., interviewed for *Apprenticeship on the Move.*

6. Robert Reade, interviewed by Julius C.C. Edelstein, tape recording, n.d. Joint Industry Board, Flushing, New York.

7. Joseph Jacobson, interviewed for *Apprenticeship on the Move.*

8. As listed in part in the JIB's *History and Organization of the Joint Industry Board of the Electrical Industry.*

9. *Electrical Union World,* July 19, 1941, p. 3.

10. Ibid.

11. Van Arsdale Jr., interviewed for *Apprenticeship on the Move.*

12. *PM,* "Van Arsdale Tripled Union's Size . . . Now He Faces Prison," by Leon Goodelman, date unknown.

13. *Electrical Union World,* July 19, 1941, p. 3.

14. Ibid.

15. When the resignation was announced at a general meeting, speaker after speaker rose to voice support for Van Arsdale who told the members and reporters afterward that he hoped the vote would show he had the full backing of the membership. A letter from an officer of Local 3 that was printed in the IBEW's *Journal of Electrical Workers and Operators* in August 1940, after the election, conjectured further about Van Arsdale's motives. The letter, cosigned by Frederick Fink, of the Educational Committee and press secretary Jeremiah Sullivan, said in part: "With all these attacks going on, the thought came to Harry, 'Possibly the membership is dissatisfied with my work; maybe I am trying to do too much; maybe they would like another business manager.' Such thoughts as these, I suppose, do come into the minds of all able men." The resignation "amazed" the membership, said Fink and Sullivan who said of the outcome: "Nothing can so upset the National Electrical Manufacturers Association, the Walter Gordon Merritts (attorney for NEMA), the Thurman Arnolds and any others of the same ilk as this overwhelming landslide for Harry Van Arsdale Jr."

16. This text, somewhat changed, was printed as a signed article in the July 1, 1940, issue of *Electrical Union World.*

17. Grace Palladino, *Dreams of Dignity, Workers of Vision* (Washington, DC: IBEW, 1991), p. 175.

Chapter 7. America at War

1. As noted in the Quarterly financial statement to the members of Local 3, Bulletin of October 3, 1941.

2. Van Arsdale, in an interview with an unidentified questioner on September 7, 1977, said that he had met with Pegler to try to temper his views about unions. Pegler indicated that he had taken some of Van Arsdale's arguments to heart, but he later continued with his union bashing, Van Arsdale said.

3. As reported in the *Electrical Union World,* November 28, 1941, p. 7, in a signed article by editor Huestis. By the same token, he pointed to the CIO and independent unions as strike instigators.

4. Armand D'Angelo, interviewed by Julius C.C. Edelstein, tape recording, December 30, 1985. Joint Industry Board, Flushing, New York.

5. Ibid.

6. The *Electrical Union World,* July 3, 1943, p. 2.

7. D'Angelo interviewed by Edelstein, tape recording, April 4, 1976. Joint Industry Board, Flushing, New York.

8. George Schruck Sr., interviewed for *Apprenticeship on the Move,* August 12, 1975.

9. Robert Reade, interviewed by Edelstein. Joint Industry Board, Flushing, New York.

10. Austin Perlow, interviewed for *Apprenticeship on the Move,* September 3, 1975.

11. Lester Velie, "The Union that Gives More to the Boss." *Reader's Digest,* January 1956.

12. D'Angelo interview, December 5, 1985.

13. Efrem A. Kahn, interviewed for *Apprenticeship on the Move,* August 1975.

14. D'Angelo interview, November 3, 1985.

15. Ibid, December 5, 1985.

16. Ibid.

17. William Blain, interviewed by Edelstein, May 11, 1987. Joint Industry Board, Flushing, New York.

18. Ibid.

19. Thomas Van Arsdale, interviewed by Edelstein, December 1986. Joint Industry Board, Flushing, New York.

20. Grace Palladino, *Dreams of Dignity, Workers of Vision* (Washington, DC: IBEW, 1991), p. 197.

21. Thomas Van Arsdale in an interview, 1990, as reported by Palladino, *Dreams of Dignity.*

22. Palladino, *Dreams of Dignity,* p. 208.

23. Thomas Van Arsdale interview, December 22, 1986.

24. Ibid.

25. Ibid.

26. Ibid.

27. As reported in the *Electrical Union World.*

28. Thomas Van Arsdale interview, December 22, 1986.

Chapter 8. The Working Man and Woman: Learning and Compassion

1. C.L. Hay, ed., From Letters of John Jay and Excerpts from His Diary, (December 23, 1863).

2. Irving Stern, interviewed by Renee Epstein, August 6, 1987, as part of the New York City Central Labor Council Oral History Collection, NS 7, Tamiment Library and Robert F. Wagner Labor Archives, New York University.

3. Said Lasher, interviewed by Julius C.C. Edelstein, tape recording, April 25, 1989. Joint Industry Board, Flushing, New York.

4. D. Bert Haring, interviewed by Edelstein, May 3, 1991. Joint Industry Board, Flushing, New York.

5. As noted by Warren Moscow in "History of Local Union 3" and Siama S. Ahmed, in her master's thesis, "Union and Housing: Harry Van Arsdale Jr. and his Contributions to Co-operative Housing," at Cornell University, Fall 1994.

6. As noted in the JIB's History and Organization of the Joint Industry Board of the Electrical Industry, p. 35.

7. Arnold Beichman, interviewed for *Apprenticeship on the Move*, August 19, 1975.

8. Harry Van Arsdale Jr., interviewed for *Apprenticeship on the Move*, September 27, 1975.

9. Ibid., November 11, 1975.

10. *New York Times*, May 14, 1949.

11. Lance Van Arsdale, interviewed by the author, July 25, 1999.

12. Harry Van Arsdale Jr., interviewed for *Apprenticeship on the Move*, November 15, 1975.

13. As attested to by Joseph Jacobson, Lance and Thomas Van Arsdale, among others.

14. Brian McLaughlin, interviewed by Edelstein, tape recording, March 18, 1990. Joint Industry Board, Flushing, New York.

15. Hy Greenblatt, interviewed by Edelstein, tape recording, August 26, 1986. Joint Industry Board, Flushing, New York.

16. IBEW *Journal*, December 1988.

17. Hy Greenblatt, interviewed by the author, March 19, 2000.

18. Austin H. Perlow, *What Have You Done for Me Lately?* (New York: Routledge, 1979), p. 124.

19. William Blair, interviewed by Edelstein, May 11, 1987.

20. Michael Smith, "The Men Who Light Up New York," *For a Change*, November 1988, p. 4.

21. William McSpedon, interviewed by Edelstein, March 27, 1987. Joint Industry Board, Flushing, New York.

22. Bertram Powers, interviewed by Epstein, June 24, 1987.

23. As reported in the *Electrical Union World*, February 1, 1951.

24. Ibid., September 15, 1951.

25. JIB, *History and Organization of the Joint Industry Board of the Electrical Industry*, p. 41.

26. According to Harry F. Fischbach, interviewed for *Apprenticeship on the Move*, October 20, 1975. Fischbach stated he saw an advertisement for the property in the *New York Times*.

27. As reprinted in the *Electrical Union World*, February 15, 1950, p. 1.

28. Harry Van Arsdale Jr., interviewed for *Apprenticeship on the Move*, November 15, 1975.

29. Ibid.

30. As printed in the *Electrical Union World*, February 15, 1950, p. 1, 8.

31. Fischbach, interviewed for *Apprenticeship on the Move*, date unknown.

32. *Electrical Union World,* July 15, 1955, p. 1.

33. Harry Van Arsdale Jr., interviewed for *Apprenticeship on the Move,* November 15, 1975.

34. Moscow, "History of Local 3."

35. JIB, *History and Organization of the Joint Industry Board,* p. 43.

36. William Michelson, interviewed by Epstein, August 1987.

37. Ibid., July 30, 1987.

38. Van Arsdale Jr., interviewed for *Apprenticeship on the Move,* September 16, 1975.

39. As reported in the *Electrical Union World,* March 1, 1953. According to former New York State AFL-CIO President Edward Cleary, the idea that led to Van Arsdale's involvement in scouting came from Governor Thomas Dewey. Dewey asked AFL President Thomas Murray for union support in the establishment of scout troops in poorer areas of the state, particularly New York City. Murray turned the matter over to Van Arsdale and the Local subsequently sponsored its first troop on the Lower East Side. Employers were then asked to partake in joint sponsorship and leadership of numerous troops in the city.

40. Van Arsdale Jr., interviewed for *Apprenticeship on the Move,* September 16, 1975.

41. James McFadden, interviewed by Terry Baker, January 14, 1986.

42. Harry Kelber, interviewed by Edelstein, June 18, 1986. Joint Industry Board, Flushing, New York.

43. Memorandum to Governor Nelson Rockefeller by Van Arsdale, July 14, 1971.

44. Bernard Rosenberg. "An Examination of the Development of the First Accredited Labor College in the United States," Ph.D. dissertation, Empire State College, May 1989, pp. 132–33.

45. As stated by Rosenberg in a letter to the author, February 22, 2000.

46. Harry Kelber interviewed by Edelstein, June 18, 1986. Joint Industry Board, Flushing, New York.

47. *Electrical Union World,* August 15, 1957, p. 12.

48. Ibid., August 16, 1957, p. 1.

49. Paul Sanchez, interviewed by Edelstein, August 26, 1986.

50. Ibid.

51. Theodore Kheel, interviewed by Edelstein, March 18, 1987. Joint Industry Board, Flushing, New York.

52. As reported in the minutes of a regular membership meeting held December 8, 1938.

53. In an interview with the author, September 1999.

54. Irving Stern, interviewed by Renee Epstein as part of the Central Labor Council Oral History Project August 6, 1987.

Chapter 9. "Mister Labor"

1. Bertram Powers, interviewed by Renee Epstein, June 24, 1987, as part of the New York City Central Labor Council Oral History Collection, NS 7, Tamiment Library and Robert F. Wagner Labor Archives, New York University.

2. Robert Wagner, interviewed by Epstein, August 1987.

3. Theodore Kheel, interviewed by Epstein, July 7, 1987.

4. *New York Times,* July 7, 1957.

5. *Electrical Union World,* September 1957.

6. Madeline Van Arsdale, interviewed by the author, September 15, 1999.

7. *New York Times,* September 4, 1981, Section B, p. 4.

8. *New York Times,* June 19, 1958.

9. Thomas Donahue, interviewed by Julius C.C. Edelstein (senior vice chancellor emeritus of the City University of New York), March 6, 1990. Donahue uses the term Central Labor Council, but means the Central Trades Labor Council (CTLC). The CLC did not come into being for another year.

10. *New York Times,* January 11, 1959.

11. *Electrical Union World,* March 1, 1959, p. 1.

12. Ibid., September 1957.

13. William Michelson, interviewed by Epstein, August 13, 1987.

14. In a speech given by Harry Van Arsdale Jr. on "The Goals of Labor" at the Cooper Union Forum in New York City on February 28, 1962.

15. Brian McLaughlin, interviewed by the author, October 6, 2000.

16. As quoted by Michael Mann, AFL-CIO regional director, in an interview with Renee Epstein, September 19, 1987.

17. Leon Davis, interviewed by Epstein, July 7, 1987.

18. Moe Foner, interviewed by the author, November 14, 1999.

19. Peter Brennan, interviewed by Epstein, September 3, 1987.

20. Struck on May 8: Mount Sinai, Lenox Hill, Beth David, Beth Israel, Bronx, and Brooklyn Jewish. Struck on June 5: Flower and Fifth Avenue Hospital.

21. *New York Times,* May 10, 1959.

22. *New York Times,* May 17, 1959.

23. McLaughlin, interviewed by the author, October 6, 2000.

24. Davis apparently was referring to the motor scooter owned by Arnold Beichman, editor of *Electrical Union World.* Beichman's motor scooter was a favorite form of convenient and quick transportation for Van Arsdale around town, especially at odd hours.

25. Davis, interviewed by Epstein, July 7, 1987.

26. Van Arsdale addressed 600 national leaders of labor, industry, and government at a dinner honoring Monsignor John P. Boland, commissioner of the New York State Board of Mediation at Utica.

27. As reported in the *Electrical Union World,* June 15, 1959.

28. *New York Times,* June 18, 1959.

29. A song was even composed and sung in Van Arsdale's honor. The song was written by Henry Foner, Moe's brother. (Henry later was elected president of the Fur, Leather, and Machine Workers' Union and worked with Van Arsdale in other efforts.) The song's title was "Tribute to Harry Van Arsdale," primarily using the melody from the popular tune, "I'm Just Wild About Harry." The melody for stanzas one and four were from the popular tune: "I'm Just Wild About Harry." For stanzas two and three the melody switched to "Mary (Tell Me Your Answer True)." The lyrics:

"We're just wild about Harry—
Harry—Harry Van A.
We were low-down.
Then came the showdown
And now we're heading for a new day.
We think it's necessary
To let him hear what we say—
For we're just wild about Harry—
Yes, we're wild about—
Just can't do without—

(Tune: Mary)
For it was Harry, Harry,
Helped us on the picket line—
We saw his motor bike
Up and down the strike,
And we felt fine.
Yes, it was Harry, Harry,
Made the labor movement hum,
That's why we make this vow,
We're with him now
Till Kingdom—
(Back to original tune)
Come on, sing about Harry,
And raise your voice to the sky.
For we're just wild about Harry.
Harry Van Arsdale's our guy."

30. *Electrical Union World,* July 1, 1959.

31. Van Arsdale's rapport with Rockefeller began during the construction of Rockefeller Center on which many Local 3 members worked, according to Leon Davis. Subsequently, Davis told of a strike that Local 1199 threatened to call against a pharmacy at the Center that barred pickets from the site. "Harry called Rockefeller and says 'Since when are you anti-labor? You know, it's just not nice for you. You've got it made and I think you ought to be sensitive to problems of working people.' And by our threat to strike, Rockefeller Center was settled positively by the union. It was an incidental event, but it showed Harry's concern and his effectiveness in pursuing a policy, a very progressive policy, on behalf of working people in this country."

32. Brennan, interviewed by Epstein, September 3, 1987.

33. *Electrical Union World*, November 1, 1959, p. 1, 3.

34. Wagner, interviewed by Edelstein, April 25, 1986. Joint Industry Board, Flushing, New York.

35. Hy Greenblatt, interviewed by Edelstein, undated. Joint Industry Board, Flushing, New York.

36. *Electrical Union World,* vol. 21, no. 1 (January 15, 1961), p. 1.

37. Lester Velie, "The Union that Gives More to the Boss, *Reader's Digest,* January 1956, pp. 2–5.

38. The *New York Times,* July 29, 1958.

39. In an interview with Brian Greenburg for the Oral History Project of the National Union of Hospital and Health Care Employees, 1977.

Chapter 10. United Federation of Teachers and the Brotherhood Party

1. Arnold Beichman, interviewed by the author, December 8, 1999.

2. A letter to Van Arsdale from Cogen, October 30, 1959, as quoted by Andrew Lorenzo in his paper entitled "Harry Van Arsdale Jr." submitted to the New York State School of Industrial and Labor Relations at Cornell University, Spring 1995.

3. As quoted by Lorenzo in his paper.

4. Philip Taft, *United They Teach: The Story of the United Federation of Teachers* (Los Angeles: Nash, 1974), p. 41.

5. *New York Times*, November 7, 1960, p. 42.

6. *New York Times,* November 9, 1960, p. 72.

7. According to Albert Shanker, interviewed by Julius C.C. Edelstein, tape recording, April 7, 1986. Joint Industry Board, Flushing, New York.

8. From a letter from Van Arsdale to local union presidents. Date unknown.

9. Telegram to Van Arsdale. Date unknown.

10. Donald Menagh, interviewed by Andrew Lorenzo, April 1995.

11. Peter Brennan, interviewed by Renee Epstein, September 3, 1987, as part of the New York City Central Labor Council Oral History Collection, NS 7, Tamiment Library and Robert F. Wagner Labor Archives, New York University.

12. *Electrical Union World*, October 1, 1959, p. 12.

13. *New York Times*, June 30, 1961, pp. 1, 4.

14. *New York Times*, July 15, 1961, p. 12.

15. Harry Van Arsdale Jr., interviewed for *Apprenticeship on the Move*, November 15, 1975.

16. *New York Times*, August 4, 1961, p. 12.

17. *Electrical Union World*, August 15, 1961, pp. 1, 8.

18. This despite a catchy song that had been written for the Brotherhood ticket: "Cast, cast, cast your vote for Wagner, Beame, Screvane/Now's the time for Brotherhood and that's our party's name."

19. In addition to Wagner, Screvane, and Beame, other candidates included: Edward Dudley, running for Manhattan borough president; Frank S. Hogan, running for Manhattan district attorney; Albert V. Maniscalco, candidate for Staten Island borough president; Joseph F. Periconi, candidate for Bronx borough president; and Judge Paul Widlitz, running for Supreme Court judge for Nassau, Suffolk, and Queens counties. Periconi was a Republican.

20. Van Arsdale Jr., interviewed for *Apprenticeship on the Move*, November 15, 1975.

21. Theodore Kheel, interviewed by Renee Epstein, July 8, 1987.

22. Kheel, interviewed by Michael Jew, a student at the New York School of Industrial and Labor Relations at Cornell University for a paper, Spring 1992.

23. Armand D'Angelo, Bert Powers, and Hy Greenblatt shared this view according to Jew in his interviews and paper.

24. *New York Times*, June 19, 1958.

25. Warren Moscow, "History of Local Union 3," p. 60.

26. *New York Times*, January 5, 1933, p. 1.

27. *Speech and Scrapbook for Speakers, A Four Hour Day Ahead* (H.H. Broach, Speakers Service Bureau, Minneapolis, Minnesota, 1924), p. 114.

28. The phrase "Harvest of Shame" referred to the famed CBS television documentary narrated by Edward R. Murrow, telling of the inequities of migrant and child farm labor.

29. *Electrical Union World*, February 15, 1961, pp. 1, 10.

30. Van Arsdale Jr., interviewed for *Apprenticeship on the Move*, November 15, 1975.

31. *Electrical Union World*, December 15, 1961, pp. 1, 4.

32. *New York Times*, December 13, 1961.

33. Ibid., September 13, 1962, p. 19.

34. Kheel, interviewed by Epstein, July 7, 1987.

35. Ibid., January 25, 1962.

36. Beichman, interviewed by the author, December 8, 1999.

37. *Electrical Union World*, June 15, 1961, p. 1.

38. *Sunday New York Times Magazine*, March 11, 1962, p. 51.

39. Ibid.

40. Ibid., p. 59.

Chapter 11. Trouble Shooting Here and Abroad

1. *Electrical Union World,* March 15, 1962, pp. 1, 9, 10.

2. Ibid., May 1, 1962, p. 8.

3. Ibid., May 15, 1962, p. 6.

4. Ibid., October 15, 1962, p. 1.

5. Ibid., November 1, 1962, p. 1.

6. Ibid., December 1, 1962, p. 1.

7. Bertram Powers, interviewed by Julius C.C. Edelstein (senior vice-chancellor emeritus of the City University of New York), February 16, 1990.

8. Bertram Powers, interviewed by Renee Epstein, June 24, 1987, as part of the New York City Central Labor Council Oral History Collection, NS 7, Tamiment Library and Robert F. Wagner Labor Archives, New York University.

9. Theodore Kheel, interviewed by the author, December 11, 1999.

10. Powers, interviewed by Epstein, June 24, 1987.

11. *New York Times,* April 1, 1963, p. 20.

12. Powers, interviewed by Edelstein. n.d. Joint Industry Board, Flushing, New York.

13. *Detroit Labor News,* March 12, 1964.

Chapter 12. Van Arsdale at the Wheel

1. Charles Vidich, *The New York Cab Driver and His Fare* (Cambridge, MA: Schenkman, 1976), p. 90.

2. Ibid.

3. Edward G. Rogoff, "History of the New York Taxicab Industry," Master's thesis, Baruch College, 1993.

4. Ibid.

5. James McFadden, interviewed by Terry Baker, January 14, 1986.

6. As quoted by Peter Brennan, interviewed by Julius C.C. Edelstein, n.d.

7. Brennan, interviewed by Renee Epstein, September 3, 1987, as part of the New York City Central Labor Council Oral History Collection, NS 7, Tamiment Library and Robert F. Wagner Labor Archives, New York University.

8. *New York Times,* September 15, 1964.

9. *Electrical Union World,* October 1, 1964, p. 13.

10. Ibid., February 15, 1965, p. 4.

11. Ibid., pp. 1, 4.

12. Ibid., March 15, 1865, pp. 1, 12.

13. *New York Times,* March 25, 1965.

14. Michael Mann, interviewed by Epstein, September 19, 1987.

15. Ibid., July 23, 1965.

16. Ibid., October 20, 1966.

17. Peter Brennan, interviewed by Epstein, September 3, 1987.

18. (New York) *Daily News,* January 11, 1971.

19. Interview with Renee Epstein, July 30, 1987.

20. As told by Lewis Stein, an assistant business manager of Local 3, interviewed by Edelstein, May 13, 1986.

21. Van Arsdale Jr., tape recording.

22. As quoted by Robert R. Barravecchio in his academic paper, "Harry Van Arsdale Jr.: His Involvement with Governor Nelson A. Rockefeller, 1979–73," Cornell University School of Industrial and Labor Relations.

23. Armand D'Angelo, interviewed by Edelstein, January 20, 1986.

24. Barbara Quill, *Mike Quill Himself: A Memoir* (Greenwich, CT: Devin-Adair, 1985), p. 312.

25. Ibid., p. 313.

26. Theodore Kheel, interviewed by the author, December 11, 1999.

27. *New York Times,* January 24, 1966.

28. Handwritten, a copy of which was made available to the author by the Harry Van Arsdale Memorial Committee. This statement was presumably published, but it is not known by whom or when.

29. *New York Times,* January 14, 1966.

30. *New York Times,* April 26, 1965.

31. *New York Herald Tribune,* March 4, 1966.

32. A view expressed by Jewell Bellush in her book, *Union Power & New York: Victor Gotbaum and District Council 37* (New York: Praeger, 1984), p. 247.

Chapter 13. A Wider Garden to Tend

1. Donald Menagh, Sr., interviewed by the author, December 15, 1999.

2. *Electrical Union World,* August 15, 1968, p. 8.

3. James McFadden, interviewed by Terry Baker, January 14, 1986.

4. Theodore Kheel, interviewed by Julius C. C. Edelstein, March 18, 1987.

5. *New York Times*, March 8, 1969.

6. Brian McLaughlin, interviewed by Edelstein, April 25, 1989.

7. Robert Wagner, interviewed by Renee Epstein, August 5, 1987, as part of the New York City Central Labor Council Oral History Collection, NS 7, Tamiment Library and Robert F. Wagner Labor Archives, New York University.

8. *New York Times,* November 15, 1967, pp. 1, 3.

9. David Rockefeller, interviewed by Edelstein, November 25, 1986.

10. *New York Times,* January 29, 1977, p. 22.

11. *New York Times,* February 9, 1968, editorial.

12. *New York Times,* February 11, 1958.

13. Ibid.

14. As quoted in "Nine Days that Shook the World," a USA publication.

15. Jack Bigel, interviewed by Terry Baker, July 30, 1987.

16. *New York Times,* February 7, 1968.

17. Kheel, interviewed by the author, December 11, 1999.

18. Robert R. Barravecchio, "Harry Van Arsdale Jr., His Political Involvement with Governor Nelson A. Rockefeller, 1959–1973," paper submitted to the Cornell University School of Industrial and Labor Relations.

19. "Statement on the Teachers' Strike," New York Central Labor Council, September 26, 1968.

20. *New York Times,* January 14, 1968.

21. *New York Times,* September 17, 1968.

22. Jack Schierenbeck, interviewed by the author, January 14, 2000.

23. As reported in *United Teacher,* January 24, 1968.

24. *New York Times,* September 4, 1967, p. 26.

25. Irving Stern, interviewed by Epstein, July 30, 1987.

26. Edwin Lopez, interviewed by the author, May 30, 2000.

27. (New York) *Sunday Daily News,* June 8, 1969.

28. (New York) *Daily News,* September 1, 1969.

29. Victor Gotbaum, in an interview for the City University of New York Oral History Project, March 26, 1997.

30. Kheel, interviewed by the author, December 11, 1999.

31. According to Bernard Rosenberg, a Local 3 business agent, who drove Van Arsdale to the meeting.

32. Bigel interviewed by H. Ron Davidson, July 16, 1999.

33. H. Ron Davidson, "Harry Van Arsdale and the New York City Fiscal Crisis," paper prepared under the guidance of Professor Lois Gray, submitted to the Cornell University School of Industrial and Labor Relations, August 1999.

34. Albert Shanker, interviewed by Baker, August 7, 1987.

35. Kheel, interviewed by Epstein.

36. *Electrical Union World,* November 1–15, 1975.

37. Rudin spoke at a symposium sponsored by the Harry Van Arsdale Jr. Memorial Committee and Cornell University at the Electrical Industry Center in Queens shortly after Van Arsdale's death.

38. From the archives of Local 3, IBEW.

Chapter 14. The Kid Goes Down Fighting

1. Thomas Van Arsdale, interviewed by Julius C.C. Edelstein, undated.

2. J.J. Barry, interviewed by Edelstein, January 29, 1987.

3. Ibid.

4. Thomas Van Arsdale, interviewed by Edelstein, December 22, 1986.

5. Theodore Kheel, interviewed by the author, December 11, 1999.

6. Jewel Bellush, *Union Power and New York: Victor Gotbaum and District Council 37* (New York: Praeger, 1984) p. 447.

7. Kheel, interviewed by the author, December 11, 1999.

8. *New York Times,* September 4, 1981.

9. Former New York State AFL-CIO President Edward Cleary believes that the incident actually occurred at a Lincoln Day dinner sponsored by the New York City Central Labor Council.

10. Frank Barbaro, interviewed by the author, December 12, 1999.

11. Harry Van Arsdale Jr., tape recording, Local 3 archives.

12. Ibid.

13. As related by Bernard Rosenberg in a memo to the author July 19, 2000.

14. *New York Times,* September 4, 1981.

15. *Electrical Union World,* October 15, 1981, p. 1.

16. *Electrical Union World,* December 1, 1981, p. 1.

17. Mario Cuomo, interviewed by the author, September 27, 2000.

18. Ibid.

19. *New York Times,* September 4, 1984.

20. Van Arsdale Jr., speaking at a seminar at Bayberry, July 7, 1982.

21. Paul Sanchez, interviewed by Edelstein, August 26, 1986.

22. *Wall Street Journal,* October 20, 1980.

23. Ibid.

24. *New York Times,* October 23, 1980.

25. *Electrical Union World,* August 15, 1983, p. 3.

26. Brian McLaughlin, interviewed by Edelstein, March 18, 1990.

27. Ibid.

28. Ibid.

29. Hy Greenblatt, interviewed by the author, February 8, 2000.

30. Harry Kelber, interviewed by Edelstein, June 18, 1986.

31. Madeline Van Arsdale, interviewed by the author, February 9, 2000.

32. Greenblatt, interviewed by Edelstein, July 8, 1990.

33. Madeline Van Arsdale, interviewed by the author, February 9, 2000.

34. Greenblatt, interviewed by Edelstein, July 8, 1990.

35. Ibid.

36. Bernard Rosenberg, interviewed by the author, December 29, 1999.

37. Dr. Alex Maurillo, interviewed by the author, March 29, 2000.

38. Ibid.

39. Madeline Van Arsdale, interviewed by the author, September 15, 1999.

40. Joseph D'Angelo, interviewed by Edelstein, July 8, 1990.

41. Ibid.

42. Ibid.

43. Rosenberg, interviewed by the author, December 29, 1999.

44. Thomas Van Arsdale, interviewed by Edelstein, December 12, 1986.

45. William Blain, interviewed by Edelstein, May 11, 1987.

46. Among those who were not there was Mayor Koch. A spokesman said Koch had "prior commitments." As reported by the *New York Times.*

47. Text made available by the New York Roman Catholic Archdiocese.

48. *Newsday,* February 17, 1986.

49. Ibid.

50. Ibid.

51. Ibid.

52. Ibid.

53. Ibid.

54. Ibid.

55. Ibid.

56. Norman William, correspondence with the author, April 7, 1986.

57. British Trades Union publication, date unknown.

58. *Electrical Union World,* March 20, 1986.

Index

About the Author

Gene Ruffini was a newspaperman in New York for nearly forty years. He was also active in union matters. His other books include *A Builder's Wisdom*, about Dr. Samuel J. LeFrak, the New York realtor and builder, and the novel, *The Power Lovers*. He is also a screenwriter and playwright, and his plays have been performed in New York City as well as throughout the United States and Canada.